THE BEING OF CHURCHES:
NEO-CONGREGATIONAL POLITY

A Teleioteti Technical Study

J. Alexander Rutherford

Paperback ISBN-13: 978-1-989560-73-0
Hardcover ISBN-13: 978-1-989560-74-7
DOI: 10.60080/eikd5738

Cover image by Louis Moncouyoux on Unsplash.

To contact Teleioteti publishing for information or to provide feedback, please visit us at **https://teleioteti.ca** or email us at **info@teleioteti.ca**

TABLE OF CONTENTS

ACKNOWLEDGMENTS

I am thankful for the many men and women over the years who have shown me what the church is and why it is important.

God has blessed my wife and me with many loving church families over the years, and I am thankful for the many opportunities I have been given to learn about the church in the context of ministry. The team at Cornerstone Foursquare Church (Calgary, Alberta Canada) gave me my first glimpse of Christian ministry, especially Chris Schollaardt, for which I am thankful. Many thanks to Doug Friesen for helping me think through the contribution I could make to the local church in my final year at Bible college. I am also grateful to Tom Jantzi for giving me the opportunity to cut my teeth on preaching at Hope Foursquare Church in White Rock, BC (Canada). To Fred Eaton, thank you for your patience towards me as you helped me to see that God is more interested in people than productivity or academic achievement. I am also thankful to Fred, his family, and The Bridge Church Vancouver, Canada (which has become Christ City Kitsilano) for the opportunities to serve in various capacities and grow in my understanding of God and his ways. In more recent years, I am grateful to have served beside Roger Chilton at St Matthews Ashbury Anglican Church (Sydney, Australia), from whom I learned much. Most recently, we are grateful for the family we have had at St Paul's Canterbury in 2022 and now at Riverwood Punchbowl Anglican Church (both in Sydney, Australia).

I am also grateful to the many families that have shown Nicole and me hospitality over the years. When I decided to stay in Vancouver and pursue further studies, the Bromiley family opened their home to me—and fed me!—until I found a place to stay. More recently, the Sholl and the Marshall families here in Sydney allowed us to live in their homes for over a month while we searched for a home to rent.

I am also thankful to the many peers I have studied alongside, first at Pacific Life Bible College, then Regent College, and now Moore College. Many thanks to Stephanie Adams who gave me some feedback on the sections pertaining to women in ministry and prophesying. It has been a pleasure to live alongside you and learn from the many traditions represented by the students at these colleges. We are richer because of the rich community God has given us.

ANALYTIC OUTLINE

INTRODUCTION

    A. WHY CONGREGATIONALISM?

    B. HOW WILL WE DO THIS?

        1. Three Principles for Constructing Local Church Polity

            a. The Principle of Sufficiency

            b. The Principle of Simplicity

            c. The Principle of Freedom

        2. Moving from Scripture to Polity

I. OF THE CHURCH AND CHURCHES

    1. That the Church Is the Key Instrument for the Application of God's Redemption of the Cosmos Decisively Achieved in Christ Jesus.

        a. Abraham

        b. The Sons of Israel

        c. The Nation of Israel

        d. The Apostates and the Remnant

        e. The Church in the New Testament

        f. The Church in These Last Days

2. That Discipline Is Gradated.

3. Censure or Discipline Is Proportionate to the Sin.

4. In Case of Private Sin, the Offended Party (where Appropriate) Ought to Confront the Offending Party in Private.

5. If an Offending Member Does Not Respond to Private Rebuke, then the Offended Party Ought to Bring Another Member.

6. If an Offending Member Does not Respond to the Presence of Another Member with the Offended Party, the Case Is to Be Brought before the Church.

7. The Elders Ought to Investigate the Matter and, Where the Breach Has Not Been Repaired, Bring the Case before a Special Gathering.

8. If the Offending Party Does not Respond to the Public Rebuke of the Special Gathering, further Censure Is to Be Prescribed, the Loss of Some Privileges of Membership and Disqualification from the Lord's Supper (Matt 18:17).

9. If the Offending Member Does not Respond to These Censures, then They Are to Put out of the Congregation and Considered a Member of Ill-Standing ("Exairtion") (Matt 18:17; 1 Cor 5:1-13; 2 Thess 3:6-15).

10. "Extra-Ordinary Fellowship" Forbidden to the Member Who is the Subject of Exairtion Is That Fellowship Unique to the Church; Ordinary Fellowship of Spouses and Guardians Is Not Restricted (Cf. CPD XIV.5).

VI. INTER-CHURCH RELATIONS

1. The Obligations of Churches to One Another.

2. The Benefits of Inter-Church Communion.

3. That Synods and Parachurch Forms of Fellowship Have No Ecclesiastical Standing; namely, They Are Not a "Church."

4. The Obligation of Other Churches in the Ordination of Ministers to a New Presbytery.

5. Of Synods (Cf. CPD XVI).

6. The Role of Other Churches in the Deposition of a Presbytery or Mediating Conflict between a Presbytery and Congregation.

INTRODUCTION

Then Peter said in reply, "See, we have left everything and followed you. What then will we have?" Jesus said to them, "Truly, I say to you, in the new world, when the Son of Man will sit on his glorious throne, you who have followed me will also sit on twelve thrones, judging the twelve tribes of Israel. And everyone who has left houses or brothers or sisters or father or mother or children or lands, for my name's sake, will receive a hundredfold and will inherit eternal life. But many who are first will be last, and the last first. – Matthew 19:27-30

"Polity" is not a word you will hear on a Sunday morning—nor is it a word the average pastor will encounter during formal theological education. However, polity (the principles and foundations for the organisation and conduct of a church) has far-ranging implications for the life of a church.

What, exactly, is a church? Who is qualified to lead a church? What is the role of denominations? How are church leaders identified and empowered? What does a church leader do? What is a congregation? Who is a member of a church? Do believers have a different role in the local church than unbelievers? Such questions and many more are questions of polity. At some point in its life, a church will need to answer these questions, and others. To do so, a church may draw on its own tradition or the Bible or develop ad hoc answers rooted in common sense or practical wisdom. Indeed, a church may do all of these in developing its own polity. The tradition of Christ's Church is rich with attempts to define the church and identify its proper organisation and function, drawing to varying degrees on the Bible, reason, and wisdom. Those of us who identify with the Protestant Reformed tradition will want to think biblically about questions of polity, yet this is in itself a polity question: to what degree and in what way does the Bible norm church polity?

Various traditions have answered this question differently: the Anglican tradition and its key proponents, such as Richard Hooker, propounded the role of natural law (itself rooted in God's self-revelation in creation) in ecclesiastical polity and law.[1] The Presbyterians and Congregationalists, along with various Anabaptist groups and the Baptists, found in Scripture significant guidance for structuring the church. Indeed, some of the latter groups forbade going beyond the forms prescribed in Scripture for corporate worship (the gathered church) and its organisation. Many in the Presbyterian and Congregational traditions have adopted the so-called regulative principle, "worship is by divine warrant, command, prescription. In worship, that is to say, we should do only what God requires us to do, and we learn his requirements only from Scripture."[2] John Cotton and others would cite the instance of God's judgment on Nadab and Abihu as proof that only God-approved forms of worship are appropriate in the church (Leviticus 10).[3] In the *Westminster Larger Catechism*, Q. 109, the principle is put in this way: "The sins forbidden in the second command are, all devising, counselling, commanding, using, and anywise approving, any religious worship not instituted by God himself."[4] All of these traditions—and many others—have

---

[1] See W. Bradford Littlejohn, *The Two Kingdoms: A Guide for the Perplexed* (Lincoln, NE: Davenant Trust, 2017). Cf. Richard Hooker, *The Laws of Ecclesiastical Polity*.

[2] John M. Frame, *The Doctrine of the Christian Life*, A Theology of Lordship 4 (Phillipsburg: P&R Publishing, 2008), 464–65.

[3] E.g. John Cotton, *The Way of the Churches of Christ in New England;* Jeremiah Burroughs, *Gospel Worship*.

[4] Given in Frame, *The Doctrine of the Christian Life*, 451.

engaged seriously with the question of church organisation.

Others have adopted the polity of those traditions from which they evolved, such as the use of episcopalian structures in many Pentecostal groups, or have adopted *ad hoc* polities rooted in convenience, tradition, or circumstances—as have many "independent" churches. But, as is evidenced by many in the latter group, all churches have a polity, whether it has been articulated, thought about in traditional terms, or discussed with the term. As will be argued below (following in the tradition of the Presbyterians, Baptists, Congregationalists, and Anabaptists), the Bible has much to say about polity, and having a biblical polity is critical to establishing healthy churches. So, in this book, we will attempt to think critically about church polity.

For reasons that will become evident, the way we will do so is rather skeletal, laying out a robust account of crucial biblical principles but something short of a sufficient statement of any single church's organisational and functional principles. We will do so because, as I will argue, the Bible only gives us a skeleton, intending that individual churches would cloth these bones with flesh appropriate for their congregation and context. We will thus follow the Puritans and other Reformed traditions in insisting that the Bible is critical to our construction of ecclesiastical polity, yet we will simultaneously reject the regulative principle (that only Biblically delivered forms are permissible to use in thinking about polity and the life of the local church). The meaning of this affirmation and denial will become clear as we proceed. We will do this, namely, lay forth biblical principles for polity, within the tradition of Congregationalism.

A. Why Congregationalism?

Many rich and rewarding books have been published on Church polity in recent decades, even under the banner of "congregational" church government, so an immediate question ought to be raised, why another? For the most part, these books have been released by Baptist brothers and sisters who write within the Baptist tradition and use its traditional resources.[5]

---

[5] E.g. Gregg R. Allison, *Sojourners and Strangers: The Doctrine of the Church* (Crossway, 2012); Mark Dever and Jonathan Leeman, *Baptist Foundations: Church*

However, Baptists are not the only group to claim the "congregational" banner, and I believe that addressing polity from within the school traditionally known as "Congregationalism" (as opposed to Baptists who have a congregational ecclesiology) will offer something new and helpful to the present conversation.

Congregationalists emerged at a similar time to the Baptists and shared with the Particular Baptists a strong Reformed, Calvinist theology. Both of their theologies embraced, with some modifications, the faith articulated by the Westminster Assembly. Many Congregationalists expressed a separatist view like the Baptists, but many others were "non-conformists," ministers who remained within the Church of England, seeking reform and ministering to their churches from congregational principles.[6] Such were John Owen, one-time chaplain to Oliver Cromwell, and the Puritans who sailed to New England and established many congregational churches. It is the latter group to which we owe several of the most thorough non-Baptist articulations of Congregational polity. In 1649, they approved the "Cambridge Platform of Discipline" (see Appendix 1), a comprehensive and mature account of congregational polity upon which I hope to draw in this book. I am not situating this study within the context of Congregationalism to suggest that I merely intend to reproduce this tradition or commend it without qualification. As will become clear, I hope to engage with Congregationalism, and the Cambridge Platform in particular, from the Bible, seeking to affirm what is good and improve what may be improved. I do so under the conviction that we all do theology within a tradition and have much to learn from those who came before us, so engaging constructively with and from

---

Government for an Anti-Institutional Age (B&H Publishing Group, 2015). See many of the resources published by 9Marks.

[6] The thesis of Timothy Haupt, "The Palace Beautiful: The Evangelical Independent Ecclesiology of John Bunyan" (PhD Thesis, Midwestern Baptist Theological Seminary, 2022) highlights some of the differences between Puritan congregationalism (though it had many forms) and Baptist congregationalism. See also his popular article on the Gospel Coalition (US) concerning the differences between Bunyan and the Baptists, Timothy Haupt, "Why John Was Not a Baptist: The 7 Irreconcilable Differences Between John Bunyan and the Baptists," *The Gospel Coalition*, n.d., accessed October 10, 2022, https://www.thegospelcoalition.org/blogs/evangelical-history/why-john-was-not-a-baptist-the-7-irreconcilable-differences-between-john-bunyan-and-the-baptists/.

within a concrete tradition is more fruitful than (pretending) to develop theology *de novo*.

It may strike the reader as odd that I will part ways with the Congregationalists on one of the most significant issues that separated them from the Baptists. The Congregationalists were, like the Presbyterians and the continental Reformers, Paedobaptists. However, I would argue that this conviction was at odds with their broader ecclesiology and eventually led to compromising positions, such as the so-called halfway covenant (whereby nominal Christian parents or believing Grandparents who were members by birth of a congregation could see their infant children or grandchildren baptised), which affected the health of the New England congregational churches.[7] Nevertheless, apart from their Paedobaptist convictions, the Congregational tradition still has something to offer us today.

In the *Cambridge Platform* and other documents, the Congregationalists set out a model of church authority that was firmly rooted in Christ's headship and upheld the equal ultimacy of the laity and the officers in the composition of a congregation's authority. Although the officers, namely, elders and deacons, are invested with genuine authority from Christ, the congregation is involved in their election, and a church's most weighty tool of discipline, excommunication, requires the joint action of the eldership and the laity. This model of authority is firmly rooted in the Bible, as we will argue, and offers clarity on many issues of church polity. The New England Congregationalists were also exemplary in their desire to uphold the biblical emphases on local congregations as the visible church (which I will argue below as the primary meaning for "congregational" in my moniker, "Neo-congregationalism") while delineating the necessary and proper relations a local church has with other local churches. They rejected the term "independent" and "autonomous" as descriptors of their ecclesiology, for this was not what they sought. They believed that God's kingdom on earth was manifest visibly only in local churches, that what we call denominations have no ecclesiological status—no being as a "church" with its concomitant authority and ministerial responsibilities—yet they never sought to be

---

[7] See the narrative of congregational history and this particular issue in Williston Walker, ed., *The Creeds and Platforms of Congregationalism*, New ed. (New York: Pilgrim Press, 1991).

divorced from other local churches and the counsel and accountability they provide. These reflections, coupled with further Biblical refining, will allow us to articulate a vision of local church being that it is neither denominational nor independent, that is genuinely accountable to other churches and able to draw on their resources in times of need but is not drawn into extra-local ecclesial structures—that does not succumb to the inertia of ever-broadening fellowships with growing powers, that is, of the urge to move from local accountability and engagement to national and trans-national denominations. These are just some of the benefits I believe justify querying the Bible for answers to polity questions within the Congregationalist framework.

For the sake of clarity, when I speak of "Congregational" (capitalised), I intend the movement within English Puritanism and its American offspring; when speaking of "congregational" ecclesiology associated with Baptist churches, I will speak either of Baptist ecclesiology or qualify "congregational" with "Baptist." When using "congregational" to describe the position I am articulating, I do not intend to recreate the beliefs of any historical Congregationalist, nor do I intend to exposit Baptist congregationalism. We will depart from Congregationalism on several vital points, such as paedobaptism and thus articulate a view that, to the best of my knowledge, was not held by any single Congregationalist. In contrast with the Baptists, "congregationalism" for us is not characterised by the twin principles of "autonomy" and "democracy," by which is usually meant the authoritative role of the congregation and the autonomy of the local church vis-à-vis broader ecclesial structures.[8] Instead, I intend merely the principle that congregations, and congregations alone, are the visible expression of the invisible church in this age, that is, before the Eschaton. That is, "congregationalism," as I am using the term, repudiates the use of the word "church" for organisational bodies above the local church (e.g. episcopalian structures [bishops, archbishops, provinces, dioceses]; presbyterian classes and assemblies; Methodist circuits; etc.). Denying that such entities are "churches" has important implications. This denial does not mean that there is no room for organisation above the level of the local church but only that such organisations have no ecclesiastical status: they are not a church and cannot express the ministerial capacities of a church, such as constituting a

---

[8] Millard J. Erickson, *Christian Theology*, 3rd ed. (Grand Rapids: Baker Academic, 2013), 888; Allison, *Sojourners and Strangers*, 226.

church gathering, ministering the Lord's supper, ordaining local church leaders (though, see Chapter 6), excommunicating individuals, deposing leaders, or dictating the doctrinal practices or polity of a local church. As we will see in Chapter 6, this claim is not the same as the Baptist principle of autonomy. However, before we begin to address important issues such as this, we must first address how we will establish the skeleton of polity we are attempting to put forth.

B. How Will We Do This?

Looking at the Old Testament, we find that God gave extensive details for how his people ought to conduct their life together. Constituted not only as a religious entity but also a socio-political one, a nation united around the worship of God and ruled by him, Israel was given the Torah, the Law, as an extensive constitution for its life and worship. The Law goes into great detail in laying out the forms of acceptable worship God's people are to bring him, and God himself lays forth a pattern for the physical buildings, cultic patterns, and roles of officers involved in worship. As has been observed by many authors, wrong or profane worship—worthy of the death penalty—was characterised not only by doing what God forbade but also by adding to God's legislated modes of worship or changing them. The archetypical example of this is the account of Nadab and Abihu, Aaron's sons.

The narrator of Leviticus tells us that these two priests "each took his censer and put fire in it and laid incense on it and offered unauthorized [lit. strange] fire before the LORD, which he had not commanded them" (Lev 10:1). In response to this "unauthorized" worship, "fire came out from before the LORD and consumed them, and they died before the LORD" (Lev 10:2). In response to this passage, I have heard it said that the problem was the heart by which Nadab and Abihu gave their offering, as is often thought to be the case for Cain's failed offering in Genesis 4:1-7. However, the narrator in Leviticus is explicit: the problem was that the sons of Aaron offered "unauthorised" (זָרָה; "strange") fire, "which he had not commanded them" (Lev 10:1). They were sentenced to death because their offering was not what God had commanded; it was a novelty. By the severe judgment Nadab and Abihu received, God makes clear, "Among those who are near me I will be sanctified, and before all the people I will be glorified" (10:3). Obedience to God in the manner of worship is about properly honouring

7

him as holy and glorifying him. There are also accounts of God's people violating God's direct commands concerning proper worship, which end similarly with death as a penalty (e.g. Exodus 32; 2 Sam 6:5-11). From these accounts, it is clear that the regulative principle applies under the Old Covenant: only what God has ordained is permissible in worship. However, establishing the presence of the regulative principle under the Old Covenant is insufficient to establish its binding nature in the present. I want to argue that the regulative principle understood this way is not active today, and this is God's good intention. Yet under the New Covenant, it is replaced by similar principles we could call the principles of sufficiency and simplicity.

The presence of the regulative principle in the Old Covenant shows us that God takes our worship of him seriously; furthermore, it shows us that where he so desires, he is able to give comprehensive instructions for right worship. The exhaustive system of worship delivered in the Old Testament is uniquely appropriate for the people the Old Covenant constituted, a socio-political entity that was meant to be distinct from all other people groups in order to radiate the glory of God before them and make known his name. The comprehensive divine ordering of Israelite society was instrumental to the purpose God had given it.

However, when we come to the New Testament, God's people have changed significantly (see Chapter 1). No longer are God's people a nation; instead, they are local embassies of a heavenly, eschatological kingdom—sojourners and exiles awaiting the future arrival of their home (1 Pet 1:1). We are told throughout the New Testament that God has ended the Old Covenant and its structures of worship (see especially Hebrews, e.g. Hebrews 8; Acts 10; Gal. 3:1-29). If God intended for the regulative principle to apply under the New Covenant, we would expect that he would deliver a similarly comprehensive account of New Covenant life and worship uniquely tailored to the Church's circumstances. However, nowhere in the New Testament do we find this. For example, teachers will need to wear clothes in the gathered church, but we are not told what they ought to wear (cf. Exodus 28). We are not told where churches should gather or what that building ought to look like (cf. Exodus 26-37). We are not told how often to practice the Lord's Supper or the exact way we are to do so (Exod. 12:1-28; Deut 16:1-8); we are not given a day to gather for worship, though an argument can be made that Christians did gather on the first day of the week (e.g. Rev 1:10); we are not told how long a gathering should go for nor all that should go into it (we are told to read the Scriptures, but not how often; we are told to sing songs, but not what instruments to use); we are told about deacons, but exact details for their role are wanting (1 Tim 3:8-13, cf. Acts 6:1-6); etc. Therefore, the lack of a comprehensive polity and directions for worship in the New Testament seems to be the most significant evidence against applying the regulative principle to the New Testament church. We can argue further that this is appropriate for the nature of the New Testament church. As sojourning and exilic assemblies, Christian churches will not have the freedom to dictate all their circumstance, as Israel would have. The day on which they are free to worship will be shaped by the prevailing culture (Christianity in the West has enabled Sundays, but in Muslim countries, churches often meet on Fridays); persecution and restricted resources often prevent Christians from building their own places of worship; appropriate clothing for a minister of a church will look different in the modern West than it will among the nomadic tribes of Niger.

However, by rejecting the regulative principle as it is found in the Old Testament, we are not opening the door to complete subjectivity in constructing appropriate polity and patterns of worship. Thus far, we have contended only that Scripture does not tell us everything necessary for constructing a thorough polity or for setting forth patterns of worship and the life of local churches. However, that Scripture does not give us everything necessary does not mean we can ignore what it does give us. The New Testament gives us extensive instructions concerning local church polity and worship. Given the Old Testament testimony that God does indeed care about how we worship him and the pervasive testimony of Scripture that God speaks expecting his people to obey him (e.g. Deut 6:4-5), we ought to obey God so far as he has spoken. This is why I speak of a "skeleton polity," for the Bible gives us critical pieces with which to construct a polity and an account of the being and function of churches. However, it leaves open the way we incarnate this skeleton—the tendons, muscles, and skin with which we furnish it. Thus, we may have an African, Caucasian, Indigenous North American, Malay, or Latino church—following the analogy of flesh and bones—with their distinctive appearances, yet we are not free to construct a possum or kangaroo church. Notice that this is not a form-content dichotomy: I am not arguing that Scripture gives us only bare content to which we are free to give form.[9] No, the Bible does dictate forms and patterns for life. It tells us not only what but often what, how, and why. However, it still leaves much left unsaid, giving local churches the freedom to contextualise the gospel as is appropriate for their context. As much as Paul is free to be "all things to all people" (1 Cor 9:22), this cannot mean the repudiation of his own apostleship, the Gospel he preaches, the commands of Jesus Christ, the overturning of the Law, etc.

1. Three Principles for Constructing Local Church Polity

a. The Principle of Sufficiency

God in Scripture *does* tell us how he wants his churches to be; we must obey him in what he has said. From this necessity of obedience, we can form a principle of sufficiency on analogy with the sufficiency of Scripture. The doctrine of Scripture's sufficiency does not say that Scripture tells us everything, full stop. Instead, the sufficiency of Scripture means that it tells us everything we need so that we may believe in Jesus and that our deeds may be pleasing to God.[10] Likewise, God has given us in the Bible everything we need for our churches to be pleasing to him. Thus, God has given us what we need in Scripture for our polity to be pleasing to him: our churches must have this skeleton, and if they have this skeleton, they will be pleasing to him (barring any other violations of his explicit word, that is, polity is not all that can be said about a church). Now, we need to qualify this: God has given a sufficient account for church polity in this sense, yet this does not guarantee that any human account of this skeleton will be sufficient in this sense.

In this book I will attempt to lay forth this skeleton, building upon the work of Godly men and women before me, yet I cannot claim inerrancy for my work. Thus, I hope only to point the reader to the riches of Scripture in this regard; it is up to you to weigh my account of the Bible's account of

---

[9] This immensely influential distinction is found, among other places, in Charles H. Kraft, *Christianity in Culture: A Study in Dynamic Biblical Theologizing in Cross-Cultural Perspective* (Maryknoll, N.Y: Orbis Books, 1979).

[10] See J. Alexander Rutherford, *The Gift of Revelation: A Biblical Perspective on the Bible*, God's Gifts for the Christian Life - Part 2: The Gift of Truth, I (Airdrie, AB: Teleioteti, 2021).

polity with the Scriptures themselves. This principle of sufficiency is what I am offering in place of the regulative principle. We can formulate it this way, *God has given us a sufficient account of the Church and its visible manifestations that our gathered life may be pleasing to him.* Correlative of this principle is the need to obey God's word in our construction of polity: *because God's word is sufficient for polity in this way, we who desire to please God ought to conform our polity to God's word.* We can also formulate a principle of simplicity from this account of sufficiency and our discussion of the regulative principle.

b. The Principle of Simplicity

If Scripture is sufficient in this sense, then we do not need to supplement the biblical testimony with any other resources for our churches to be pleasing to God. That is, we will need to put flesh on these bones, yet where Scripture has not spoken, there can be no normativity to this flesh. If someone is to argue from common sense, reason, natural law, or some other avenue for a particular mode of church practice, and if this practice is neither commended by Scripture nor forbade, it is at best *adiaphora*, a matter indifferent. One is free to employ it or not. Moreover, because God does care about our worship of him and has chosen not to give us more instructions than he has, we should refrain from adding superfluous practices and forms to what is given in Scripture and necessary to enflesh the biblical skeleton. In other words, the restraint of the Biblical account of polity is not meant to promote novel invention but flexibility and freedom to contextualise the Gospel: we are not given absolute license but are invited to be wise in the use of our freedom. God could have given us further instructions if he so willed, but in his beneficent wisdom, he has not. We gather from this that he has not desired to lay any further binding legislation upon his people.

The reason for this freedom can be gathered from passages such as 1 Corinthians 9, namely, that God wants us to be free to contextualise the Gospel so as to make it commendable to all people. Adding layers of unnecessary complexity to our worship and polity will not please God more, for he has given us a sufficient Word for this purpose. Moreover, adding further layers of complexity increases the likelihood of unintended error, of multiplying the opportunities for the unintentional contravention of Scripture or offence to those we seek to reach. For these reasons, I think we can formulate a principle of simplicity, that *we ought not to needlessly multiply church practices and structures.* The warrant for practices and structures is what we have seen thus far, what is necessary to enflesh the Bible's skeleton of polity. As we develop an account of the church and its polity, we must therefore always ask two questions, is this mandated by Scripture (interpreted for the New Testament context)? And, is this helpful for embodying the Church in this context? The drafters of the Cambridge Platform describe the principle in this way,

> The necessary circumstances (as time and place etc.) belonging unto order and decency are not so left unto men as that under pretence of them, they may thrust their own inventions upon the churches. Instead, they are circumscribed in the word with many general limitations. Where they are determined in respect of the matter to be neither worship itself nor circumstances separable from worship in respect of their end, they must be done unto edification. In respect of the manner, they are to be done decently and in order, according to the nature of the things themselves and civil and church custom. (CPD I.4)

We could consider the matter of the teacher's clothing in the gathered congregation. In the Old Testament, God dictated the appropriate garb for the priesthood; however, we are not given explicit instructions in the New Testament. We are told that Christians should not adopt flashy or ostentatious clothing (1 Tim 2:9; 1 Pet 3:3-4; though addressed primarily to women, I think by analogy these passages may be applied to all Christians), and (arguably) a man should not have long hair (1 Cor 11:2-16), but we are not told positively what any Christian should wear, let alone the teacher. We are thus permitted, within these bounds, to employ various forms of clothing in the role of teacher. Suppose a special garment would reinforce the biblical role of a teacher in the local church without implying favouritism towards the rich, flaunting wealth, or violating the distinctive roles of biological males and females. In that case, I see no reason to forbid the practice of using elder-specific garments in the local church. Conversely, if doing so would establish a barrier to effectively communicating the gospel, such as indicating favouritism towards one socio-economic stratum over another (cf. James 2:1-7), then we must not do so. Similar reasoning would apply to the level of formality an elder and congregation should adopt with their clothing.

c. The Principle of Freedom

From our discussion thus far, we can set forth three principles for thinking biblically about polity, namely, the principles of sufficiency, simplicity, and freedom. The Bible gives sufficient instructions for our churches to be pleasing to God—we ought to obey God's instructions and do not need to supplement them. We ought to strive for simplicity, not needlessly multiplying church practices and structures. Finally, we are free to be the church in an endless variety of ways as conforms to the former two principles and is oriented to the end of magnifying the glory of God through commending the Gospel, namely, making disciples of all nations, baptising them in the name of the Father, Son, and Holy Spirit, and teaching them to obey everything Jesus has commanded them (Matt 28:19-20).

Thus far, we have talked in general about the role of Scripture in constructing a biblical polity, yet one issue remains before engaging in the constructive task before us. Much of the biblical testimony to questions of polity is found in highly contextualised forms, such as the accounts of the early church in Acts or the detailed instructions in the New Testament epistles, often addressed to specific churches and their issues.

2. Moving from Scripture to Polity

We don't find a detailed treatise on polity in the New Testament. We are not given universal principles that can be applied to every church everywhere, yet this does not mean that Scripture does not say something to every church everywhere. As Christians, we believe that God has spoken to us in Scripture to guide us in all things; Scripture is meant to teach us so that we can obey him. We ought to affirm with Paul that the Scriptures, Old and New, are written for us, upon whom the end of the age has come (Rom 4:23; 15:4; 1 Cor 10:6, 11).[11] With John Frame, I think it is dangerous to treat the Bible as if it were a poorly organised or overly particularised treaty from which we are to abstract general principles and then organise and re-apply them.[12] The Old Testament demonstrates that God is capable of delivering relatively abstract

---

[11] See Rutherford, *The Gift of Revelation*.

[12] In John M. Frame, *The Doctrine of the Knowledge of God*, A Theology of Lordship (Phillipsburg: P&R Publishing, 1987). See my argument against this sort of thinking in J. Alexander Rutherford, *God's Gifts for the Christian Life — Part 1: The Gift of Knowledge* (Airdrie, AB: Teleioteti, 2021).

laws such as the ten commandments and particularised instructions such as is found in the prophets, yet he has chosen to give us instructions for the New Testament church primarily in the latter form (though there are, of course, significant exceptions, etc. Matt 18:15-20; 28:18-20). The Prophets give an important analogy for what we find in the New Testament as particular applications of the Torah with specific and vivid divine insight into the present circumstances of Israel. This divine insight teaches future generations simultaneously about God, his expectations, and their present state.[13] The Torah itself also gives us a helpful analogy for the mode of revelation God has given us in the Epistles and their authoritative function for our churches, namely, the case laws.

Case laws can be defined as specific legal judgements intended to give examples of the application of more general laws. For example, "you shall not murder" does not tell the reader what constitutes murder and what the penalty should be for different degrees of "murder"; for this purpose, there are case laws. Consider Exodus 21:12-14,

> Whoever strikes a man so that he dies shall be put to death. But if he did not lie in wait for him, but God let him fall into his hand, then I will appoint for you a place to which he may flee. But if a man willfully attacks another to kill him by cunning, you shall take him from my altar, that he may die. (ESV)

This is a series of case laws that explicate what "you shall not murder" means and how transgressions of this law should be punished. There is a distinction made between premeditated and spontaneous killing: both are punishable, yet only premeditated murder earns the death penalty. These correspond to distinctions in degrees of murder in various Western countries. There are also laws showing that this command includes "manslaughter" and legislating its consequences (e.g. Exod 21:28-32). Notice how the New Testament epistles serve a similar function, demonstrating the application of Jesus' teaching or the Old Testament to the New Testament churches. We find something similar in the Prophets and the Wisdom literature. In the latter case, specific circumstances are given as an example of how Scripture governs particular behaviour. Consider, for example, the Book of Job. The Torah, the Prophets,

---

[13] Cf. Rutherford, *The Gift of Revelation*.

and the Psalms have much to say about God's goodness and sovereignty, especially in times of trial and despair. The Book of Job takes these truths and embodies them in a specific story about a man who loses everything. It illustrates the nature of wisdom in light of brutal realities, the sovereign goodness of God despite horrible circumstances, the nature of foolish counsel, and the response of the righteous to God's providence. Instead of listing these things in the form of proverbial sayings or theological statements, it unpacks them over many chapters of narrative and poetic reflection on a man's experience of suffering and the counsel he receives from his friends. Like the case laws, it takes the general theological and ethical truths of Scripture and particularizes them, gives them flesh and bones so that the reader might learn how they apply in his or her own life.

The Epistles do this even more evidently. The New Testament gives instruction to churches facing the real circumstances of life in the World. Instead of merely repeating the Beatitudes and the Ten Commandments, Paul and the rest of the New Testament authors apply these general instructions to specific circumstances. For example, Jesus tells His disciples that they will face persecution but should find joy in this (Matt 5:3-12); Paul, James, and Peter all make specific applications of this truth to the circumstances facing the churches (Rom 5:2-5, Jam 1:2-4, 1 Pet 1:6-7). Paul also makes particular applications of the laws against adultery and immorality to the circumstances of the Corinthian church in general and those of specific believers (1 Cor. 5:1-2, 6:12-20, 7:1-40). All these examples are similar to the case laws: they embody in specific circumstances truths taught elsewhere in Scripture, giving particular examples of what they look like lived out. Though not being "joined with a prostitute" (1 Cor 6:16) has always been implicit in the nature of sexual union (1 Cor 6:16) and the law against adultery (Exod 20:14; Matt. 5:27-30), examples such as those given in Leviticus and by Paul in the letter to the Corinthians are essential for our understanding of these implications.

Consider with me the New Testament accounts of polity. Jesus spoke of a threefold process of dealing with unrepentant sin and conflict in the church; Paul sheds light on this practice by giving counsel for particular cases (1 Cor 5:1-13; 2 Cor 2:5-11; 2 Thess 3:6-15; cf. 1 Tim 1:20). Jesus appointed apostles to teach his people after his ascension; these apostles would bear his authority, following the Old Testament examples of Moses and kings relying

15

on subordinates to manifest their authority. The apostles themselves did not legislate the continuation of their role. However, as the early church became churches, the apostles appointed elders in every local congregation, laying forth a pattern of local church leadership mirroring the Old Testament structure of elders representing the congregation and varying layers of socio-political structuring in Israel (such as the tribe, city, and family). Because the New Testament Church is only visibly incarnated on one level, the local church, elders are only installed in local churches. The pattern of election and ordination, where the people put forward a leader and ordained leaders invest their authority in these leaders (Acts 1:12-26; 6:1-7; 14:23; 1 Tim 4:14, 5:22; 2 Tim 1:6; Titus 1:5), provides specific examples by which we can understand the process we ought to employ in ordaining local church leaders (see Chapter 3). As with the case laws, the specific examples given in the epistles and in Job are necessary for appropriately understanding and using the more general laws given in Scripture. Furthermore, like the case laws, the specific examples cannot be reduced to the principle they embody: they are themselves authoritative. This is important as we consider the application of the specific moral instructions found throughout Scripture, particularly the instructions concerning polity.

Case laws were essential to properly understand and apply the Ten Commandments in the personal and political life of Israel. It is vital to observe that the case laws cannot be replaced by the Ten Commandments: each one implies one of the commandments yet says more than that commandment does on its own. It gives an authoritative application of it: both the case law and the law are equally authoritative, the difference being the particular nature of the case law and general nature of the law. The point of case laws, those found in the Torah and the analogous literature in the rest of Scripture, is not to restate in a memorable way propositional legal or theological truths. Each expression of more general truths is itself an authoritative exposition and application of the general truth.

Thus, guided by the analogy of the case laws, our question as we approach the New Testament examples of polity in practice should not be, "What general truth does this text convey"? Instead, we ought to ask, "How does this text give authoritative guidance for similar situations or help me better understand God and His commands"? Because the case laws are themselves authoritative, their decisions are binding on identical and analogous situations. They also shed light on the meaning of the laws and truths they reflect and so can be used to better understand how the more general teachings of Scripture apply to situations not discussed in Scripture. Thus, where our circumstances are the same as the immediate addressees of the New Testament teachings, we are obligated to employ the commands and instructions directly. Where our situation is different, we are invited to draw on the various case laws given in the New Testament (and, where applicable, the Old Testament) to establish God's instructions for particular circumstances or questions. In what follows, we will move back and forth between generalisations and concrete cases, following the pattern laid forth in Scripture. The concrete instances are to be understood as expositions of the general principles and the general principles as distillations of what goes on in specific; both are mutually implicated in each other (various specific cases are always subject to generalisation, and no generalisation exists apart from particular instances).

It should go without saying that in a treatise such as this, there are some things that Scripture speaks about clearly and others where we employ biblically informed reason to make extrapolations. The Bible warrants such applications and gives them authority so far as they conform to the Scriptures they apply, so this movement is not necessarily one that diminishes authority. However, where such extrapolations are made, there is a higher margin of error, so such judgments ought to be measured by you, the reader, against Scripture. Such is the task I hope to perform. I pray that the results will be edifying to you, the reader, and will contribute to strengthening churches.

I. OF THE CHURCH AND CHURCHES

I hope to come to you soon, but I am writing these things to you so that, if I delay, you may know how one ought to behave in the household of God, which is the church of the living God, a pillar and buttress of the truth. – 1 Timothy 3:14-15

1. That the church is the key instrument for the application of god's redemption of the cosmos decisively achieved in Christ Jesus.
2. That there is an invisible Church.
3. That the visible church consists of congregations.
4. That congregations are demarcated, local composites of believing laypersons and officers that engage in the life of the local church.
5. That the invisible church has global expression in the communion of local churches.
6. That this global expression has no ecclesial authority.

1. That the Church Is the Key Instrument for the Application of God's Redemption of the Cosmos Decisively Achieved in Christ Jesus.

God created humanity in his image,

in the image of God he created him,
male and female he created them. – Genesis 1:27
(Author's Translation)

I will put enmity between you and the woman,
and between your offspring and her offspring;
he shall bruise your head,
and you shall bruise his heel." – Genesis 3:15 (ESV)

The God of peace will soon crush Satan under your feet.
– Romans 16:20a (ESV)

The Church is God's people, those who love him and are loved by him with his personal, redemptive love. The church stands in a special relationship to God, to those who are part of the Church, and to all those outside the Church. The Church begins with Adam and Eve. In the beginning, the man was alone and could not complete his commission to rule the world in God's stead without a helper fit for him. Thus, God created the woman, a partner equal to him; the church was constituted by a relationship of mutual partnership in a shared mission, with the man as the head leading their partnership and the woman as the necessary help to see this purpose accomplished. They were created in right relationship with God, enjoying the pleasure of his presence and the responsibility of serving him. God entrusted to them the tasks of ruling over his creation as his representatives. Together they were to live before God, with one another, and outwardly in fulfilment of the kingdom mandate, to be fruitful, multiply, and subdue the earth.

Things, of course, went terribly wrong. The result of the curse was division in each of these relationships. Humanity was estranged from God (Gen 3:23-24, 4:1-7), one another (Gen 3:16), and their task (Gen 3:16-19). However, even as God announced the curse, he was working a plan to undo what had been done; through the woman would come a serpent crusher (Gen 3:15) who would end the opposition of the serpent and humanity. The Fall and the curse necessarily change the dynamics of the Church. Before the Fall, the Church was co-extensive with humanity. However, after the Fall, humanity was no longer united before God; they were divided in opposition to him and one another. There are the righteous, such as Abel—the offspring of the woman—and the unrighteous, such as Cain—the offspring of the

Devil. The church was now specifically that portion of humanity that was in a right relationship with God. From the beginning, there has been a righteous remnant, a remainder of humanity that has, by God's grace, followed him. Their story is the story of the Church; in it we see the evolution of the entity we call the Church, the New Testament ἐκκλησία (*ekklesia*, "church"). We will thus trace this story to elucidate the Church as a character in redemptive history before elucidating her nature.

Despite the Fall, God's purpose will still be accomplished, yet it will now go forth in opposition to fallen humanity and their king, the Serpent. Marked by warfare between one another, sin and thus separation from God, and Satanic opposition, God would act in all three dimensions to bring healing: he would bring healing in the Church's relationship to God, to the World, and one member to another. From Seth through Noah, a faithful remnant of God's people continued. Only with Abraham does this people begin to take on more defined contours and the solution to these problems, hinted at earlier, gain clarity.

a. Abraham

Through Abraham, God would bring about a multitude of people; God would fulfil the kingdom mandate through Abraham, multiplying his descendants and establishing a king over them (Gen 12:1-3; 17:5-8). Genesis 15 indicates that because of God's own actions on his people's behalf—even his death—relationship with him would be maintained. Through the multitude of Abraham's descendants, all the peoples of the earth would be blessed (Gen 12:1-3). That is, God would unite divided humanity, make them a kingdom, and reconcile them to himself.

b. The Sons of Israel

God's hand of favour is demonstrated throughout the narratives of Abraham and Isaac, even when both acted sinfully. With Jacob, we are confronted with a character who is corrupt and yet the object of God's special purpose. Through sinful means, Jacob receives his father's blessing and is singled out as the one through whom God will accomplish his kingdom purposes. God works extraordinarily through Jacob's children, especially Joseph, yet Judah receives particular mention. Among other moments, the narrative of his unrighteous behaviour with Tamar highlights the continuation of his line (Genesis 38). In the final blessings of Abraham and Jacob, Judah receives special attention. Through him will come a king (Gen 49:8-12).

c. The Nation of Israel

Through the Exodus, God's redemptive purpose leaps forward in dramatic ways. God enters a covenant with his people, dramatically demonstrating his power and his goodwill towards them. He makes them his very own people, a prized possession (Exod 19:1-6). The Law instituted in the Torah reveals an answer to all three of the needs introduced by the Fall.

God's people were to conduct themselves towards one another with love and faithfulness. They were to give justice to the widow and orphan and take care of the poor among them. Justice was to be swift towards the evil doer, yet not without mercy.

To provide for a relationship with him, God instituted the priesthood and the sacrificial system. He would dwell in their midst through the Tabernacle and Ark. A sacrificial system would be a constant reminder of sin, discouraging intentional sins and displaying the cost of unintentional ones. God's abhorrence towards sin was viscerally demonstrated by the bloody death of an animal. A life for a life, such was the cost of sin.

The Torah also constituted Israel in contrast with the nations. The extensive purity laws made every aspect of life, from food and dress to burial practices, an intentional demonstration of the distinctiveness of this nation. They were to be a kingdom of priests, mediating God to the world. Even at the time of the Exodus, some were already drawn by God's glorious power (Exod 12:38).

However, though the Torah was good and holy, it was an impermanent solution (e.g. Hebrews 8). Especially in its sacrificial system, it had no clear map for victory. Its institutions would hold off sin but not end it, invite the nations but not persuade them, and provide for justice but not end human distress and social strife. Most fundamentally, it would not provide that which was most needed, a heart remedy. Deuteronomy ends with a testimony to Israel's future failures; their future apostasy is memorialised in a song as a warning to a future generation. Yet this immanent apostasy promised something better. In Deuteronomy 29-30, God showed his people that they would fail and be sent far from their homeland, yet something would change. They would return and be restored. Why? Because God himself would change their apostate hearts (Deut 30:6). Because of their sinful hearts, they were incapable of fulfilling the Torah, yet God would bridge the chasm and bring his law into their hearts, where they could act on it. God would give them hearts to love him, yet it was unclear how this would be accomplished.

d. The Apostates and the Remnant

Because not all of God's covenant people had these new hearts, they were a mixed people: the wicked and righteous lived side by side. National Israel would never succeed in its mission because the offspring of the woman and of the serpent coexisted. As Paul puts it, not all Israel was Israel (Rom 9:6). Yet God preserved a remnant of the faithful throughout Israel's history.

When the people rejected God's rule and demanded a king, God granted them Saul. Nevertheless, he was already raising up a king of his own choosing, David. David was far from perfect, yet he was nevertheless loyal to God. His sons were, for the most part, not cut from the same cloth. From their leadership to the poor peasants, Israel and Judah were rife with apostasy. Yet through his prophets, God continued to speak, setting aside a remnant for himself. Through the prophets, he shed further light on a day when he would enable his people to serve him. Through Babylon, he saved a remnant of Judah. However, when they returned to the land under Cyrus and subsequent Persian kings, it became apparent that full spiritual restoration and the promised new covenant had not yet been granted (e.g. Ezra 3:12; 10:1-44; Nehemiah 13). With the closing of the Old Testament narrative in the late 5th century BC, God's people still awaited the day when he would permanently bridge their relationship with him, provide a faithful community united in purpose and peace, and crush the serpent, completely establishing his kingdom.

e. The Church in the New Testament

Roughly 400 years later, something happened. In the time between the closing of the Old Testament and the beginning of the New, many things transpired, yet God's plan to institute his kingdom on earth made no progress. Then something remarkable happened. A faithful priestly couple became pregnant, and Zechariah was made mute for questioning the angel, Gabriel. Their son, John, was declared in prophecy to be the forerunner of the Messiah. To the attentive listener, echoes of the story of Samson and Samuel's births and Isaiah's prophecies were invoked (Jdgs 13:1-25; 1 Sam 1:1-28). Then their relative Mary, a young, betrothed woman, was told she would bear a son before she would be with her husband. This child would be Immanuel, who would save his people from their sins (Isa 7:10-17).

Like Samuel, Jesus grew in wisdom and stature, yet he would prove to be far greater than his predecessor. Along with the witness of the Father and the Spirit, he revealed himself to be God himself incarnate, the long-awaited king who would rule on God's throne. Yet he would not conquer through military might or political prowess. No, as a humble servant, he set his face towards Jerusalem and went to his death. The spotless lamb of God bore the sins of his people on the cross, drinking in full of the cup of his Father's fury against sin. The serpent had snapped at the offspring's heel, yet what appeared to be victory for the serpent was transformed when Christ rose from the dead. The price was paid; the power of sin and death conquered. Satan was stripped of his power, bound, and cast to the earth. On Calvary, the hill of skull, the Serpent's head was crushed. Christ had delivered the fatal blow. Yet though dying, the serpent was not yet dead. As Christ ascended to his Father's right hand, he entrusted his people with the job of enacting the victory he had secured. There was still work to be done, "filling up what was lacking in Christ's afflictions" (Col 1:24): Christ had secured the victory but would work through the Church, his body, to bring it to completion. God would crush the serpent under their feet (Rom 16:20). This would reach its climax when Christ comes again on the clouds, ready to judge the living and the dead.

Christ gave his church the charge to build his kingdom. He was on the throne; he commanded them to "go therefore and make disciples of all nations, baptizing them in the name of the Father, the Son, and the Holy Spirit, teaching them to observe all that I commanded you" (Matt 28:19-20). Under the leadership of the apostles and filled with the power of the Holy Spirit, the Church made amazing progress. Thousands in Judea were saved at first, then many more in Samaria, across the Roman Empire, and beyond.

Jesus had torn down "the dividing wall of hostility" (Eph 2:14), so all were welcome; Jew and Gentile, slave and free, all were one in Christ Jesus (Gal 3:18). Jesus restored the relationship among people, he restored the relationship between humanity and God, and he guaranteed the success of God's kingdom in the world. By the end of the 1st century, Christians were found witnessing to and dying for Christ, their Lord, across the known world.

However, all was not glamour and glory. For as much as God has filled all his people with his Spirit and guaranteed their faithfulness, Satan would not go without a fight. As Jesus had warned, the enemy had sown weeds among the good harvest of the saints; there were sheep and wolves among God's people. The apostolic letters testify to the reality that the church was not perfect. The seven letters to the churches in Revelation 1-3 are a sober diagnosis of the trials and troubles facing the churches, and an indictment of those that fell short of God's call. Yet, despite these troubles, Revelation reveals that all is unfolding according to God's perfect plan. The Lamb is worthy and unleashes God's plan to bring the old to an end and usher in a perfect new creation. "Endure," Christ tells his people through John, "hold fast my promises." He assures us that he is coming quickly: labour now, for rest and restoration are coming. The Church has fallen short of its ideal, but the beautiful hope of Revelation 21 is that the bride will descend from heaven in perfected glory: the full number of the saints will be called and preserved. Christ's bride will be prepared.

This is the tension of the "latter days," in which we now live. God's promises have been enacted yet not brought to completion. The Church has been called and given life by the Spirit yet remains imperfect. Its mission goes forth with the assurance of victory, yet there is no shortage of disheartening testimonies. Yet Christ's proclamation remains true: "Behold, I am coming quickly!" When he comes, his bride will be prepared in all her beauty and receive a crown and eternal life.

f. The Church in These Last Days

A sober look at church history from the 2nd century AD reveals the same picture we see in the New Testament: God's purpose is going forward, but it does not achieve perfect progress. The 2nd and 3rd centuries are filled with amazing testimonies of martyrs giving their all for Christ alongside theological trajectories that should trouble us. The 4th and 5th centuries witness different struggles, different stories of victories, and different defeats. We could pick several highlights, yet in each case, the fruit is ambiguous. The Apologists, and Origin after them, produced monumental feats of the intellect in defence of their Christian faith, yet when weighed against the Bible, many of their works contain problematic theological conclusions. Nicaea in 325 AD was, in many ways, a monumental victory in favour of the biblical testimony to Christ. Some of the language used in this creed would be decisive in shaping enduring conflicts and the trajectory of theology for centuries to come. Yet this language was, arguably, ambiguous when used and invited the synthesis of biblical theology with Greek metaphysics that characterised the so-called Cappadocian settlement.[14] Chalcedon in 451 seemed to be a triumph for a biblical doctrine of Christ, yet it triggered severe division within the Eastern church, within churches that were eager to maintain the full humanity and deity of Christ but used different metaphysical categories and terminology.[15]

The following centuries saw rapid developments in theology and the Church's life, including division among the Eastern churches and, then, between the East and the West. In the later Middle Ages, the church in the West grew more and more corrupt; in the East, the growing presence of Islam produced unique challenges and opportunities for ministry.

The Reformation was a response to corruption in the Western Church, producing much fruit. However, it was followed by more division and led to monumental shifts in Western culture. In the immediate aftermath, Reformed, Anabaptist, and Catholic churches were all responsible for atrocities inflicted on their Christian brothers and sisters. Though much good can be said about the Reformed intellect, the intellectual approach to theology that was nurtured within Reformed denominations blossomed into

---

[14] See J. Alexander Rutherford, *The Trinity and the Bible: How All Scripture Testifies to One God in Three Persons* (Campbell River, BC: Teleioteti, 2022). Cf. J. Alexander Rutherford, "Whose Fall? What Hellenism? Christianity's Fall into Hellenistic Philosophy Revisited," *The Teleioteti Journal for Christian Ministry* 1, no. 1 (2023): 1–40, https://doi.org/10.60080/cliw1201.

[15] See James Rutherford, *Rightly Defining the Son of God*, forthcoming PhD thesis (Moore Theological College, 2023).

the academisation of church ministry in the post-Enlightenment West. Church groups persecuted one another, and others drifted into stagnant faith. Stagnation was sometimes interrupted by bursts of renewed spiritual vitality, yet the endurance of this vitality in following generations is questionable. In the 19th and 20th centuries—and now the 21st century—good and beautiful things have happened in the Church across the globe alongside saddening developments. The Western church shows signs of severe degradation in its spiritual vitality, biblical fidelity, and even its sense of purpose.

Once the driver of world missions, it has now become a vast mission field. It has also been responsible for propagating some of the worst false doctrines, including the so-called "prosperity gospel," which has had a devastating impact worldwide, especially in the majority-world countries. Though the Church in every nation faces its own struggles, the African, Asian, and South American continents have experienced amazing growth. However, even here, the story of North Korea has been a tragic one; before the 1960s, the entire peninsula experienced the phenomenal growth of the Church as a result of late 19th-century and early 20th-century Presbyterian missions. Since the Korean War, the North has heavily persecuted Christians and the South has been plagued with cults. China has also witnessed phenomenal growth in churches and converts, despite waves of intense persecution. Africa tells a similar story. The African Church has proved to be a bulwark against doctrinal decay for many Western churches, holding their ground on biblical teaching while churches in England, Canada, Australia, and the United States have drifted.

The 20th and 21st-century developments in the Church give us an important insight into prior generations. Often, success and failure in the early church has been measured in terms of key events and figures. There are the colossal intellectuals of the early church, such as Athanasius, Augustine, and Cyril, and later leaders, such as Aquinas, Luther, Calvin, and Wesley. There are key victories and defeats, such as the conversion of Constantine, the councils of Nicaea, Constantinople, and Chalcedon, the Great Schism, the Crusades, and the Reformation. There are parallels in the 20th century, with the Barman Declaration, the Lausanne Covenant, and the ministries of Billy Graham and John Stott in the English-speaking world. However, for all its faults, the flourishing of global media has allowed us to look beyond these few events to witness the real causes of the Church's failures and successes.

I don't believe we have to ignore the serious deficits in the greatest moments and brightest minds of the early church to recognize God's continuing work in history. We can and must learn from our past, reading alongside our predecessors to grow in our understanding of Scripture while soberly evaluating their judgments and doctrines in order to hold fast what is good but not perpetuate error.[16] The results of such judgments need not threaten our understanding of God's purpose working out in history, for church councils and towering intellects are not the key players in God's strategy to win the world.

Behind the scenes are everyday pastors and parishioners serving with zeal or falling into stagnancy, and every state in between. The failures and successes of the Western Church are not traceable to distinct moments or towering figures; there are stories of minor compromises and cut corners alongside stories of God's amazing work through faithful men and women labouring for his name. The successes in the worldwide Church are similar. Surely this has been the case throughout Church history. Nicaea, Chalcedon, Augustine, and Calvin are parts of a broader tapestry of God's work in local congregations and their leaders to see his kingdom come and his will be done. This is where the Bible's concern lies. Here, the victories are won and battles lost each day. It is here that his victory will assuredly be won. After God himself, the Church is the key player in redemptive history, yet the biblical model for the visible life of the church is not found in trans-global institutions, in national or denominational "churches," but in local congregations.

2. That There Is an Invisible Church (Cf. CPD Ch. II).

> As for you, you shall keep my covenant, you and your offspring after you throughout their generations. This is my covenant, which you shall keep, between me and you and your offspring after you: Every male among you shall be circumcised. You shall be circumcised in the flesh of your foreskins, and it shall be a sign of the

---

[16] Cf. Rutherford, *The Trinity*, 183-270.

covenant between me and you. – Genesis 17:9-11 (ESV)

And no longer shall each one teach his neighbor and each his brother, saying, 'Know the LORD,' for they shall all know me, from the least of them to the greatest, declares the LORD. – Jeremiah 31:34 (ESV)

Our survey of Church in Redemptive history concluded with an eye to the local church, yet before we consider the local church and its significance, we need to back up a bit and consider God's people from a different perspective. It may seem odd to some readers that I will discuss the concepts of "covenant community," the "remnant," and the "invisible church" together under the heading "invisible church," for the first and the last term are ecclesiological— they are regularly discussed in the context of a theology of the Church—yet the middle term is biblical-theological: we talk about the "remnant" when we speak of the Old Testament and apostate Israel. Moreover, these categories do not, at first glance, seem to line up, for the remnant is only a portion of the covenant community, and it may not be clear how the "invisible church" corresponds to either category. However, these terms have significant overlap when we read them across the narrative of Scripture; grasping their connection is important for our understanding of the Church today, under the New Covenant. We will begin by looking at all three terms as they pertain to the Old Testament and then the New Testament.

a. Under the Old Covenant

"Covenant" is a key concept in the Bible; it features prominently in Old Testament theology, yet it is essential to understanding both Testaments. A covenant refers to a formal relationship enacted between two parties, whether individuals or groups. A covenant usually involves obligations for both parties, with corresponding rewards or blessings and punishments or curses for fulfilling or failing one's obligations. Covenants were common throughout the ancient world, but all these features are attested in the Bible. We find covenants between Abraham and Abimelech (Gen 21:22-34), and covenants enacted by the Jewish leaders (Jeremiah 34), yet the covenants that are most significant are those that God enters into with humanity. Here we are particularly concerned with the covenant variously called the Sinaitic, Mosaic, Israeli, or Old Covenant. This is the covenant after which the Old

Testament is named, "Testament" and the Latin *testamentum* being translations of the Hebrew and Greek words for a covenant (בְּרִית, *berit*; διαθήκη, *diatheke*). The Old Testament is particularly the covenant constitution or "Law" (תּוֹרָה, *torah*) governing the relationship God establishes with Israel at Mount Sinai. This covenant has two parties, God, who initiates the covenant, and Israel, who are bound in faithfulness to God, their covenant Lord. The "covenant community" refers to all those who constitute "Israel," all those governed by this covenant.

i. The Covenant Community

The Old Covenant is a sweeping institution, constituting a socio-political nation and establishing various social and ceremonial statutes along with the religious *cultus*. We will talk more about the institutional dimension of the Old Covenant in the following section (§3); here, I want to focus on the covenant community. In particular, I want to answer the "who" and "how" questions.

As I said above, the OT covenant community is the entire nation of Israel, regardless of anyone's personal regard for Yahweh, the God of Israel. Faithful and unfaithful Israelites were under a Covenant and stood to gain life from obedience (Lev 18:6; Deut 28:1-14) or curses for disobedience (Deut 13:1-5; Deut 28:15-68). These blessings can be seen on both the individual and corporate levels: individually, faithfulness to the covenant meant a right relationship with God and the hope of resurrection life, whereas faithlessness meant death and punishment. Corporately, the nation's obedience would lead to numerous blessings, health for humans and animals alike, peace from warfare, economic stability, etc.; disobedience would result in war, plagues, and exile. Because the OT covenant community was mixed in this way, containing the faithful and the unfaithful alike, its history is a roller coaster ride of blessings and curses. The books of Kings and Chronicles bring out this reality in different yet complementary ways: in Kings, we see the trajectory of Israel's unfaithfulness leading to the divided kingdom, the end of the Northern Kingdom, and the exile of the Southern Kingdom. Chronicles illustrate blessing and curse in the life of individual kings, showing how obedience to God resulted in blessing and disobedience resulted in curses. So, when we speak of the "covenant community" with reference to the Old Testament, we mean all of physical Israel.

Most people were born into this covenant, symbolised by the circumcision of every male (who would represent all female members of their family under the covenant): circumcision was a visible sign of covenant commitment, analogous to the severed animals lined up by Abraham in Genesis 15. Circumcision was a sign of blessing and curse in the area of reproduction, a key aspect of God's promises to Abraham and the whole narrative of Scripture: God would crush the Serpent, Satan, through the offspring of Eve; this offspring would come through Abraham. However, though entrance into the covenant was primarily through birth, we also find examples of those who willingly entered into the covenant. Many leave Egypt with Israel, a "mixed multitude" (12:38); we also read of Rahab and Ruth (perhaps also Tamar), who marry into the covenant and demonstrate fidelity to Yahweh (Genesis 38; Joshua 2:1-21, 6:17; Ruth, especially 4:13-22; Matt 1:3-5; Heb 11:31; James 2:25). Presumably, males who chose to join the covenant would be circumcised (cf. Exod 12:44).

ii. The Remnant and the Invisible Church

So, the covenant community was co-extensive with physical Israel, yet as Paul tells us in Romans 9:6, "not all who are descended from Israel belong to Israel." That is, there was always a minority of those faithfully following God within the covenant community; these are identified as a "remnant" throughout the prophets—sometimes amounting to a minuscule portion of the population (e.g. 1 Kgs 19:18). These are true Israel, those who receive God's covenant blessings and are the object of his saving affections from eternity past. Thus, the remnant is only a portion of the Old Testament covenant community. The term "invisible church" is usually used in discussions of the New Testament Church or the Church without reference to either covenant; however, we can apply the term specifically to our discussion of the Old Covenant. The "invisible church" can refer to the entire universal church, all believers from the beginning of creation until its consummation, alive on earth or in heaven, or to believers—those who are in right relationship with God—on earth at any one time. Used in this later sense, for all believers on earth at some time (classically, this was called "the church militant"), the invisible church under the Old Covenant was co-extensive with the remnant.

iii. The Problem of a Mixed Community

The division between covenant community, remnant, and invisible church in the Old Covenant is not presented as the ideal state; indeed, it is treated as a significant problem. The covenant blessings, including land and peace, rely on the people and their leadership being faithful to Yahweh, so a mixed community jeopardises the fulfilment of God's promises. God's purpose to demonstrate his glory through these people as they stand forth distinct from their neighbours would fail if the community were mixed—faithful and apostate alike (Lev 20:22-26). Much of Israel's ceremonial life was intended to mirror the ideal of a pure, faithful community: they were to eat unmixed food, wear unmixed fabric, etc. (Lev 11:1-8; Lev 19:19; Deut 22:9-11). They needed to do so if they were to have God dwelling in their midst, as Paul brings out in a compound of several Old Testament passages,

> "I will make my dwelling among them and walk among them,
>   and I will be their God,
>   and they shall be my people.
> Therefore go out from their midst,
>   and be separate from them, says the Lord,
> and touch no unclean thing;
>   then I will welcome you,
> and I will be a father to you,
>   and you shall be sons and daughters me,
> says the Lord Almighty." (Lev 26:12; Isa 52:11; and others [e.g. 2 Sam 7:14, Exod 4:22]) in 2 Cor 6:16-18)

In pursuit of holiness, those who taught the worship of other gods or practised pagan religion were to be driven out and put to death (Deut 13:1-18; 18:9-14; Lev 20:27). However, Israel never achieved this ideal; they remained a mixed community.

The problem lay in their hearts; the majority of Israel lacked the ability to obey God; they were hardened towards him at the very centre of their being (Deut 5:29; 10:16). As Moses tells them, "to this day the LORD has not given you a heart to understand or eyes to see or ears to hear" (Deut 29:4).[17]

---

[17] See J. Alexander Rutherford, *Prevenient Grace: An Investigation into Arminianism*, 2nd Revised Ed., Teleioteti Technical Studies 2 (Vancouver: Teleioteti, 2020).

For Israel to obey God and receive his blessings, they needed to have soft, obedient hearts, yet they were unable to circumcise their own hearts as God commanded them to (Deut 10:16). As of yet, God had not given them obedient hearts. For this reason, the curses were sure to fall upon Israel (Deut 30:1), yet after they had fallen, something would change; Israel would then remember the words of blessing and curse (Deut 30:2), and they would return to God and obey him (Deut 30:3, Hebrew).[18] Thus far, they were hardened in sin, and God had not yet given them obedient hearts. What has changed to bring about obedience? Deuteronomy 30:6 tells us, "And Yahweh, your God, will circumcise your heart and the heart of your offspring so that you will love Yahweh your God with all your heart and all your soul, so that you may live" (my translation). Because of their sin, the law was impossible to keep (Deut 30:11-13), yet in this future day—after they were sent into exile— "it will be very near to you, in your mouth and in your heart, so that you will do it" (Deut 30:14, my translation). God would one day give Israel obedient hearts, yet that day had not yet arrived. So hardened were they in their sin that God gave them a song to sing, anticipating the day when they would turn away from him and receive the covenant curses; this song was a witness to their brazen rebellion (Deut 31:1-29, esp. v. 19; 31:30-32:47). The hope of Deuteronomy 30:6-14 is picked up throughout the Old Testament, and it is clarified: God would not give believing hearts to *some* of his covenant people. No, he would give it to everyone:

> For this is the covenant that I will make with the house of Israel after those days, declares the Lord: I will put my law within them, and I will write it on their hearts. And I will be their God, and they shall be my people. And no longer shall each one teach his neighbor and each his brother, saying, 'Know the Lord,' for they shall all know me, from the least of them to the greatest, declares the Lord. For I will forgive their iniquity, and I will remember their sin no more. (Jer 31:33-34)

> All your children shall be taught by the Lord,

---

[18] "And when all these things come upon you—the blessing and the curse, which I have placed before you—then you will return these things to your heart among all the nations where Yahweh your God scattered you." My translation, in ibid. 260. See *Prevenient Grace* Appendix 1 for a translation of Deuteronomy 30:1-14 and a defence of the interpretation presented above (also printed in, *The Gift of Reading – Part 2* in *The Gift of Knowledge*).

and great shall be the peace of your children. (Isa 54:13)

> I will sprinkle clean water on you, and you shall be clean from all your uncleannesses, and from all your idols I will cleanse you. And I will give you a new heart, and a new spirit I will put within you. And I will remove the heart of stone from your flesh and give you a heart of flesh. And I will put my Spirit within you, and cause you to walk in my statutes and be careful to obey my rules. (Ezek 36:25-27)

No longer would God's covenant community consist of believers and unbelievers alike, unregenerate and regenerate alike. No, under the New Covenant, "they shall all know me, from the least of them to the greatest." As a result, because of God's new covenant work to ensure faith and blessing for his people, "great shall be the peace of your children."[19] No longer would curses be visited on God's covenant people. Thus, with the New Covenant will come a new understanding of the covenant community; there is some overlap in these categories but also important differences.

b. Under the New Covenant

Under the New Testament, the covenant community, the remnant, and the invisible church are co-extensive. The New Covenant has arrived, secured by Jesus' sacrifice (Luke 22:20); the Old Covenant has passed away (Hebrews 8). The promise of the Holy Spirit giving true faith to God's people has come, as Jesus tells those who grumble about his teaching, "No one can come to me unless the Father who sent me draws him. And I will raise him up on the last day. It is written in the Prophets, 'And they will all be taught by God.' Everyone who has heard and learned from the Father comes to me" (John 6:44-45). The Spirit is calling, and all who are called respond; they all become part of God's covenant community. After Pentecost, Peter declares the fulfilment of Joel's prophecy about the pouring out of the Spirit, his miracle-working power being closely associated with his life-giving power,

> And in the last days it shall be, God declares,

---

[19] On this aspect of the newness of the New Covenant, see Peter J. Gentry and Stephen J. Wellum, *Kingdom through Covenant: A Biblical-Theological Understanding of the Covenants*, 2nd Ed. (Wheaton: Crossway, 2018), chaps. 12–14.

that I will pour out my Spirit on all flesh,
and your sons and your daughters shall prophesy,
and your young men shall see visions,
and your old men shall dream dreams;
even on my male servants and female servants
in those days I will pour out my Spirit, and they shall prophesy.
(Acts 2:17-18)

In the New Covenant, all who are part of the covenant are enabled to believe; they are grafted into Christ and in him enjoy "every spiritual blessing in the heavenly places" (Eph 1:3).

However, though the covenant community is now identical to the invisible church (two things divided under the Old Covenant are now united), a new division is created by the arrival of the New Covenant. From our experience—and throughout the New Testament—not everyone who claims to be a Christian is so (Matt 7:21-23), and not every "church" is a manifestation of Christ's body. Jesus, through John, warns the church in Sardis that though once alive, it is now dead and would miss out on the resurrection of life if it did not repent (Rev 3:1-6). Under the Old Testament, the covenant community was visible; it had a discreet location, and its participants were physically marked by circumcision or usually related to a man so marked. Thus, the covenant community was identical to the *visible* church, which we will discuss in the next chapter. However, in the New Testament, the covenant community is identical to the invisible church: God's promises are all yes in Christ for all those in this covenant (2 Cor 1:20), but this does not mean this is the case for every person who calls themselves a Christian or every so-called church. The covenant community is not visible. Paul, for example, warns of false teachers arising from within the churches (Acts 20:29-30). John identifies false teachers in the church to whom he writes (1 John 2:19). So, we must keep these two realities distinct: the covenant community consists of all those who are drawn by the Father through the Holy Spirit, respond in faith, are united with Christ, and will be raised on the last day. When someone formerly identifying as a Christian walks away from the faith, never to return, it is thus demonstrated that they were never part of the invisible church and covenant community.

The invisible church or covenant community is what I mean when I write of the "Church," though "Church" with a capital C has sometimes been used in the tradition for the visible or global church (which we will discuss in the following chapter). The invisible church is always visible to some degree, yet it is visible in a mixed form, so the visible, global church (as opposed to the local church) is not co-extensive with the invisible church; it represents the invisible church in an impure or mixed form. The Church invisible is what the Bible speaks of as the bride of Christ, the New Jerusalem which will descend from heaven, clothed in beautiful garb and prepared for the eschatological wedding feast. The New Covenant is like a marriage covenant, with a betrothal now and the wedding to come; because the invisible Church is the bride, this marriage covenant is unstained by the faithlessness and adultery that characterised the Old Covenant. The Church invisible is also the body of Christ, the visible presence of the invisible God. The *invisible* Church is the *visible* presence of the invisible God because the *invisible* Church is always instantiated in a physical, tangible form in local churches and their interrelationships (the global church). We don't collapse the invisible Church into its visible instantiations because it is always instantiated imperfectly; there is always a mixture in the visible church, believers and unbelievers side-by-side. This will be the case until the final day when God's angels will come and separate the weeds from the wheat, the sheep from the goats. However, while the Bible is clear that the local church always contains a mixture and that among local churches there will be false teachers and, as a result, false congregations, it also sets forth an ideal of the New Covenant Church. The ideal, visible Church is pure, perfect in righteousness, prepared for her groom, our Lord Jesus Christ:

> Then one of the seven angels who had the seven bowls filled with the seven final plagues came and spoke with me, saying, "Come, I will show you the bride, the wife of the lamb." [10]He carried me in the spirit up to a great and tall mountain and showed me the holy city, Jerusalem, descending from heaven from God. [11]The city had the glory of God. Its radiance was like most precious stone, like jasper as clear as crystal, [12]and it had great and tall walls. It had twelve gates, and upon the twelve gates were twelve angels, and the gates had names written on them, which were the names of the twelve tribe of the sons of Israel. [13]On the east side were three gates; on the north side, three gates; on the south side, three gates; and on the west side, three gates. [14]The walls of the gates had twelve foundations and upon them were the names of the twelve apostles of the lamb. (Rev 21:9-14)

This is where we are heading, yet we are not there yet. The New Covenant has arrived, so the perfected community spoken of by Isaiah, Jeremiah, and Ezekiel is here, yet it has not fully arrived. New Testament scholars speak of an already-not-yet tension in the New Testament: God's promises have arrived, yet they await their fulfilment at Christ's second coming. Because of this already-not-yet tension, we speak of the invisible Church in distinction from the visible church. The reality of the invisible Church is the "already": God's promises have been fulfilled; the Spirit has been poured out; all who the Father draws respond and will be raised to new life; we are sanctified, saints already; we, the Church, are the bride of Christ, for whom Christ died.

In Ephesians, Paul writes that the Church "is his body, the fullness of him who fills all in all" (Eph 1:23). The Church is "the fullness of Christ," who is God (cf. Eph 2:18-22; 3:19). This Church has received "every spiritual blessing in the heavenly places," seated as we are with him in heaven (Eph. 1:20, 2:6). For this Church, "all things work together for good," from calling through to glory (Rom 8:28-30). These things are all true now, yet when we zoom in on the local church and all those communities who call themselves a Christian church, we are confronted by individuals and communities for which these things are not true. There are clearly unbelievers in our gatherings—and there are some who look perfectly faithful on the outside and yet will hear "I never knew you" on the day of judgment (Matt 7:21-23). So, the "invisible Church" refers to that invisible reality known only to God—the elect throughout the ages. We get a glimpse of this perfect congregation in Hebrews: after recounting the saints throughout the ages surrounding believers as they run their race—as if cheering them on (Heb 12:1-2)—the author then paints a picture of this invisible community encompassing all the righteous, angels and humans. The covenant community is contrasted with the physical Mount Sinai; Israel arrived at this mountain in the wilderness, and they were terrified by fire, lightning, smoke and dark clouds, by the trumpet sound "a voice whose words made the hearers beg that no further messages be spoken to them." At these sights, even Moses trembled in fear (Heb 12:18-21). This is not the Mountain that Christians have come to:

> But you have come to Mount Zion and to the city of the living God, the heavenly Jerusalem, and to innumerable angels in festal gathering, and to the assembly of the firstborn who are enrolled in heaven, and to God, the judge of all, and to the spirits of the righteous made perfect, and to Jesus, the mediator of a new covenant, and to the sprinkled blood that speaks a better word than the blood of Abel. (Heb 12:22-24)

No matter how mixed the global church appears, this reality remains: there is a faithful remnant, an invisible community that has received all of God's promises and is empowered by the Spirit for faithful ministry. Though the external reality in the time before Christ's return may look like the Old Covenant, where God's promises are not fulfilled because of the unfaithfulness of his people, this is not the real picture. Behind the veil of brokenness and falsehood stands this grand reality, an assembly enrolled in heaven, ransomed by God, purchased by the blood of his son; a community empowered and filled with the Spirit, strengthened by God through their faith to endure and receive all his good promises at the end of this age. They are the firstborn of the new creation, the inbreaking of the future, perfect reality into this old, broken one. Because the invisible church exists and is the recipient of God's promises in Christ, the purpose God has given his church will succeed.

The Church is not the fullness of Christ if they obey; they are the fullness of Christ now because they do obey—however imperfectly that obedience may be. The Church is not the body of Christ when they obey him; they are his body now to those with the eyes to see the truth. God is working a plan of reconciliation in this world through his people to bring those who are now far off close to him (Eph 2:11-22; 2 Cor 5:11-21). This plan will succeed. Its success has been purchased by the precious Lamb of God; "He who did not spare his own Son but gave him up for us all, how will he not also with him graciously give us all things?" (Rom 8:32) Even now, God is working to defeat the ancient serpent, and "The God of peace will soon crush Satan under your feet. The grace of our Lord Jesus Christ be with you" (Rom 16:20). This victory is portrayed in Revelation 5 with a scroll, God's plans for the ages bound up; John cries out in sorrow for no one was found worthy to open the scroll and bring God's plan of redemption and judgment to completion (v. 4), but an elder approaches John and points him to the "Lion of the Tribe of Judah," who has achieved victory and thus can open the scroll and its seals. All heaven breaks out in praise, responding to this Lion, the sacrificial lamb who was slain,

> Worthy are you
>   to take the scroll
>   and to open its seals
> for you were slain
>   and you redeemed us for God by your blood,
>   people from every tribe and tongue, people, and nation.
> You made them a kingdom and priests to our God,
>   and they will rule upon the earth. (5:9-10)

Victory is certain; God's people will rule. For all who are in Christ, all the promises of God are "yes" in Christ Jesus (2 Cor 1:20). This is true of the invisible church, the New Covenant community.

3. That the Visible Church Consists of Congregations (Cf. CPD Chs. II)

> I hope to come to you soon, but I am writing these things to you so that, if I delay, you may know how one ought to behave in the household of God, which is the church of the living God, a pillar and buttress of the truth. – 1 Timothy 3:14-15

When we read the New Testament closely, we perceive a picture that confronts our modern (and ancient) sensibilities. The fundamental players in God's purpose and plan for this world are neither individuals nor nations. Nowhere in the New Testament are we permitted to think that the Christian life is about any one of us and God, nor can we accomplish God's purposes as lone wolves. Descriptively, we find the apostles working with a vast number of compatriots in their ministries, and Jesus himself gathered to himself a great number of disciples whom he sent out to do the work of ministry. God himself in the flesh was not a one-man army (e.g. Luke 10:1-12). The task of church leaders is to train Christians for the work of ministry (Eph 4:11-14), which has its end not in the endurance or growth of the individual but in the mature stature of the whole body of Christ bound together in unity. The life of a Christian is eminently social and relational: in Ephesians 4, it is speaking the truth in love (4:15-16). Elsewhere, it is any number of the "one another" commands. 1 Corinthians 12 and Romans 12 both capture this vision with the picture of a body and its parts: it takes each part of the body for it to function.

In the first part of this chapter, we saw how God's purposes are not tied to nations; Acts 1 reminds us of this point. The Jews in Jesus' day were expecting him to come and conquer their Roman oppressors with brute force, to establish God's kingdom on earth in purity. Even after the resurrection, Jesus's disciples asked him, "Will you at this time restore the kingdom to Israel?" (Acts 1:6) Restoration will come, yet God's plan was not to initiate a political revolution then, nor is it to do so now. Instead, Jesus tells them, "You will receive power when the Holy Spirit has come upon you, and you will be my witnesses in Jerusalem and in all Judea and Samaria, and to the end of the earth" (Acts 1:8). This echoes Christ's great commission,

> Going forth, make disciples of all peoples, baptising them into the name of the Father, the Son, and the Holy Spirit, teaching them to keep all of which I commanded you; behold, I am with you always, until the end of the age. (Matt 18:19-20, author's translation)

We also saw that God's purpose and plan involve the whole Church—the Church universal. The Church is Christ's body, the fullness of him who fills all things (Eph 1:23). Yet, we also saw that this invisible reality encompasses all the believing community from the beginning of creation until today with no one-to-one counterpart in the present. Below, we will see how the global church is not a discreet entity but rather the communion of local churches (I.5-6). Thus, when we consider the instantiation of the Church in the present day, the entities fulfilling its purpose, we are left with local churches. This is exactly the picture we find in the New Testament, of local churches as the fundamental players in God's plan for the ages under the New Covenant, as instantiations of the Invisible Church today. Between the Invisible Church and the individual Christian is the myriad of local churches spread across the globe.

When I speak of "the local church," I refer to local, delimited groups of Christians with recognised leadership and regular gatherings. Each of these components is necessary for a local church to exist, and they are recognisable throughout the New Testament and the last two millennia. Defined in this way, we immediately recognise the local church as the fundamental entity in the New Testament. In this section, I only hope to establish my contention that the local church is the fundamental entity in God's dispensation of the New Covenant. This is the central contention of congregational ecclesiology, so it is worth being clear about our argument on this point. The argument that the only ontological items in the visible church—the only thing that may be called a "church" in this tangible, temporal age—is based on two facets of the New Testament teaching: first, local churches are the context for the New Testament exhortations and the objects of all its instructions, that is, the whole New Testament attests to the centrality of the local church. Second, the only global expression of the invisible church is the communion of local churches: the Bible does not address, describe, or prescribe any trans-local, visible entity that may be called the "church" in this age. If the Bible is sufficient as we argued in the introduction to this book, then this is not an argument from silence but an argument from conspicuous absence. If God desired a visible, organisational "church" transcending local churches, he would have given us instruction for establishing such an entity. Instead, we find only instructions for the proper functioning of local churches and their communion with one another. In this section, we will focus on the local church as the object of the New Testament's address. The nature of a local church or a congregation will be delineated in the following section (I.4), and then the global expression of the church in local church communion will be shown (I.5).

a. The Content of the New Testament Is Addressed to the Local Churches

When we consider the pages of the New Testament, we find no abiding trans-local "church" or institution that bridges local congregations. The Apostles performed a trans-local role, but their office is not an abiding one (see I.5-6, III, VI); indeed, the book of Acts portrays their role as establishing local churches. Everywhere they go, they leave behind local churches; the rest of the New Testament consists of letters written either to particular churches (1-2 Corinthians; Philippians; 1-2 Thessalonians), groups of churches close together (Romans; Ephesians; Galatians), or individuals as parts of churches (1 Timothy, 2 Timothy, Titus, Philemon). We will discuss Paul's letters further in the following section, but the rest of the New Testament affirms that the local churches are the objects of biblical exhortation and instruction.

James and Peter appear to be writing to more than one local church, yet they are clearly writing to churches, neither individual believers nor larger entities. The content of Philemon appears to be a personal matter, yet it is addressed to Philemon's entire family and the church meeting in their house; after Philemon, 2 Timothy is the closest the New Testament has to a personal letter. Hebrews is addressed to a local church, though we cannot be sure of the details of its recipients (10:25). It is not clear who the recipients of Jude and 2 Peter are, yet the details are consistent with a discreet local church or group of local churches being addressed. The recipients of 1 John are not specified, and the style appears to be consistent with a group of churches; 2:19 and other verses suggest that it is again intended for local congregations. Revelation is addressed to seven local churches (chs. 1-3).

In Galatians, Paul writes not to "the church" but to the "churches" in Galatia (a region, not a city) (Gal 1:2; 1 Cor 16:1). Though the introduction of Philippians speaks generally of the saints (Phil 1:1), not "the church" (like the letters to the Roman and Colossian churches), Philippians appears to be addressed to a single congregation. Philippians 4:15 refers to them as a church, and Philippians 1:1 speaks of "the overseers and deacons." The letter of Ephesians does not give us sufficient evidence in itself to determine if it is addressed to one church or several, yet in Acts, Paul meets with the "elders of the church" from Ephesus (Acts 20:17); in Revelation, Jesus speaks of "the church in Ephesus" (Rev 2:1). The letter has a general style suggesting that it could be addressed to multiple congregations; manuscript evidence suggests it was a circular letter, the same letter being sent to multiple churches in different cities.

Thus, the New Testament is primarily interested in local churches; it's instructions not only pertain to the life of local churches, but it is also primarily addressed to these churches. Furthermore, when we look closely at redemptive history, two facts emerge that support our argument that the local church is the key entity in God's purpose for the ages. The whole Bible concerns the Church Invisible, but as the Scriptures progress, this focus zooms in on the local church. Throughout the New Testament, allegiance to Christ our Lord manifests in a concrete commitment to a local church.

b. The Manifestation of the Invisible Church in the New Testament Is Local Churches

In God's plan for creation, the Church is preeminent. It is not the family, the state, or nature but the Church. The Church was established in the beginning and is the heart of God's plans for creation. The Bible begins and ends with a marriage, of Adam and Eve (Genesis 1-2) and Christ and his bride, the Church (Revelation 19-22). Juxtaposed with final judgment is the marriage feast of the lamb and the Church, prepared with glory for her wedding day (cf. Eph 5:25-32). In an important way, the marriage of Christ and his people, our eternal union with him, is the purpose of all creation. Earlier, we saw that God gave Adam and Eve the charge to expand his kingdom on earth, so in a sense, the kingdom of God is the goal of creation. And, of course, the whole purpose of the kingdom is to display God's glory in all its facets. The kingdom is the context for this display, yet it is not the sum of it. In Ephesians 5 we are told that Christ died to prepare for himself a bride, perfected in glory (5:25-32). Paul draws on the language of Genesis 1-2 and echoes the Old Testament theme of Israel as God's wife; however, the great mystery revealed in these last days concerns Christ and his Church (5:32).

God's people, the Church, are not an afterthought in his creation, merely plan B after the fall. The Church is the whole point of the creation. In light of the fall, many things needed to happen for God's purpose to be completed; the bride needed to be redeemed from her sins. From the beginning, the Church was charged with preparing the earth for the eternal reign of God; in light of the fall, this necessitated warfare. Nevertheless, from Genesis to Revelation, the Church is next to God at the centre of history; she is the object of his affection and redeeming actions and is the tool of his redemptive work.

If the Church is at the centre of God's plan for the ages, does it not follow that it should be at the centre of our lives? In the New Testament, Allegiance to Christ manifests in prioritising his Church, and his purpose through the Church is manifest as allegiance to a local church. It may be odd, at first, to say that we have allegiance to a local church, for we would usually say that our allegiance is with God and God alone. This is very true, but not the whole story. We are united with Christ, yet the Church is Christ's body, so our allegiance to him manifests in allegiance to her. We are loyal to Christ, yet the Church is his bride, and we cannot have him without her. God is our primary allegiance; we could say he is our allegiance on the vertical axis. To him alone we owe fidelity and submission. Yet God is present on earth in the Church, his work is accomplished through the Church, and his purpose for creation revolves around the Church. So, the Church is also our primary allegiance; we could say she is our allegiance on the horizontal axis. We do not get Christ apart from the Church, and God's mission will not be accomplished apart from her.

Consider several ways the Bible flips our conventional understanding to drive this point home. No area of life escapes being re-oriented to the Church in Scripture. In each case, this re-orientation will be manifested as our participation in the local church. Though not so much the case in the West, most cultures hold the family to be central to human life. However, the Bible calls for a radical re-orientation of this most fundamental commitment. When Jesus' physical family comes to speak with him, he informs those around him that his true family are his disciples (Matthew 12:46-50). Later, he describes his ministry in this way,

> Do not think that I have come to bring peace to the earth. I have not come to bring peace, but a sword. For I have come to set a man against his father, and a daughter against her mother, and a daughter-in-law against her mother-in-law. And a person's enemies will be those of his own household. Whoever loves father or mother more than me is not worthy of me, and whoever loves son or daughter more than me is not worthy of me. And whoever does not take his cross and follow me is not worthy of me. Whoever finds his life will lose it, and whoever loses his life for my sake will find it. (Matt 10:34–39; cf. Luke 14:26)

Notice the radical repudiation of traditional familial allegiance for the sake of the Gospel. This transformation perhaps explains an interesting scene in John's Gospel. At the cross, Mary alone of Jesus' physical family follows him. Instead of entrusting his mother's care to his unbelieving brothers (cf. John 7:5), Jesus entrusts her care to John, part of his spiritual family (John 19:26-27). Jesus states that it is possible, even likely, that Christians will lose their families for his sake. If one must choose between family and the Lord, allegiance to him takes precedence. Yet "there is no one who has left house or wife or brothers or parents or children, for the sake of the kingdom of

God, who will not receive many times more in this time, and in the age to come eternal life" (Luke 18:28-29). This here-and-now recompense is juxtaposed with the future inheritance of eternal life: it is through the local church that we Christians receive houses and family (cf. Matt 12:46-50, 19:29; Mark 10:29-31).

According to 1 Timothy 5:8, Christians are still expected to provide for their family (at least within the Church, notice how the reason is that the Church would not be burdened). However, Paul conceives of a radical reorientation at the heart of the family. This continues into his account of marriages between believers and unbelievers; when he touches upon this issue, his language differs significantly from his account of the Christological mystery of marriage in Ephesians 5:25-32. Paul encourages Christian spouses to remain with an unbeliever not because of the inviolability of marriage (cf. Matt 19:6; Eph 5:31) but because God may use it for a redemptive purpose (1 Cor 7:14; cf. 1 Pet 3:1). If an unbeliever leaves, Paul declares the believer free, that is, they may remarry (1 Cor 7:10-16). Paul also permits only marriage to believers: this closest of unions is only permitted "in the Lord" (1 Cor 7:39, cf. 2 Cor 6:14-7:1). Becoming a Christian, therefore, transforms even this closest union, subordinating it to the union with Christ and his body.

Not only is family reoriented, but ethnic and national allegiances are shattered (Rom 2:9-11; 11:11-24; Gal 3:28; Eph 2:11-3:13; Col 3:11; Heb 11:8-16, 13:13-14; 1 Pet 1:1, 1:17, 2:11), work is radically re-oriented (e.g. Eph 4:28; 2 Thess 3:6-12), and our relationship vis-à-vis secular authorities are relativised (Acts 4:18-20; 5:27-32; 39-42; cf. Exod 1:15-22, Exod 2:1-2 and Heb 11:23; Dan 3:1-18). Because we are drawn to familiarity and the comforts it avails us, we tend to be drawn toward those with the same experience and presuppositions. Humans tend towards tribalism, building closer relationships with those of the same ethnic group and society. Indeed, there is a Biblical account for this behaviour: social fragmentation is the result of the curse God poured out on humanity at Babel. United, humanity could achieve much, and with sinful hearts, that "much" would be sin, so God divided humanity through the barrier of language (Gen 11:1-9). However, through the Holy Spirit and the coming of the Gospel, God began to undo this curse,

When the day of Pentecost arrived, they were all together in one place. And suddenly there came from heaven a sound like a mighty rushing wind, and it filled the entire house where they were sitting. And divided tongues as of fire appeared to them and rested on each one of them. And they were all filled with the Holy Spirit and began to speak in other tongues as the Spirit gave them utterance. Now there were dwelling in Jerusalem Jews, devout men from every nation under heaven. And at this sound the multitude came together, and they were bewildered, because each one was hearing them speak in his own language. And they were amazed and astonished, saying,

> Are not all these who are speaking Galileans? And how is it that we hear, each of us in his own native language? Parthians and Medes and Elamites and residents of Mesopotamia, Judea and Cappadocia, Pontus and Asia, Phrygia and Pamphylia, Egypt and the parts of Libya belonging to Cyrene, and visitors from Rome, both Jews and proselytes, Cretans and Arabians—we hear them telling in our own tongues the mighty works of God.

And all were amazed and perplexed, saying to one another, "What does this mean?" But others mocking said, "They are filled with new wine." (Acts 2:1-13)

The Church is explicitly designed to abolish this tendency toward fragmentation. "There is neither," Paul tells us, "Jew nor Greek, slave nor free, no male or female, for you are all one in Christ Jesus" (Gal 3:28, cf. Col 3:11). Jew and Greek were baptized by the same Spirit into the same body (1 Cor 12:13). This leads to the beautiful scene in Revelation where a people gathered from "from every nation, from all tribes and peoples and languages" fall down and worship the Lamb in unity (Rev 7:9-17). The most significant division witnessed in the Bible is between Jew and Gentile, but with the coming of the New Covenant, the distinct role of Israel as a nation set apart for God has ceased (though, Rom 11:25-36). Now God's people are drawn from every nation on Earth, from Israel and the Gentiles. There are now also deeper lines of connection and unity than anything that separates us: we are united in covenant with Christ, part of his very bride, and share the same fundamental purpose, hope, king, and family. Speaking of Christ's work to abolish all that would previously distinguish one people from another in terms of superiority or radical differentiation, Paul writes that in Christ the "dividing wall of hostility" has been torn down (Eph 2:14). By uniting us to himself, Christ has bridged all potential points of division between believers.

However, this uniting work does not end merely with breaking down ethnic and national barriers. By uniting us to himself, Christ also re-orients the entire Christian life around himself. There is the kingdom mandate or great commission, which centres the life of God's people on going forth and creating disciples. The commands and instructions concerning this mandate throughout the New Testament are all-inclusive, touching upon every area of life. Consider Paul's instructions in Ephesians 4:28—a telling indicator of the pervasive transformation Christ's calling mandates. To the Christian who was once a thief, Paul writes, "Let the thief no longer steal, but rather let him labor, doing honest work with his own hands, so that he may have something to share with anyone in need" (ESV). Theft is a sin (Exod 20:15), so a Christian should obviously stop. However, Paul does not instruct the thief to stop his thievery because it is a sin: he redirects the thief's work toward the local church. In this context, Paul is unpacking the mutual ministry of believers within the local church (cf. Eph 4:11-32); Paul instructs the thief to work honestly and hard "so that he may have something to share with anyone in need" (cf. Acts 2:42-47, 4:32-37; 1 Cor 16:1-4; 2 Thess 3:6-12). Work, which in the West is treated with such centrality, is relativised to the mission of the Church. There is also our relation to the government and society around us. We are to pay taxes (Matt 22:15-22), submit in every way unless doing so would mean disobedience to our Lord Jesus Christ (Acts 4:18-20; 5:27-32; 39-42; cf. Exod 1:15-22, Exod 2:1-2 and Heb 11:23; Dan 3:1-18)—which is a high bar to meet —and to honour the emperor (Rom 13:1-7; Titus 3:1; 1 Pet 2:13-17). We are to do these things in submission to Christ so that our lives might be exemplary, not thwarting but aiding the purpose of the church (2 Cor 8:21; Phil 2:15; 1 Tim 2:1-4; Titus 2:8; 1 Pet 2:12, 3:16).

More significantly, when confronted by injustice within a local church, Paul prioritises the body and its leadership to resolve such crises, not the civil authorities (1 Cor 6:1-11; Matt 18:15-20). Now, it is crucial to observe that in 1 Corinthians 6, Paul is speaking of what we would call civil lawsuits, and Matthew 18 speaks of sins one believer commits against another; in neither case is Jesus or Paul suggesting that we should not seek the prosecution of illegal activities committed by Christians: God has explicitly entrusted the civil authorities with that role, and we ought to submit to them in this regard (Rom 13:1-7, see Ch. V below).

In all these ways, the local church becomes the Christian's closest company; it is the believer's primary allegiance. As considered above (I.2), the Bible does give us a doctrine of the Universal Church, but it is essential to observe that in their biblical context and practical outworking, each of these spheres where Christian allegiance is aligned with the church finds its manifestation in the local church. Therefore, because the concrete expression of a believer's relation to Christ's body on earth is consistently oriented to the local church, the visible manifestation of the Universal Church is local churches. This is reinforced by the absence of any concrete embodiment of the universal, invisible church in this age apart from the local church (I.5-6).

c. Conclusion

All of life is oriented to the Church. However, orienting ourselves to God's purpose on earth, aligning ourselves fully with the Church, happens in the context of the local church. "The Church" and its mission is not nebulous: aligning ourselves with the Church and God's purpose through it cannot mean isolating ourselves and doing whatever we think would further God's purpose, no matter how selfless. At every point in the New Testament, allegiance to Christ and the fulfilment of his purposes happens in the context of the local church. The necessity of the local church is an inevitable result of the nature of the people God has constituted. If they are to make him known as a "city" on a hill, they must be working together (Matt 5:14-16). If they are to practice discipline, there must be defined boundaries of "inside" and "outside" in a physical location (cf. 1 Cor 5:1-13, cf. Deut 13:5; 2 Thess 3:6-15; 1 Tim 1:18-20). Teaching, as required in the Kingdom Mandate, requires commitment and relationship (Matthew 28:18-20). The command to love, with its specific focus on the relationships among believers, requires believers to be together (Eph 4:15-32; Gal 5:13, 6:9-10). The salvation Jesus accomplishes is not simply deliverance from sin, though it is not less than this; it is the institution of a kingdom under his rule, within which his subjects work together to accomplish his purposes. The New Testament is primarily concerned with individuals in local "churches," or defined groups; God's purpose is primarily accomplished through local churches. It is in allegiance to a local church that our allegiance to Christ and participation in his Church is expressed. The word often used for the local church is a congregation, though this term is also sometimes used for the laity in contrast with the officers of a local church. However, "congregation" appropriately captures the nature of a local church as a group of people *and* an institution, a socio-political entity. I will use local church and congregation interchangeably throughout this work.

4. That Congregations Are Demarcated, Local Composites of Believing Laypersons and Officers That Engage in the Life of the Local Church (Cf. CPD Chs. II-IV).

> And they devoted themselves to the apostles' teaching and the fellowship, to the breaking of bread and the prayers. And awe came upon every soul, and many wonders and signs were being done through the apostles. And all who believed were together and had all things in common. And they were selling their possessions and belongings and distributing the proceeds to all, as any had need. And day by day, attending the temple together and breaking bread in their homes, they received their food with glad and generous hearts, praising God and having favor with all the people. And the Lord added to their number day by day those who were being saved. (Acts 2:42-47)

> The instituted Church of the New Testament is an organic body of diverse members, of eyes, ears, feet, hands, of elders governing and a people governed. – Samuel Rutherford, *The Due Right of Presbyteries* (1644, p. 175, language updated)

Words in all languages are flexible; they evolve over time and often become detached from whatever rationale justified their original use. The Greek and Hebrew words that we translate as "church" or "congregation," ἐκκλησία (*ekklesia*) and קָהָל (*qahal*), follow this pattern, yet they never stray too far from the regular or non-technical use. Both words are used in the Old and New Testaments and secular literature for an assembly or gathering. In the New Testament, the use of ἐκκλησία extends beyond a physical or spiritual assembly (whatever that latter concept might mean) but never strays too far from it. Though the "Universal Church" has not yet gathered in its entirety, it has as its end an eschatological gathering, a gathering in the clouds to meet the Lord (1 Thess 4:13-18; 2 Thess 2:1; Jude 14-15), a wedding feast (Luke 14:15, 22:14-16; Rev 19:6-10), and an eternal city (Rev 21:9-27); in the interim, Hebrews and Revelation speak of a heavenly gathering of all the departed saints with the righteous angels in the presence of God (Heb 12:22-24; Rev 4:1-11, 5:1-14, 7:9-17). So, though the term ἐκκλησία (ekklesia) neither means "gathering" in any direct sense nor refers immediately to something gathered, an "assembly" is certainly appropriate for the entity to which it refers, an invisible plethora of believers who will one day gather in endless worship before their triune God. Similarly, those local entities called "churches" in the New Testament are not merely gatherings nor primarily gatherings. Yet in every case, gatherings are an indispensable feature of what makes them what they are. Not only does Hebrews warn against "neglecting to meet together" (10:25), but we are given a glimpse of regular church meetings on the first day of the week—the "Lord's Day" (Acts 20:7; 1 Cor 16:2; Rev 1:10). A gathering is presupposed in the context of reading the Scriptures, teaching, and reading the apostolic letters as attested throughout the Epistles (e.g. 1 Tim 4:13; Col 4:16). In 1 Corinthians 11, Paul speaks of the Corinthians coming together as a church and partaking of the Lord's supper; they were doing so in such a way that denied with their actions the unity they proclaimed with the symbols of the bread and the wine (1 Cor 11:17-34, cf. 1 Cor 5:4). In 1 Corinthians 14 Paul addresses the spiritual gifts and their use or abuse in the context of the church gathered (1-25), then he addresses how the regular gathering is to be orderly (26-40). James also addresses the gathered church, rebuking churches that showed partiality towards the rich when they gathered (2:1-13). Though the local church gathering is explicitly mentioned many times, it is more often presupposed as a regular rhythm of Christian worship, as 1st-century Jews would regularly meet in their synagogues on the Sabbath. Christians regularly gathered in cities across the known world to worship, encourage one another, share fellowship, read Scripture, be taught, and share the Lord's supper. However, a single gathering of Christians did not constitute a church—the Jerusalem council was not a church (Acts 15); no, the above passages present the practice of regular gatherings, presupposing stability among the constituents of a local church. This stability is found in two dimensions, recognised leadership and a demarcated group of Christians being led.

In each of the above cases, the Apostles address groups of individuals concerning their regular gatherings, presupposing that these individuals will regularly gather and that they are a group. Paul can speak of outsiders (presumably unbelievers), indicating that there is enough rigidity to this group to speak of clear demarcation; therefore, a church is a recognisable group of Christians. I specify above that they are not only demarcated in terms of their gathering, for this group that regularly gathers is also presented as regularly engaging in a shared life, building one another up, serving one another, and collaborating in daily life to meet each other's needs and reach the World with the Gospel. The Bible does not conceive of local church leaders, to which we will turn shortly, as CEOs of an abstract corporation or as organizers of an event—even a regular event—but as shepherds of a flock (Ch. III). That their leadership over a church is the leadership of persons means that the church is thus constituted—of persons, specific sheep with these shepherds. As the Cambridge Platform puts it in II.5,

> Elders being appointed to feed, not all flocks, but the particular flock of God over which the Holy Ghost had made them the overseers, and that flock they must attend, even the whole flock (Acts 20:28): and one congregation being as much as any ordinary Elders can attend, therefore there is no greater Church then a congregation, which may ordinarily meet in one place.

Moreover, there are distinctions between churches within a local area, further emphasising the demarcation of a specific group. Paul's letters to Rome and Colossae appear to address several distinct local churches in these cities. In Colossians, Paul asks the recipients to greet the church in Nympha's house (Col 4:15), indicating there is more than one "church" in Colossae (the one in that house and those who will greet that church). This is reinforced by the Epistle to Philemon, who lives in Colossae (cf. v. 10, Col 4:9). In this epistle, Paul greets Philemon and "the church in your house" (v. 2). There are, therefore, at least two churches in Colossae, the one in Nympha's house and the one in Philemon's house. In the Epistle to the Romans, Paul asks them to greet the church in Prisca and Aquila's house (Rom 16:5; cf. 1 Cor 16:19); this presupposes at least two churches, the church in their house and those who will greet them. Romans 16:14 and 15 may also suggest two more churches in Rome. As will be established in the following two sections, there is no evidence of organised cooperation among these churches other than the assumption that these churches will encounter one another, pass around, and read the letter, nor is there said to be *a* church in Rome or Colossae (cf. Rom 1:7; Col 1:2). So local churches are characterised by both a regular gathering and demarcated membership (to use the term "membership" loosely). It is because the church is demarcated in this way that church discipline can have an effect: to be put outside of the church is not to be excluded from a gathering but from a group of Christians who are committed to one another and function as a concrete whole in their fulfilment of God's purposes (1 Cor 5:1-13; 2 Cor 5:-8; 2 Thess 3:6, 13-15).

The final aspect of the local church is identifiable leadership. God used the Apostles to establish local churches, and it appears that the Apostles and their co-workers established leaders over each local church, leaders identified as elder-overseers (as we will discuss below, ch. III). We read of elders over the churches throughout Judea (Acts 11:30) and Jerusalem specifically (Acts 15:6). In Acts 14:23, we are told that Paul and Barnabas "appointed elders for [the disciples] in every church" (Acts 14:23). In Acts 20:17-38, we read of Paul's meeting with the elders of the Ephesian church; in 1 Timothy, we read of Paul's instructions to Timothy concerning this church, with specific instructions for its elder-oversees (which includes Timothy). In Paul's letter to Titus, we read that Paul charged Titus with appointing "elders in every town" (Titus 1:5), and James incidentally refers to elders of the church in his letter (James 5:14). Finally, in 1 Peter 5:1-11, Peter addresses the elders leading the churches he writes to. Thus, the New Testament gives a consistent picture: local churches have appointed leadership. This appears to be mirrored in the heavenly reality of the Church, for John portrays the Church in terms of 24 elders gathered before the throne of God (Rev 4:4). Therefore, a minimal definition of a local church (without considering what makes it genuinely Christian or healthy) is a local, demarcated group of Christians. This group will have officers and laity; thus, it is composite. They will be demarcated by their active participation in the church's life together, including regular gatherings.

Those who drafted the Cambridge Platform argued that the church exists prior to the appointment of officers, that its being is constituted by a group of Christians but its well-being by the presence of leaders. Thus, a church may not have leaders, but a healthy church will have leaders:

A Church being a company of people combined together by covenant for the worship of God, it appears thereby, that there may be the essence and being of a church without any officers, seeing there is both the form and matter of a church, which is implied when it is said, the Apostles ordained elders in every church [citing Acts 14:23]. (VI.1)

Nevertheless, though officers be not absolutely necessary, to the simple being of churches, when they be called: yet ordinarily to their calling they are, and to their well-being: and therefore the Lord Jesus out of his tender compassion has appointed, and ordained officers, which he would not have done if they had not been useful and need full for the church. (VI.2)[20]

We must depart from our esteemed brethren on this point, as they themselves set the foundations for in their discussion of congregational authority. Their argument is as follows: in Acts 14:23, the narrator speaks of "churches" *before* the appointment of elders, "and appointing elders for them in each church, praying with fasting, they committed them to the Lord in whom they had believed" (my translation). We will discuss the dynamics between the officers and laity to a much greater extent in the following chapters. For now, we will make two observations on this passage.

First, the verse does not clearly indicate that the church existed before elders were appointed. That is, there is no mention of a church until the appointment of elders in this verse; beforehand, the narrator speaks only of the disciples. In this verse, "them" refers not to churches but to the disciples previously mentioned. Thus, the distributive phrase "[in] each church" (κατὰ ἐκκλησία) is not necessarily indicating the pre-existence of churches (notice how the preposition "in" is supplied for clarity, not being explicit in the Greek). Second, what this verse does establish is that each church has elders. Indeed, given the absence of any mention of "churches" before this verse, it is better to read it not as indicating the being of a church before the

---

[20] The discussion here and at several points involves Scholastic logic and metaphysics. Though the drafters of the Cambridge Platform are admirable in their adherence to Scripture, their reasoning at times requires these presuppositions for its validity. I offer an alternative account of metaphysics and logic in my book *The Gift of Knowledge,* one that I believe stands on better foundation than that employed be these brothers.

appointment of officers but as the constitution of these disciples as churches through the appointment of elders for each congregation.

If it is appropriate to speak of a church before the appointment of its officers (and I can think of no instance in the New Testament where this is the case [the apostles having an eldership role when the church began, cf. 1 Pet 5:1; 2 John 1:1]), then it is only appropriate as is speaking of conversion without baptism. That is, conversion is pictured in the New Testament as a matrix of regeneration, faith, repentance, and baptism. However, though all four elements will be present given that no circumstances circumvene, it is possible that someone may be regenerated and express faith yet not reach a point of complete repentance (confessing and turning away from sin) or being baptised. The classic example is the thief on the cross, who professes faith and is assured of salvation but does not live long enough to demonstrate repentance unto holiness and receive baptism (Luke 23:39-43). Thus, *if* we may speak of a church without officers, it is only because circumstances have prevented the full being of the church from being expressed in the organisation of disciples under the leadership of elders.

5. That the Invisible Church Has Global Expression in the Communion of Local Churches (Cf. CPD Chs. XIII, XV-XVI).

> Now concerning the collection for the saints: as I directed the churches of Galatia, so you also are to do. On the first day of every week, each of you is to put something aside and store it up, as he may prosper, so that there will be no collecting when I come. And when I arrive, I will send those whom you accredit by letter to carry your gift to Jerusalem. If it seems advisable that I should go also, they will accompany me. – 1 Corinthians 16:1-4

If the local church is the only manifestation of the Invisible Church under the New Covenant, then there is no space for intermediary ecclesiastical entities such as denominations or parachurch organisations *functioning as or identifying themselves as the churches*. The inverse claim of congregational polity made above (§I.3) is that there is no global church institution under the New

Covenant. However, this claim is simultaneously controversial and readily misunderstood, so we will undertake to explain and defend it in this and the following section. We are not claiming that there is no expression of cooperation or unity between local churches, nor that there wasn't a global church institution under the Old Testament. In this section, we will explain the positive claim that there is a global expression of the invisible church in the communion of congregations; we will then establish the negative side of the claim, that this communion has no ecclesiastical authority or status in the following section. I will use the term "global church" to discuss this communion in the discussion below, but this should be understood as shorthand for the global expression of the Invisible church.

The Invisible Church is the foundation for what I call the "global church," or the sum of all local churches worldwide; the Invisible Church is also its end, that which it seeks to become. The global church is not just a mathematical claim, the sum of all the local churches added up, but a description of their shared behaviour, of all the inter-church relationships that arise out of our union in Christ, out of the reality of the Invisible Church. Because there is a reality that stands above and behind all local churches—a universal gathering of the saints in heaven, throughout the ages, and identified with faithful communities here on earth—all Christians are united. They are united by a shared identity: they are those who follow Christ. They are united by a shared reality: they are the body of Christ. They are also united by a shared purpose: they have been given the great commission. This underlying unity creates a platform for collaboration and communion, for the shared life of Christians beyond the local church (See further §VI below; CPD §§XIII-XVI). Because we are united together in Christ, local churches across the globe welcome each other's members as their own, they share resources with one another, and they work together in concrete ways. Though its expression comes with greater difficulty, it is nevertheless true that, because of this unity, local churches hold each other accountable, addressing false teaching and teachers outside of their local church community. The expression of the Invisible Church globally is a significant difference between the Old and New Covenant.

a. Under the Old Covenant

Under the Old Covenant, the visible church was co-extensive with the covenant community but not with the invisible church, the remnant. Instead, the remnant or invisible church existed within the visible, covenant community. Under the Old Covenant, the visible church was a kingdom, a socio-politico entity to be ruled by a king, with a distinctive political and social programme and delimited land. The Old Covenant was legislated by the Torah or the Covenant Law, found in the Pentateuch (Genesis – Deuteronomy). Much of this Law defines the kingdom of God in its external form, in its physical, spatial, and temporal instantiation. It was common in the Reformation to divide the Law into moral, civil, and ceremonial laws; the Reformers recognised that the Law had dimensions addressing how civil life was to be conducted, how one's personal life was to be conducted, and how one's religious life or ritual life was to be conducted. However, these clear-cut divisions are neither taught in the Bible nor evident there. For instance, the Ten Commandments legislate moral, ceremonial, *and* civil life, forbidding idol worship, mandating the Sabbath, and laying down fundamental moral laws for the proper function of society. Rather than seeing three distinct bodies of statutes in the Law, it is perhaps more accurate to see one set of legislation containing abstract laws such as the Ten Commandments and the case laws, explaining the application of these principles. Every commandment has civil, ceremonial, or moral dimensions, legislating the Old Covenant community in its external life. Perhaps we could revise the Reformation's three categories and say that every law has an upward, inward, and outward dimension. Every law pertains to the corporate and individual relationship with God, the relationship of one member of the community to another, and the purpose to which God has called the community.

Take, for example, the Ten Commandments. It is clear how these commandants serve an upward purpose; they display God's will for obedient living, for a life shaped by love for God and as a reflection of his character. They also serve an inward purpose, legislating a community that is focused on loving God and neighbour—fulfilling the two great commandments (Mark 12:28-34). Doing these things also fulfils their outward purpose, marking Israel as a distinct community centred on God and radiating his character through righteous and obedient lives. It is a community characterised by a distinctive purity of worship and Godward communal life, namely, a morality structured by the character of the creator God.

Turning to an example of civil legislation, the Law makes provision for a king (Deut 17:14-20). The provision of a king served to lead the people in faithfulness to God: he was to produce a copy of and read the Law regularly, living according to it. His personal life needed to reflect the spiritual and physical separation to which Israel had been called, upholding the purity of marriage, not going back to Egypt, and he must be a member of the covenant community, an Israelite. His life was to reflect the inward and upward purposes of the Law, godly living towards his neighbour and right worship of God, but also to contribute to God's purpose for Israel, exemplifying the purity to which Israel was called and leading them in right worship and living before God. The laws concerning civil punishment for apostates ensured that no one was encouraged to abandon God and be unfaithful, so they served the purpose of upholding right community, reflected the purpose of right worship and honour towards God, and would ensure the nation was a pure light shining forth among the Gentiles (Deut 13:1-18).

The laws sometimes called "ceremonial" are those concerning sacrifices (Lev 1:1-7:38), food laws (Lev 11:1-47), ritual purity (Lev 12:1-15:33), feast days (Lev 16:1-34; 23:1-44), etc. These laws have a significant upward purpose, illustrating the cost of sin and postponing punishment through the sacrificial system (which, of course, pointed forward to a once for all sacrifice that would not postpone but end punishment); they served to maintain a right relationship with a holy and just God, his loving gift to the people he had made his treasured possession. Yet these laws often have a communal purpose, to testify to one's children, family, and friends of God's faithfulness and kindness shown in the salvation of Israel, the provision of the land, and his presence among them (e.g. Deut 6:1-25). As a testimony to one another, they would encourage and promote right worship and faithful living before God, ensuring that the whole community received God's blessings. The corporate sacrifice of the Day of Atonement (Lev 16:1-34) would ensure that God's judgment was put off despite the people's failures. These rituals also served a significant outward purpose, providing a constant reminder to the people of their unique calling as God's treasured possession and a holy people, entrusted with a unique relationship with God and commissioned as a nation of mediators or priests; they also provided a constant reminder of Israel's distinction from their neighbours. Various food laws and strange regulations about not wearing clothing of mixed fabrics or not mixing grains were designed by God as tangible symbols of Israel's calling and the ideal to which they were to conform: Israel was never intended to be mixed. They were a reminder that God's purposes would only be fulfilled, and his blessings only be bestowed, when they put off unbelief together as a community, drove out the apostate, and maintained faithfulness to their covenant Lord.

However, as we know, Israel failed on every count: failure in any dimension—upward, outward, or inward—would mean a failure in the rest. Israel as a nation failed to honour and worship God exclusively; as a result, they failed to treat one another with the loving-kindness legislated in the Torah; they also failed to shine forth as a light to the Gentiles, as a distinct people dedicated to God. Instead, like the prophet Jonah, they ran from their calling and despised their neighbours; they failed their prophetic, priestly call. A mixed community simply would not do; if God's people were divided amongst themselves, and their allegiances distributed in every direction—to this or that god—God's saving mercy would not extend forth as he intended it to. However, the Old Covenant was never Plan A—at least not Plan A in its entirety: instead, the Old Covenant was a type and a shadow, an arrow pointing forward to the fulfilment of God's saving plan in Christ's New Covenant.

b. Under the New Covenant

As we saw above (I.1-2), the Bible has much to say about the Church universal, the unseen body of believers stretching across time and space—all who possess the Spirit, love God, and will receive his kingdom. I argued that this universal church is instantiated in local congregations (I.3-4): this marks a significant break with the Old Covenant. Under the Old Covenant, the Church's primary—if not the only—realities were the invisible and the global, visible church. We could talk about the tribes, clans, and families that composed the visible church under the Old Covenant, or the exilic community and the remnant in the land, yet none of these entities is given ecclesiological significance in the Old Testament; they exist and have important roles in redemptive history, yet the role they play is not discussed in the Old Testament along the lines of ecclesiology, of considerations of God's people and God's purpose for that people as a corporate entity in the dimensions of its leadership, structure, and gathered life.

Under the Old Covenant, the visible, global Church was the primary entity in God's plan for Israel; Israel failed to fulfil its purpose because, despite the faithful remnant, it was unfaithful on the global, visible level. In comparison to the vision of the people of God in the Old Testament, as a kingdom, as a socio-politico entity with a concrete location and a civil and religious programme, the global, visible church in the New Testament appears almost as an afterthought, a footnote on a portrait painted of the local church and the universal, invisible reality it instantiates. There is a visible, global church in the New Testament, yet it is neither developed as much nor given the same priority as the church local and universal. It is essential to recognise this reality for two reasons: first, this marks a significant break with the Old Covenant and should lead us to ask why there is such a change; second, much ecclesiology throughout the history of the New Covenant Church has been dedicated to the idea of the global, visible church—to "Christendom" and denominations or worldwide Church structures (on which, see the following section).

i. The global, visible church in the New Testament

When confronted by the reality that New Testament does not discuss God's people on its global level in the categories we usually use, such as a socio-political kingdom or an analogous ecclesiological structure (such as denominational structures), the response of some might be to say that the New Testament does not talk about the Church at this level at all: all that exists is the Universal Church and local churches. Others might (and have) turned to the Old Testament and its covenant community for the model of a Christian global church, using wisdom to fill in the gaps. Still, others have latched on to one model of global church behaviour in the New Testament, namely, the role of the 12 apostles, and sought to implement that in the contemporary church, usually alongside structures developed in light of the Old Testament, tradition, and reason. The latter approach would be that of the so-called New Apostolic Reformation, particularly prominent among Pentecostal groups. Independent churches take the first approach, and the middle route is adopted by all denominations (though to varying extents). Congregationalists have tended to focus on the precedent of the Jerusalem Council for the pattern of synods. However, the global church appears in several ways in the New Testament: we will examine each of these in turn. In Chapter VI below, we will unpack these relations further.

1) The apostolic ministry

First, we find the global church through apostolic ministry: the Apostles were not heads of any local church body but expressed oversight of and ministered to many different local congregations. This is evident in their itinerant ministry, such as Paul's missionary journey. Paul and Barnabas not only planted churches but also appointed leaders over them (Acts 14:23). Paul continued to minister to the churches he planted and some, like the churches in Rome, that he did not plant. He visited these churches and wrote letters to them, even enacting discipline (e.g. 1 Cor 4:21; 2 Cor 1:23-2:4). James and other apostles remained in Jerusalem and, if we accept the premise that there was not one church but several churches in Jerusalem, they appeared to exercise a level of leadership above the local level (Acts 6:1-7; 8:1-2; 9:26-31; 11:20; 15:1-25). Through the Jerusalem Council, the Apostles and the elders in Jerusalem engaged with and acted towards churches worldwide, acting on a global level.

It is generally agreed that the Apostolic ministry expressed by the Twelve and Paul was unique; it was part of God's work to establish the invisible church and its local instantiations (and some global structures, as we will see). Among others, two reasons for this are Paul's own criteria for his apostolic ministry, beholding the risen Christ and receiving the apostolic commission from him (1 Cor 15:1-11; Gal 1:1; 1 Tim 1:1; Titus 1:3), and the lack of instruction concerning the appointment of and role of such leaders— in contrast to that given for elders and deacons (e.g. 1 Timothy 3). Observe how in the first set of texts, Paul's appeal to his direct commission from Christ is used to establish his apostolic authority; without such a commission, this authority would be lacking. The apostles are also given, alongside the Old Testament prophets, a unique role as the foundation for the New Covenant Church (Eph 2:20, 3:5; cf. Rev 21:14). One could argue that there are some called "apostles" who serve a different role than Paul and the Twelve, a role similar to contemporary missionaries or itinerant preachers: they do not bear the unique apostolic role or authority and nowhere is it suggested that they need the apostolic commission Paul and the Twelve received. However, the evidence is not clear cut in this matter; Barnabas (Acts 14:14) could qualify for either understanding of "apostle," and the references in 1 Corinthians 12:28-29 or Ephesians 4:11 could be interpreted either way. Romans 16:7 is sometimes used in this context, but the ESV's "well known to the apostles" seems to be the appropriate translation. So, the global church existed as the apostolic ministry to local churches and between local churches in the 1st century, but we are not to expect this ministry to continue. However, the global church exists in further ways as well.

2) The Jerusalem Council

Closely related to the apostolic ministry, we also find the church acting globally in the Jerusalem Council (Acts 15). Here, an issue among the new Gentile churches threatened the unity of the Church; the conversion of the Gentiles raised problems for many Jewish believers. So the elders and apostles in Jerusalem, in conjunction with "the whole church" in Jerusalem (Acts 15:22), gathered together and produced a letter instructing Gentile believers on specific issues troubling Jewish believers. The instructions appear to be an expression of apostolic authority, yet the whole Jerusalem church, particularly its leadership, is involved in the decision (Acts 15:2); the Jerusalem church acted towards other churches. In addition to its significant role as the first church and residence of most apostles, the Jerusalem church was also the centre of Jewish Christianity. This was particularly relevant given that the issues arose from the conflict between Jewish and Gentile believers and the presence of Jews alongside converted Gentiles (Acts 15:1, 5, 21; cf. Gal 2:11-12). The Jerusalem church settled on a position among themselves and then communicated this to those churches initially affected by the confusion. This passage neither mandates the pre-eminence of the Jerusalem church nor a role for church councils as they were understood in the 4th century and afterwards, but it does show how churches interacted, sometimes with negative ramifications, requiring actions such as that taken by the Jerusalem church.[21]

In this and the former case, the unique apostolic ministry and the Jerusalem council, the global church is not codified; it is not given structure nor a programme for the ages to come. Instead, we see the interaction of local churches through temporary measures, sending and sitting under the apostles and working out theological growing pains under the apostolic

---

[21] For a further treatment of this council in relation to later "ecumenical" councils, see J. Alexander Rutherford, *The Trinity and the Bible: How All Scripture Testifies to One God in Three Persons*, Teleioteti Technical Studies 3 (Campbell River, BC: Teleioteti, 2022), ch. 20.

oversight. We could envision scenarios like the Jerusalem council without apostolic authority, yet we have no reason to believe that any church can lay even the minimal burden the Jerusalem church lays on the gentiles. How Jerusalem responded with its letters appears indicative of apostolic authority, yet the process of convening a local church to address an issue between itself and other churches could clearly happen apart from that authority. So, the council is demonstrative of how local churches may interact. However, turning further elsewhere in the New Testament, we see more prescriptive actions demonstrated between local churches.

3) The support of one church for another

In Acts, we are confronted by the Church acting with incredible generosity— a generosity and care for one another that is foreign to many of our churches today (hence, *confronting*). Not only was there a deliberate effort to meet the needs of widows (Acts 6:1-7), but the Christians were regularly selling their possession to meet each other's needs (Acts 2:42-47; 4:32-5:11). We see a similar concern for widows in Paul's first letter to Timothy (5:3-16), indicative of an attitude throughout the early church (cf. Matt 25:31-46). In 1 Timothy and Acts, we see this care expressed at the level of the local church. However, this care is expressed between local churches elsewhere in Scripture. In Paul's ministry to the Corinthians, he organises a generous gift to be given to the Jerusalem church (1 Cor 16:1-4; 2 Cor 8:1-24, 9:1-5). This was a "collection for the saints"; Paul had organised a similar collection in Galatia, Macedonia, and Achaia (1 Cor 16:1; 2 Cor 8:1-5; Rom 15:25-29). Thus, local churches are led to support one another with the same generosity they show within the local congregation.

4) Hospitality and itinerant ministry

Finally, the global church is displayed in the active itinerancy of non-apostolic Christians throughout the New Testament. In addition to Paul's apostolic ministry and the ministries of Barnabas, Silas, Peter, and the rest of the Twelve, we read of Christians travelling from church to church, often teaching. In Acts, several deacons travel and have itinerant evangelistic ministries, particularly as Saul persecuted the Church (Acts 7:1-16, 8:4-8). However, the ministry I have in mind is that of Christians such as Apollos. We first meet Apollos in Ephesus; he was evangelising in the synagogue (Acts 18:24-25). After receiving further instruction from Priscilla and Aquila, he went on to Achaia and "greatly helped those who through grace had believed" (Acts 18:27). Next, Apollos was at Corinth (Acts 19:1); we learn in 1 Corinthians that he had a formative influence on at least some of the congregation there (1 Cor 1:10-17; 3:1-9). Paul recounts encouraging Apollos to return to Corinth (1 Cor 16:12). We meet Apollos for the last time in Titus 3:13, once again being sent to another church. Some Christians travelled from church to church out of necessity; Priscilla or Prisca and Aquila were driven out of Italy because of persecution (Acts 18:2-3, 18; Rom 16:3-51; Cor 16:19; 2 Tim 4:19). A prophet, Agabus, is also mentioned similarly (Acts 21:7-14). In addition to the positive accounts of itinerant ministers above, we also read of travelling false prophets and teachers (Gal 2:4-5; 2 Cor 11:1-15; 1 John 4:1-6). So, there is a global, visible expression of the Church in the interrelation of Christians coming from one church to another, whether because of local upheaval or intentional ministry. For the church that receives these believers, the apostolic writers call for "hospitality." The word translated "hospitality" in the New Testament is used not for entertaining, as it often is in our society, but for welcoming in and caring for the Christian stranger (in a non-Christian context, Acts 28:7; in a Christian context, Rom 12:13; 1 Tim 3:2, 5:10; Titus 1:8; Heb 13:1-2; 1 Pet 4:9). Christians are commended for and instructed to welcome the foreign brother or sister, thus acting out the sort of inter-congregational activity we are discussing.

The epistles of 2 and 3 John are the most direct treatment of hospitality in this sense. Both are presumably written by the Apostle John, who identifies himself as "the elder" (2 John 1; 3 John 1). In 2 John, John writes to a local church, "an elect lady"; the short body of the letter echoes the themes of the Gospel of John and 1 John, warning, in particular, about false teachers. In the context of this warning, John exhorts the church to practice hospitality with care: "If anyone comes to you and does not bring this teaching, do not receive him into your house or give him any greeting, for whoever greets him takes part in his wicked works" (2 Jn 10–11). Local churches are to welcome their fellow believers, including itinerant preachers, yet they must do so with great care, lest they partake of the teacher's sins. 3 John addresses the same theme of hospitality, writing to an individual named Gaius,

> Beloved, it is a faithful thing you do in all your efforts for these brothers, strangers as they are, who testified to your love before the church. You will do well to send them on their journey in a

manner worthy of God. For they have gone out for the sake of the name, accepting nothing from the Gentiles. Therefore we ought to support people like these, that we may be fellow workers for the truth. (3 Jn 5–8)

In addition to commending Gaius for his hospitable behaviour, John condemns a certain Diotrephes for the opposite behaviour (vv. 9-11).

Thus, what I call the global, visible church finds expression in the welcoming reception of believers from one local church to another and through inter-congregational ministry seen in the itinerant teachers. However, this welcoming and sending behaviour is grounded in the ideal of the Invisible Church: hospitality is to be discerning, promoting healthy, right faith and not welcoming and, thereby, abetting false teaching. As in the local church, the Church in its global function ought to express discernment, testing the spirits lest the work of the "antichrists," that is, false teachers, be promoted and sinful behaviour be commended (1 Thess 5:20-22; 1 John 2:18-27; 4:1-6)—lest cooperation with "Belial" be entertained (2 Cor 6:14-7:1).

5) Conclusions: The global church and its invisible ideal

To the best of my knowledge, the New Testament never uses the word "church" (ἐκκλήσια) to refer to what I am calling "the global church." It is not the same sort of tangible reality as the Invisible Church or the local church, yet it is real, nonetheless. Its reality is not that of a thing, an entity, but a function, a relationship. The global church is the practical outworking of the invisible reality of the Church in the cooperation of its local instantiations: the Church exists as an invisible reality across time and space, finding its concrete here-and-now existence in local churches. Because of the unity of local churches as the one Body of Christ, his blood-bought Bride, local churches ought to and often do work together. In the New Testament, local churches exchange resources, both gifted persons and physical necessities. Local churches also provide a home away from home for the sojourning Christian, someone detached for a time from the local family of which they are a part.

As we have seen, the global church exists in the New Testament, yet the contrast between the Testaments should be apparent. In the Old Testament, there was neither a local/global distinction nor a covenant community/global distinction. In the Old Testament, the kingdom of Israel was the covenant community and the whole reality of God's people, though it was terribly mixed with believers and unbelievers side-by-side. This kingdom was manifest as a single, socio-political reality; its nature as a kingdom was central to its purpose. For the Old Testament kingdom, the fragmentation of exile signalled defeat; it was a curse that held no promise for God's purpose to be fulfilled. In the New Testament, the difference could not be starker: though there is a universal reality, an invisible church, its only instantiation is a fragmented one—local churches. Individual churches constitute the universal Church's concrete, temporal reality. The Church Global is not a socio-political reality, nor is it analogous to one; there is a global reality to the visible church, yet this global reality in the New Testament is the interworking of local churches, their realisation of the universal ideal in care and cooperation, in hospitality, and in the mutual ministry of sending and receiving brothers and sisters for a season. Exile is not a curse but is central to the Church's mission: as elect exiles (1 Pet 1:1; 2:11; Heb 11:13), Christians are able to engage in a ministry of reconciliation (2 Cor 5:11-6:13), calling those who are far off, who separated in a different kingdom, to draw near to God in his kingdom (Eph 2:1-10, 11-22). Their kingdom is an eschatological one, present now as the invisible Jerusalem and as hope for a city that will come (Heb 11:10, 13-16; 12:18-24; 13:9-16), of the invisible Jerusalem come visible in the New Creation (Rom 8:18-25; Rev 21:1-27).

c. Conclusion

There is, therefore, a prescription for the Church's global, visible activity in the New Testament. However, the global church under the New Covenant is not identical to the global, visible church in the Old Covenant. The differences between the two dispensations of God's one people are remarkable. However, minding these differences is essential if we are to grasp God's unique purpose for the Church in the New Covenant as ambassadors and embassies of a heavenly and eschatological kingdom spread throughout the hostile kingdoms of the earth, beckoning all who would hear to come and receive new citizenship, new family, and new purpose.

6. That This Global Expression Has No Ecclesial Authority (Cf. CPD Chs. II, VII-X).

Not only is there no mandate for an institutional unity between local churches, an ecclesiastical trans-congregational entity, but the vision of the Church global in the New Testament is also incompatible with such a mandate, with a vision of Christendom. The New Testament does not lend support to the view that Christian unity requires organisational unity encompassing all local churches and Christians in the word. Indeed, it does not support the position that Christian unity requires any organisational structures above the local church. This does not mean that denominations or any organisational structure above the local church are wrong or unhelpful; we will consider positive ways trans-local relationships can be developed in Chapter VI. However, such relationships ought to be distinguished from the view of a "denomination" that attributes it with ecclesial authority. Because these relationships are not the equivalent of a denomination in the contemporary sense, denominations should not be understood as a necessary expression of Christian unity (according to the sufficiency principle established in the Introduction).

Christian unity is expressed at the global level not through pan-church leaders, cross-church bureaucracies, formal ties, or identical theological formulations, practices, and church cultures but through the collaboration of local churches working together to see God's purpose fulfilled through sharing resources, providing a home away from home, and providing accountability and support in the battle against false teaching and moral decay. This collaboration is discriminatory; it does not welcome all who call themselves Christians but all who display true faith in the way they live and in the Gospel they profess (cf. VI.8). However, this is broad ecumenicism that is not eager to create division and shows Christ's patience even where Gospel fruit is wanting (2 John 10; Rev 2:5; cf. VI.8). The New Testament's vision of the global church presupposes that the fundamental realisation or instantiation of the Invisible, Universal Church before Christ's return is local churches.

a. Alternate Views

Not only does this vision of the Universal Church's visible, global reality contrast with that of the Old Testament (§I.5), but it also contrasts with various visions of the global church throughout church history. Many (though not all) denominations and theologians see the structural unity of all local churches—a global "church" with a shared confessional and structural reality—as an ideal to strive for. From a Tridentine Roman Catholic perspective, to be outside of the Roman Catholic Church (notice that "Church" here means neither the invisible nor the local church) is to be outside God's salvific will: salvation is found in this church alone, *sola ecclesia*. In this position, the Roman Catholic Church is the only true Church, and its reality is the bureaucracy of the Catholic ecclesia.[22] The Eastern Church has traditionally held a similar position. John Frame, in his book *Evangelical Reunion*, argues that structural unity on a global level is a necessary goal for true Christian unity: "We must first be assured that Jesus Christ established on earth one church, not many denominations. Further, the unity of the church is not merely 'spiritual,' but also organizational."[23] To a lesser extent, all Protestant denominations see a structural unity of local churches as beneficial and even necessary. The Early Church, the Roman Catholic Church, the Eastern Churches, and many denominations in the "Magisterial" Reformed tradition (such as Anglicans, Presbyterians, Lutheran, and Reformed churches) also seek the realisation of a "Christendom," an earthly, Christian kingdom.[24]

Following the model of Old Testament Israel with its visible, global unity, these denominations see God's kingdom here-and-now as having both an ecclesiastical and civil reality, both the global, universal church and the state, which uses the sword under God's authority to support the Church and uphold righteousness. Though they understand God's governance of these two kingdoms differently, they agree that both kingdoms are unified in their allegiance to Yahweh and ought to share the purpose of maintaining and furthering Christ's kingdom on earth. For some, the continuity between the

---

[22] This is true for Tridentine Catholicism, though this stance has softened somewhat with the rise of the ecumenical movement and Vatican II.

[23] John M. Frame, *Evangelical Reunion: Denominations and the One Body of Christ* (Grand Rapids: Baker, 1991), ch. 1.

[24] On the topic of "Christendom" from a congregational perspective, see J. Alexander Rutherford, *The Gift of Purpose: Orienting the Christian Life to the Western World.*

Old Testament kingdom and the New Testament is strong, such as the Theonomy movement pioneered by Rousas Rushdoony.[25] More often, Christians rely on Natural Law to develop their understanding of Christ's earthly, civil kingdom.[26]

b. The Incompatibility of Christendom and a Global, Visible Church Institution with the New Testament Global Church

Whether it is the model of Christendom or the organizational unity of the Church visible, both models of the global church are considerably different from what I have presented above as the New Testament model. It is important to recognise that the Bible says something about the global activity of local churches, yet this activity looks nothing like Christendom or a global, organisational church. Indeed, what the New Testament says appears incompatible with these views. In addition to the absence of any prescriptive model of global church unity, the New Testament presents several themes that seem contrary to this vision.

i. The earthly kingdom of God is an eschatological reality

For one, the earthly instantiation of God's kingdom on earth is understood not only as future but eschatological, inaugurated when Christ returns (e.g. Eph 1:14; Heb 11:10, 12:22-24, 13:14; Rev 21:1-27). The unity that currently exists, for which Christ prayed in the Garden and is now ours (John 17:1-26), is the unity of the Invisible Church, a heavenly reality that extends across time (encompassing believers who have died and are still alive) and space (e.g. Gal 4:21-31; Eph 1:3, 1:22-23, 2:11-22, 3:17-14, 4:4-5; Heb 12:22-24; Rev 21:9-27). What was presented as a single event in the Old Testament—the coming

---

[25] E.g. Rousas J. Rushdoony, *The Institutes of Biblical Law*, 3 vols. (Phillipsburg: P & R Pub, 1973).

[26] E.g. David VanDrunen, *Natural Law and the Two Kingdoms: A Study in the Development of Reformed Social Thought*, Emory University Studies in Law and Religion. (Grand Rapids: Eerdmans, 2010); David VanDrunen, *Divine Covenants and Moral Order: A Biblical Theology of Natural Law*, Emory University Studies in Law and Religion (Grand Rapids: Eerdmans, 2014); Douglas Wilson, *Empires of Dirt: Secularism, Radical Islam, and the Mere Christendom Alternative* (Moscow, Ida.: Canon Press, 2016); Littlejohn, *The Two Kingdoms*.

of the Messiah or the Christ and the inauguration of the final age, the end of sin, and a pure kingdom—is split across two moments in the New Testament, Christ's first and second coming. New Testament scholars and Biblical Theologians call this an inaugurated eschatology or the already-not-yet tension: what seemed to be promised all at once in the Old Testament has now arrived in part but is not entirely ours until Christ returns (e.g. Deut 30:1-14 [Heb]; Isa 53:1-12, 54:1-17, 61:1-11, 65:17-25, 66:15-24; Jer 30:1-31:40; Ezek 36:1-37:28; Joel 2:18-38; Matt 8:17, 24:1-25:46; John 3:5-15, 6:44-45, 12:36-43; Acts 2:1-24; Eph 1:3; Heb 8:1-13; 1 Pet 2:24; Rev 19:1-21:27).[27]

ii. There is discontinuity between New and Old Covenant ecclesiology

Second, though I would affirm with John Frame that there is much more continuity between the New and Old Covenants than old-school Dispensationalism would acknowledge, a clear point of differentiation between the covenants is in ecclesiology.[28] For one, the earthly kings of the Old Testament pointed forward to Christ, God's true king who presently reigns (e.g. 1 Cor 15:20-28; Eph 1:15-23).[29] They were signs pointing to one who is to come; now that Christ is on the throne and ruling his kingdom, there is no place for earthly rulers over an earthly kingdom.[30] Not only is

---

[27] E.g. George Eldon Ladd, *A Theology of the New Testament*, Rev. ed., reprinted (Grand Rapids: Eerdmans, 1994), 368; G. K. Beale, "The Role of the Resurrection in the Already-and-Not-Yet Phases of Justification," in *For the Fame of God's Name: Essays in Honor of John Piper*, ed. Sam Storms and Justin Taylor (Wheaton: Crossway, 2010); G. K. Beale, *A New Testament Biblical Theology: The Unfolding of the Old Testament in the New* (Grand Rapids: Baker Academic, 2011); G. K. Beale, *Handbook on the New Testament Use of the Old Testament: Exegesis and Interpretation* (Grand Rapids: Baker Academic, 2012); Graeme Goldsworthy, *The Goldsworthy Trilogy* (Milton Keynes: Paternoster, 2012).

[28] Frame, *Evangelical Renunion*, ch. 1. Cf. Craig A. Blaising and Darrell L. Bock, *Progressive Dispensationalism* (Grand Rapids: Bridgepoint Books, 2000); Gentry and Wellum, *Kingdom through Covenant (2nd Ed)*.

[29] See J. Alexander Rutherford, *God's Kingdom through His Priest-King: An Analysis of the Book of Samuel in Light of the Davidic Covenant*, Teleioteti Technical Studies 1 (Vancouver: Teleioteti, 2019).

[30] See J. Alexander Rutherford *The Gift of Reading – Part 1* in *The Gift of Knowledge* (Airdrie, AB: Teleioteti, 2021) and *The Gift of Purpose*.

there a difference in the presence of God's true king, but the Old Testament also promises that a radical revision of the Covenant Community would accompany the New Covenant. No longer would brother say to brother "know YHWH" (Jer 31:34), for they would all know him (Jer 31:34; Isa 54:13). God would give the circumcised heart promised in Deuteronomy 30:6, thereby enabling obedience within the covenant (30:6-14 [Heb]). This promise has already come, yet we encounter a mixed church at the level of the local and global church; therefore, we need to see this promise inaugurated in the heavenly gathering of which true believers are part (Heb 12:1, 22-14; Eph 1:3, 2:6) awaiting its consummation when Christ returns, when the Church is prepared in all her glory (Eph 5:25-27; Rev 19:6-10, 21:9-27). Because the Bible presents discontinuity on this very issue, we must explore the differences between the two covenants regarding the constitution of God's people, as we have been doing here in Part 1 (Chapters 2-4). Considering the matter in this way, we see a profound difference not in the way believers are saved nor their future eschatological blessing, as Covenant theologians are right to insist upon, but in the dispensation or administration (οἰκονομία) of God's covenant, that is, in how he administrates the Covenant made with his people and how he will fulfil his purpose with them.[31]

iii. Exile is instrumental to the New Testament Church, not a curse

Third, selecting one final theme, the way the New Testament treats the exilic nature of the Church is vastly different from the Old Testament, and this difference is telling. In the Old Testament, God's people awaited a land promised to them; this land was essential to their purpose and constitution as a covenant people. Exile was a curse for disobedience, imposed upon them for their apostasy (Deut 29:1-30:2). When Israel was in exile, they were instructed not to seek to build a kingdom, to fulfil their God-given commission, but to live humbly in their exilic state, remaining loyal to God, until he would restore them to the land (Jer 29:1-23). Though Israel returned to the Land under Cyrus, king of Medo-Persia (see Ezra-Nehemiah), they

---

[31] Cf. Gentry and Wellum, *Kingdom through Covenant (2nd Ed)*; Peter J. Gentry and Stephen J. Wellum, *God's Kingdom through God's Covenants: A Concise Biblical Theology*, 2015.

remained in spiritual exile. By the close of the Old Testament, the rebuilt temple was not the glorious restoration of right religion prophesied in Ezekiel (e.g. Ezekiel 40-48). Instead, it was a pale imitation of the original temple (Ezra 3:12-13). Moreover, Israel was not righteous through a Spirit-wrought new heart; they remained as unfaithful as before (e.g. Neh 13:1-31). For this reason, the Old Testament canon in Hebrew does not end with a note of victory but with the hope of fulfilment,

> Thus says Cyrus king of Persia, 'The LORD, the God of heaven, has given me all the kingdoms of the earth, and he has charged me to build him a house at Jerusalem, which is in Judah. Whoever is among you of all his people, may the LORD his God be with him. Let him go up.' (2 Chron 36:23)

Thus, the Old Covenant ended with an incomplete, physical return from exile but the continuation of spiritual exile.

In the New Testament, the Covenant curses are completed with the utter destruction of Jerusalem in AD 70 (e.g. Matt 24:3-28). The promise of a physical return from exile is pushed forth into the eschaton when Christ returns and makes all things new (Heb 13:14; Rev 21:1-27). However, spiritual exile has ended; the new heart has been given; all God's people under the New Covenant know him (John 3:1-15; 6:44-45; Eph 2:1-10; etc.). Not only has the physical return from exile—the promise of land—been put off into the eschaton, but this is also presented not as a curse but as an instrumental part of God's plan through the church.

In Hebrews 11-13, the language of sojourning and exile is used to model New Testament faith, awaiting the fulfilment of God's promises, including the land promise (typified by the city to come, see Heb 11:10). It should strike us that Peter writes to the "elect exiles of the Dispersion" (1 Pet 1:1), for "elect" brings in the promises of a new, faithful Israel (e.g. Rom 9:1-10:4) but "exile" reminds us of the curse Israel received for disobedience. However, the theme of exile is transformed in Peter's epistle; no longer is it a mark of shame but a description of the Christian identity. They are exiles because they await the imperishable inheritance stored for them in heaven (1 Pet 1:3-5). Life is exile now because we are strangers in the old creation, suffering various trials (1 Pet 3:6-9, cf. Rom 8:18-39). Their calling is not foreign to their exile but realised in it. They must, therefore, be holy: "conduct yourselves with fear throughout the time of your exile" (1 Pet 1:17). It is in this context of exilic faith that these Christians are identified as a "holy priesthood," "chosen race," and a "holy nation" (2:5, 9)—language originally used of Israel's calling to be a socio-political entity shining forth the light of God's goodness (Exod 19:6). They are the recipients of God's eschatological promises, while in exile (1 Pet 2:9-10, cf. Hos 1:6, 9, 10, 2:23; Rom 9:25-26, 10:19). They are not told to seek the end of exile but to endure through it until they receive the goal of their faith (see 1 Peter 1). Being among the Gentiles as exiles is essential to God's purpose for the Church as a city on a hill, an embassy of reconciliation to those far off (2 Cor 5:11-6:13; Eph 2:11-22), so Peter exhorts them,

> Beloved, I urge you as sojourners and exiles to abstain from the passions of the flesh, which wage war against your soul. Keep your conduct among the Gentiles honorable, so that when they speak against you as evildoers, they may see your good deeds and glorify God on the day of visitation. (1 Pet 2:11-12)

Instead of seeking a kingdom, they are to submit to the kingdoms in which they sojourn as exiles (1 Pet 2:13-17; cf. Rom 13:1-7). As in the Old Testament, no authority exists that is not under God's authority, yet this does not mean they will be benevolent nor favourable to God's people, only that they are installed by God and under his control (e.g. Isa 45:1-7; Hab 1:5-11) (cf. Ch. VII). Christians will suffer in exile, yet they must do so as those doing good and for Christ's sake, not for any evildoing on their part (1 Pet 4:12-19). Peter's picture of an exilic Christianity is precisely that which Jesus presents in Matthew 5, where the blessedness of the Christian life is found not apart from suffering but in the midst of it (Matt 5:2-12). Exile is, therefore, not the state of curse it was in the Old Testament but an opportunity for the blessed life and the occasion to fulfil God's calling upon the Church. The exilic reality of the Church is likewise presupposed in Jesus' juxtaposition of those who seek to lead earthly kingdoms and the leaders of his church: the former seek prestige and power; the latter seek to lay down their lives, not to pursue power (Matt 20:20-28).

b. Conclusion

Positively, local churches express their invisible unity through cooperation in ministry, sharing resources, counsel, and welcoming each other's members.

Negatively, there is no room for a global, institutional church: this is the eschatological reality towards which we are moving, but it will only be instantiated when Christ returns. In its place, we are commended to embrace our exilic life as God's means to achieve his salvific purposes. Local churches are thus embassies of an eschatological kingdom that mediate its power and promise in the present within a broken, sinful world. As instantiations of the same eschatological congregation, local churches are to engage in intentional communion. However, this communion is not intended to become that eschatological kingdom. There is no explicit command in Scripture to engage in such institutionalising behaviour. Such behaviour contradicts the Biblical portrait of the New Covenant church, and we are given no instructions on how such an institution ought to be structured and governed. Thus, we can employ the principles of simplicity and sufficiency to say involvement in a global, institutional church is unnecessary for any church to please God (via sufficiency), and there is great danger in establishing a global, institutional church (via simplicity). Moreover, because we are not given a mandate for a global church, nor instructions concerning its ecclesial ministry, we conclude that it is not right to identify trans-congregational communions as "churches," for they do not bear sufficient similarity to the two biblical authorised bodies called "church" (viz. the Invisible Church and local churches), nor can they bear ecclesial or ministerial authority.

That is, trans-congregational communions or "denominations" cannot bear the authority 1) to excommunicate individuals or churches, 2) to elect and ordain ministers, or 3) to administer the Lord's Supper. Such authority abides in congregations. 1) The excommunication of individuals in the New Testament is seen as a whole congregation (laity and officers) decision (see. Chs. III-V). The decision to disfellowship from false teachers and so, presumably, entities falsely called "churches" rests with congregations— though they are to follow Christ, who only after great patience threatens to remove a church from his presence (see VI.8). 2) The election of officers is an act of the congregation and their ordination of officers, either those of the relevant congregation or of other local congregations (there being no trans-local ordained role that continues beyond the initiation of the Church) (see Chs. III, VI). 3) Though the Lord's Supper carries with it the declaration of one's participation in the Invisible Church (1 Cor 10:16), the implications for this declaration are for the localised relationships of the little bodies or temples that are local churches (1 Cor 11:17-34, 12:12-31)—microcosms of the whole (John 2:19-22; 1 Cor 3:16-17; 1 Cor 6:19; 2 Cor 6:14-7:1).[32] Paul's exhortation to discern the body in 1 Cor 11:17-34 addresses the right perception of one's relationship with others likewise united to Christ in the local congregation, suggesting that the local congregations are the appropriate context for this declaration of unity in Christ in remembrance of his sacrificial death and in anticipation of the wedding feast. Other than the institution of the supper, before the Church was instituted after Christ's death, we have no example of this supper being practised other than within the local church. Thus far, we have mostly considered what the global church is not, but we will turn to the positive functions of inter-congregational communion in Chapter VI.

---

[32] Notice the use of the temple metaphor for the body universal, the local church, and the individual.

II. OF LOCAL CHURCH MEMBERSHIP (CF. CPD XII)

Therefore, having put away falsehood, let each one of you speak the truth with his neighbor, for we are members one of another. – Ephesians 4:25 (ESV)

1. A member of a local church is a believer who regularly participates in the life of the church; thus, an ordained leader is a member.
2. Members of a congregation are mutually accountable to one another and are responsible to hold one another to account.
3. The genuineness of faith is to be judged according to the principle of charity.
4. Members of a congregation are obligated to serve their brethren in the local congregation according to the gifts entrusted to them by God.
5. Members of a congregation willingly submit to one another according to the position given them by God.
6. To ensure the health of the local congregation and the salvation of each individual, a congregation is obligated to practice discipline towards members who are found in continuing sin.

If local churches are the locus of God's work in this world, and they are to strive for the pure ideal prophesied in Jeremiah 31:34, then the question "who is a member of a local church?" becomes highly important. In the parish understanding of the localised church, the members of a church parish are all those who live within the parish boundaries; for legal purposes, one is officially a member of the parish and, therefore, able to vote on church matters after some time (6 months here in Sydney). However, according to the Biblical understanding of the local church, the local church is meant to be an instantiation of the invisible Church and, so far as is possible, express the pure nature of that invisible reality (see Ch. I.3-4, 5.b.i.5; V.8). The local church in the New Testament refers to believers; each local church is a discrete set of believers. The question of membership thus asks who the members of a church are, how they become a member, if one can lose membership, the obligations and responsibilities of such members, and other such questions. As we will address in this chapter, 17th-century Congregationalists believed that infants may become members of a local church and that church covenants were essential for constituting a local church. We will reject the former claim and accept the latter in a modified way, that a covenant is a useful tool for achieving what the Bible lays forth without a covenant.

1. A Member of a Local Church Is a Believer Who Regularly Participates in the Life of the Church; Thus, an Ordained Leader Is a Member.

a. The Qualification for Membership

Because a local church is more than a gathering, regular participation in a local gathering is not sufficient to qualify a person for membership in a congregation. Though we are not given a measure of the frequency with which this occurred, Paul speaks of unbelievers being involved in the gatherings of the Corinthian church. This supports our point: being in the gathering, even regularly, is insufficient to qualify for membership (1 Cor 14:20-23). In this passage, and according to our definition of the local church discussed above (I.4), being a believer is a qualification for church membership. Because much of the life of a local church identified in the New Testament happens outside of the regular gathering, being a believer who attends a local gathering appears to be an insufficient condition for membership (indeed, *mere* attendance of a gathering would seem to be evidence against the genuineness of professed belief given the corporate dimension of the good works that true faith ought to manifest (e.g. Eph 4:28; 2 Thess 3:10-12)). It is involvement in this more wholistic life of the church that Scripture has in mind when it speaks of a congregation and its individuals, members of one another (Eph 4:25). Therefore, those believers who regularly participate in the life of a local church are qualified as its members. I add the term "qualified" to bring out the element of intentionality that was insisted upon by our Congregational brethren.

b. On the Propriety of Church Covenants

A congregational covenant was a way to bring the obligations and rights of church membership to the fore, to make it explicit and ensure that people understood the cost of committing to Christ in a local church. It was the Congregational way of ensuring that people counted the cost of following the Christ who established local congregations as the expression of his Lordship. It was argued that as the church is analogous to a marriage or a city, both of which (as the Congregationalists understood it) involved commitment under a covenant, so also a local church required an explicit covenant for its convocation (see CPD V.3-6). I do not find their arguments persuasive on this matter: I cannot establish a biblical warrant for requiring a covenant for membership in a local church. However, given the significant demands of local church membership (see Chs. II.2-5, V), it seems wise to make these demands and responsibilities explicit and have members express verbal assent to them. The obligations and requirements appear to be explicit in the New Testament (that is, there are no secret members of the congregation); therefore, if a covenant secures the intentionality of local church commitment, then it seems permissible.

c. The Officers and Laity as Two Categories of Members

We can distinguish two subcategories among the broader category of congregational members (which is itself a subcategory of those found in the local church, to be discussed below): officers and laity. It is important to recognise that officers and laity are both members; thus, congregational authority is found in the whole congregation, excluding neither the elders nor the laity. Officers are members in the same capacity as the laity and, therefore, are subject to the same rights and responsibilities. Their election and ordination add additional responsibilities onto those that are theirs as members. Therefore, to qualify for office, an elder or deacon must first be a member. Elders and deacons must, therefore, be regular participants in the life of the church to which they are to serve and, as judged on the principle of charity (the external measure of determining the genuineness of professed faith), they must be believers. This qualification, that officers must *first* be members will receive significant objection, so we will dwell on this point a moment longer. We can establish this based on the election process, Scriptural precedence, and membership non-transferability.

The election process involves the church members putting forth one of their own for the role of a leader (Acts 2:21-23, 6:3; see Ch. III), so membership would seem to be a prerequisite for election. The wisdom of this is apparent: participation in the life of the local church is necessary to ascertain whether the candidate possesses the qualifications for the role.[33]

In addition, there is no biblical precedence for bringing in an outside candidate for election and ordination. In addition to the two occasions of an election mentioned above, the most natural reading of Acts 14:23 and Titus 1:5 is that those appointed were among the disciples that were to become churches.

Finally, this is supported by the non-transferability of membership. If membership involves some period whereby we might distinguish the transient association with a church from full participation required for membership, then electing and ordaining non-members means that for some time while they possess their office, they would not be members of a church. This conclusion being unsatisfactory—namely, the church's leaders should not be exempted from the proper accountability and horizontal obligations of membership, should they?—it would seem that membership is a prerequisite for possessing office. If membership is non-transferable, then this membership must be acquired *first* before election and ordination may occur. In the Cambridge Platform, the primary argument for the non-transferability of membership is the responsibility of each church to maintain the high standard of pure membership and fitness of its leaders. A church must not, they argue, outsource this process of vetting to another, lest a wolf be admitted owing to the mistake of another. We could perhaps support this weighty argument with 1 Timothy 5:22, where Paul instructs Timothy to be

---

[33] Cf. Martin Bucer, *Concerning the True Care of Souls*, trans. Peter Beale (Edinburgh: Banner of Truth Trust, 2009), 62–64.

slow in ordaining an elder lest responsibility for their transgression fall on the ordaining leaders. Those who elect and ordain a leader are, to some extent, responsible for that leader's actions. Therefore, the electing and ordaining members must take thorough measures to ensure those they elect and ordain are appropriately qualified. The test of membership seems to be an appropriate way to do this, supported as it is by biblical precedence.

Someone may object that this places an onerous burden on churches in the modern world. That is, many churches are insufficiently resourced to raise up their own leaders and, until an alternate method of training is implemented, are reliant upon students who have received pastoral training in major city centres. Sometimes these students are forced to switch churches regularly during their studies. How can we insist on membership before office in such situations? Until a better solution is attained, namely, the equipping of churches to raise their own leaders, introducing a period of probation as a part of the hiring process may be prudent. That is, instead of restricting the hiring process to a select committee based on interviews and references, it may perhaps be insisted that prospective ministers join a church and attain membership towards an appointment to office; this period of probation would give the congregation time to test the prospective minister before being complicit in his appointment through an election. This will certainly be unsatisfactory to many, yet it seems to be necessitated by the high standard of appointment in Scripture.

d. Members Are a Category of Those Who Are Associated with a Local Church

A "member" is not the only category we will find in association with a local church; there are several more. There are unbelievers, members in bad-standing, believers from another church, and probationary members (including children).

First, there may be persons who regularly participate in the congregation's gatherings but are not believers, therefore not qualifying for membership. Unless there is reason to suspect that their participation in the gathering would be a hindrance to the health of the body (such as someone who does not engage in illegal behaviour yet encourages sexually immoral behaviour), their participation in the gathering does not seem to be prohibited by Scripture (1 Cor 14:20-23); with prayer, a congregation may hope that God's Spirit, at work through the reading and teaching of Scripture and the testimony of the saints, will convert such a person.

Second, there may also be members in bad standing before the church. Such are believers who have qualified and submitted to membership yet have acted so as to put themselves under church discipline. As is determined at the elders' discretion with the support of the members, such persons may be prohibited from some of the rights of memberships, such as participation in the election of officers, voting on matters of church business, receiving financial care and support, or participating in the Lord's Supper, or they may be prohibited from all rights through the extreme measure of "*exairtion*." As argued below, "*exairtion*" is the highest act of church discipline, cutting off a member from all membership privileges (Ch. V). The purpose of such actions is that such a person would be soon welcomed back as a full member of the congregation (1 Cor 5:5; 1 Thess 3:14-15).

Third, there may be those who are members of another church or are judged to be a believer yet who only join the congregation's gathering for a season. As argued in Chapter 1.5.b.4-5, a congregation is obligated to welcome such persons with care, being eager to demonstrate hospitality but acting with discernment lest they become complicit in the works of darkness (Eph 5:11). *The Cambridge Platform* required letters of commendation be carried by such persons, declaring their good standing in their home church (ch. XIII, cf. Acts 18:27; Col 4:10; Rom 16:1; 2 Cor 3:1); because such is not a common practice in our age, such a requirement seems unreasonable, yet it agrees with the biblical testimony that congregations are responsible to "judge" their brothers, as Paul puts it (1 Cor 5:12, see the discussion in Ch. I).

Finally, there may be believers who are in the process of becoming members. Such are ministers in the process of becoming members (as discussed above, II.1.c) or anyone who has begun to participate in the life of the local church and has been judged a believer but has yet to be formally recognised as a member. In this category, I would venture, are infants and some, but not all, children. In the case of infants, the ideal of a pure church as laid forth in Jeremiah 31:34 and elsewhere (see our discussion in Ch. I), argues against accepting infants as members on account of their parents. This can be supported by the position of credobaptism, as defended in Chapter IV.B. That is, if union with Christ is through faith, and baptism is a symbolic demonstration of that union granted to those who, on the principle of charity, are to be counted as members of Christ's body, then a child who is unable to profess faith through belief in the resurrection and the confession of Christ's lordship, along with repentance from sin (Rom 10:9-13), would seem to not yet be part of the New Covenant. They do not yet *appear* to be a member of Christ's body and the invisible Church (Christ alone knows their true state). As discussed below, the principle of charity relies on such evidence to identify those who are "believers" and so prima facie part of the Invisible Church, the prerequisite for church membership; thus, children would be excluded from church membership because it is impossible to determine in charity if they have joined the Invisible Church. However, because of the believer's prayer that God would incorporate their children into his Church, and their confidence that a believing parent has a sanctifying influence on their children (1 Cor 7:14; Titus 1:6; cf. 2 Sam 12:23), we ought not to count our children as unbelievers until they demonstrate this with their lives. That is, the Bible does not give us a certain age after which a person may become a believer; we have no reason to believe young children cannot genuinely believe in Jesus Christ (as some of us have experienced, with no conscious memory of moving from unbelief to belief). However, the church is obliged to seek evidence of faith before granting membership, and children will often be unable to put forth sufficient evidence. Therefore, though we cannot judge whether a child is genuinely a believer, this does not mean they are unbelievers. It would seem prudent, therefore, to treat children as probationary members until such a time as they demonstrate themselves to be unbelievers, either through their behaviour or by verbally renouncing the Lord; until they withdraw from regular participation in the life of the church, thereby disqualifying themselves from membership; or until they can give evidence of belief, receive baptism, and intentionally commit themselves to the rights and responsibilities of memberships. The Bible provides us with no indication at which age a child may do this (and in the case of a person with an intellectual impairment, we may also consider adults); therefore, judgments should be made on a case-by-case basis.

e. Concerning Degrees of Membership

An issue we have not yet discussed is the gradation of membership that has been employed by some in Baptist churches (undoubtedly, others have also employed such a practice). We can imagine a scenario where someone is a genuine believer (as judged by the principle of charity), they have regularly participated in church life, yet they deny the validity of a critical tenet of the church's constitution. Perhaps they believe that infant baptism is appropriate and children are total participants in Christ's Church and, therefore, the local congregation. Suppose such a person were to express an interest in becoming a member in a church that accepted the entire model of polity outlined here, including as it does credobaptism. Should they be permitted to do so? The ecumenical desire to welcome all of Christ's sheep would push us to answer in the affirmative, yet doing so may lead to unacceptable consequences. Namely, as such persons as members would be eligible to elect leaders and participate in corporate judgments, it is conceivable that they could be instrumental in achieving substantial constitutional changes. Should membership be withheld to avoid such outcomes? We could imagine more significant doctrinal issues among genuine Christians, which could lead to a schism in a local congregation. For want of biblical evidence, I am reluctant to give a definitive answer to this conundrum, but I think several courses of action are biblically permissible.

First, a congregation may welcome such persons, trusting that the Holy Spirit will have his way and work such reformation as he wills. Perhaps such a congregation would seek to discern whether such a person, though a believer, conducts themselves in a schismatic, divisive manner and factor such behaviour into their judgment (cf. Titus 3:10-11). Second, a congregation may welcome such a person on analogy with the probationary member, granting them certain membership benefits, such as financial support, teaching, and discipline, but not voting privileges. This would appear to be an unhappy arrangement; perhaps it would be best used where no Gospel-centred, faithful congregations are available for such a person to join. Third, a congregation may deny such a person membership but treat them as a Christian from a different congregation. This is similar to the second option; however, given the recognition of the transitory nature of such hospitality, the congregation should actively seek to help such persons settle in another congregation. Surely there are other alternatives, but these three stand out to me as the most likely courses of action.

2. The Genuineness of Faith Is to Be Judged according to the Principle of Charity

If membership is contingent on belief, and the hearts of men and women are known only by God, how can we judge whether someone has faith? How are we to identify who is part of Christ's invisible Church and who is not? There are at least two inadequate responses to this question.

On the one hand, someone might accept a person's statement of faith at face value; if someone claims to trust in Jesus, we should accept them to be in Christ based on this profession alone. The reasons for the inadequacy of this position are, minimally, that the Bible is clear that many will claim to know Christ but actually do not (e.g. Matt 7:21-23; 1 John 2:19) and that the Bible itself calls for evidence of the genuineness of faith (e.g. Matt 3:7-10, 7:15-20; Gal 5:16-26; Jam 2:14-26; 2 Pet 1:3-15; 2 John 8-11; 3 John 11-12).

On the other hand, someone might set forth an objective test or standard of holiness and measure all persons by that same measure. The inadequacy of this position is that all Christians will be at different stages in their walk before Christ: we recognise that sanctification is a lifelong journey, children will not be as far along as mature, adult Christians, and new Christians will not be as far along as mature Christians (e.g. Rom 14:1-23; 1 Cor 8:7-13).

Therefore, a judgment of charity is necessary: we are to seek evidence corresponding to a person's confession of faith, yet we do so with charity— with great patience, with gentleness, with attentiveness to the person and their circumstances, with cognisance of the individual nature of sanctification. We ought to seek genuine fruit, yet we ought to presume the best (that a profession of faith is honest) unless such a profession is not accompanied by fruit appropriate for this person's maturity and life circumstances. *The Cambridge Platform* spoke of this principle in this manner,

> The things which are requisite to be found in all church members are repentance from sin and faith in Jesus Christ. Therefore, these are the things whereof men and women are to be examined at their admission into the church, and which then they must profess and

hold forth in such sort as may satisfy rational charity that the things are there indeed. John Baptist admitted people to baptism, confessing and bewailing their sins: and of other it is said that they came, confessed, and shewed their deeds.

The weakest measure of faith is to be accepted in those that desire to be admitted into the church because weak Christians, if sincere, have the substance of that faith, repentance, and holiness which is required in church members and such have most need of the ordinances for their confirmation and growth in grace. The Lord Jesus would not quench the smoking flax, nor break the bruised reed, but gather the tender lambs in his arms and carry them gently in his bosom. Such charity and tenderness are to be used as the weakest Christian, if sincere, may not be excluded nor discouraged. Severity of examination is to be avoided. (XII.2-3)

3. Members of a Congregation Are Mutually Accountable to One Another and Are Responsible to Hold One Another to Account.

We now move from the nature of membership and how someone is to be accepted to the rights and obligations of members to each other. Fundamental to a healthy congregation is the accountability of its members to one another. To be a congregation member is to subject oneself to God's means of sanctification, one of which is the corporate work of God's people in identifying and rebuking sin and restoring those who have repented. We will later consider the formal means of church discipline, but before these formal means, members of a congregation are called by God to render to one another informal acts of accountability.

In his letter to the Colossians, Paul urges them, "Let the word of Christ dwell in you richly, teaching and admonishing one another in all wisdom, singing psalms and hymns and spiritual songs, with thankfulness in your hearts to God" (3:16). Letting Christ's words indwell their community meant they ought to serve one another not only through instruction but also admonishment, giving a warning concerning sin. This same command to hold one another accountable and offer a timely rebuke, if necessary, is found in Hebrews 3:13, "exhort one another every day, as long as it is called "today," that none of you may be hardened by the deceitfulness of sin." In Ephesians, Paul uses the phrase "speaking the truth in love" (Eph 4:15, 4:25) for this mutual ministry of the word of Christ—of the Scriptures—in warning, encouragement, and teaching. In Ephesians 4:25, he specifies that we do this because we are "members one of another." Speaking the truth in love is not only offering timely admonishment but also encouragement, as Paul commends the Thessalonian church, "encourage one another and build one another up, just as you are doing" (1 Thess 5:11). Part of this mutual ministry of the Word obligated of all members one to another is the confession of sin and extending Christ's forgiveness to those who so confess. In Luke 17:3-4, Jesus exhorts the disciples to rebuke a brother or sister found in sin and to forgive them when they repent; this is couched in the command to keep watch closely on oneself so as not to lead another believer into sin. Confession in Scripture is most often vertical, before God (1 John 1:9; Psalm 32:5; Prov 28:13), but it has a horizontal dimension, as in James 5:16. After instructing Christians to pray for the sick and for the sick to seek the prayers of the church elders (Jam 5:14), James then turns to the whole congregation, "confess your sins to one another and pray for one another, that you may be healed" (Jam 5:16).[34] Acts 19:18 also reflects this confession of church members to each other, though here it appears to be in a public context. Therefore, there is a warrant for both private, one-to-one confession and public confessions of sin. Some churches express this sense of mutual confession through corporate prayers of confession, which seems to be warranted by the Lord's Prayer in Matthew 6:9-13, involving as it does a request for forgiveness in the context of corporate prayer.

This ministry of mutual accountability expressed in the ministry of the word and in the confession and forgiveness of sin is described by Paul in Galatians 6 in this way,

> Brothers, if anyone is caught in any transgression, you who are spiritual should restore him in a spirit of gentleness. Keep watch on yourself, lest you too be tempted. Bear one another's burdens, and so fulfil the law of Christ [cf. John 13:34]. (Gal 6:1-2)

The gentle restoration of those in sin fulfils Christ's command to love one another (John 13:34) and can be described as bearing "one another's burdens." The final verses of this section remind us that we are individually responsible before the Lord and ought not to let ourselves be deceived through comparison to others who we might have the opportunity to serve

---

[34] The healing he has in mind here is physical; see the context.

(Gal 6:3-5). Bearing another's burdens does not excuse us from our own responsibilities before God, nor should the presence of a brother or sister in sin become an opportunity for someone to boast their own (supposed) holiness; instead, the presence of a brother or sister in sin is an opportunity to express the selfless love modelled by Christ.

4. Members of a Congregation Are Obligated to Serve Their Brethren in the Local Congregation according to the Gifts Entrusted to Them by God.

Though there are general obligations placed upon all members of a congregation, such as those considered in §3, members are also expected by Christ to serve one another with the unique gifts he has entrusted to them. To conform more accurately to the Biblical language, it would be better for us to say that each member is a gift to the congregation equipped to serve their brothers and sisters as God has created them to do so. Recognising that each of us is a gift given by Christ for the growth and perseverance of our brethren, we see that there is weight to our responsibility; God forbid that we would withhold the grace he would administer through us and, thereby, see one of our brothers or sisters stumble. Consider the words our Lord,

> Again, it will be like a man going on a journey, who called his servants and entrusted his wealth to them. To one he gave five bags of gold, to another two bags, and to another one bag, each according to his ability. Then he went on his journey. The man who had received five bags of gold went at once and put his money to work and gained five bags more. So also, the one with two bags of gold gained two more. But the man who had received one bag went off, dug a hole in the ground and hid his master's money. After a long time the master of those servants returned and settled accounts with them. The man who had received five bags of gold brought the other five. "Master, he said, "you entrusted me with five bags of gold. See, I have gained five more." His master replied, "Well done, good and faithful servant! You have been faithful with a few things; I will put you in charge of many things. Come and share your master's happiness!" The man with two bags of gold also came. "Master," he said, "you entrusted me with two bags of gold; see, I have gained two more." His master replied, "Well done, good and faithful servant! You have been faithful with a few things; I will put you in charge of many things. Come and share your

master's happiness!" Then the man who had received one bag of gold came. "Master," he said, "I knew that you are a hard man, harvesting where you have not sown and gathering where you have not scattered seed. So I was afraid and went out and hid your gold in the ground. See, here is what belongs to you." His master replied, "You wicked, lazy servant! So you knew that I harvest where I have not sown and gather where I have not scattered seed? Well then, you should have put my money on deposit with the bankers, so that when I returned I would have received it back with interest. So take the bag of gold from him and give it to the one who has ten bags. For whoever has will be given more, and they will have an abundance. Whoever does not have, even what they have will be taken from them. And throw that worthless servant outside, into the darkness, where there will be weeping and gnashing of teeth." (Matt 25:14-30, NIV)

We need not linger on the details of this parable here, but the import for our context is clear: we ought to use what God has entrusted to us. If we withhold what has been given to us by not exercising it in the Church context, we will receive judgment.

Three critical passages in the New Testament consider how members are gifted to the congregation so that the Church, through its local manifestations, might be built up to full maturity. In Ephesians 4:1-16, Paul speaks of key leaders given to the Church so that God's people ("the saints") might be equipped "for the work of ministry." Notice how these leaders are gifted so that God's people might do something, "the work of ministry"; thus, it is God's people as prepared by Church leaders doing something that will see "the body of Christ" built up, "until we all attain to the unity of the faith and the knowledge of the Son of God, to mature manhood, to the measure of the stature of the fullness of Christ" (ESV). Notice the corporate language here: it is not about any one of us being fully mature, but Christ's body—the whole encompassing us all—becoming a mature man: as Christ grew as a boy into a man that he might die for our sins and rise to reign forever as king, so his body in the present age, the Church, is to grow to full maturity, that it might complete its work.

This work of building up is described throughout the rest of the chapter as "speaking the truth in love" (see §3 above). There is some debate over the roles Paul speaks of, but it should suffice for our purpose to identify them as the key equipping ministries of the corporate Church, with some ministries expressed across congregations and some within specific congregations (see Ch. III): the leadership equips God's people so that the whole congregation may accomplish God's work, by which also the whole Body of Christ, composed as it is by local congregations, may accomplish its work in this world. We have discussed this purpose above, but we can reiterate it here as the upward, inward, and outward posture God has granted his Church and the churches that compose its temporal instantiation to present its members as living sacrifices in the worship of God (Rom 12:1-2), to build up its members for so that they would persevere in holiness to become the perfected bride of Christ (e.g. Heb 3:13; Eph 5:25-32), and to reconcile the hostile word to the God of all mercy and grace (2 Cor 5:11-21).

In 1 Corinthians 12 and Romans 12, Paul uses the analogy of a body and its parts to describe the role of congregation members in the Body of Christ. 1 Corinthians 12:14-26 reminds us that none of us are an accident; God has made us perfectly fit to contribute to the body of Christ, as the various bodily members are appropriately suited for the role granted to them. Like Ephesians, we are given a brief taxonomy of gifts, but this is not meant to be exhaustive; unlike the list in Ephesians, 1 Corinthians mixes functions or offices a person might have (such as "apostles" and "prophets") with acts performed or received. As in Ephesians, there are apostles, prophets, and teachers (the Book of Ephesians also speaks of pastors, but they are identified with teachers, see Ch. III below); then there are moments or gifts of healing God may grant to the person who is sick, the skill necessary for administration or helping those in need, miracles performed by and for his people, and languages (the nature of which has been a topic of much controversy in the last century). All of these gifts, persons or moments of grace granted to God's people attesting to God's presence and kindness, are given for the building up of the Church, as we saw in Ephesians. Romans 12 tells us that Christians are members of one another with distinct functions given to them by God within Christ's body (Rom 12:3-4). Paul exhorts the Romans to use these gifts, which "differ according to the grace given to us" (Rom 13:6),

> if prophecy, in proportion to our faith; if service, in our serving; the one who teaches, in his teaching; the one who exhorts, in his exhortation; the one who contributes, in generosity; the one who

leads, with zeal; the one who does acts of mercy, with cheerfulness. (Rom 12:6-8)

5. Members of a Congregation Willingly Submit to One Another according to the Position Given to Them by God.

All members of a congregation are responsible to one another for mutual accountability and the expression of the grace God has given them according to their faith, but there are also discriminating obligations, fitting to the roles God has given to each member. The relations of authority and submission (being the appropriate response to authority according to the nature of that authority) that exist between members, particularly between the laity and the ordained officers of a congregation, are not negated by the fact that each member of the congregation is a member of Christ, an heir of grace, a son of God the Father (sonship being the role of the inheritor, whether a male or female is accounted as such, Rom 8:14-17), and, as united with Christ and a constitutive part of the Church and a local congregation, bears authority alongside their brothers and sisters (1 Cor 12:13; Gal 3:28).

In Ephesians 5:18-21, Paul describes what it means to put off the works of the darkness, here drunkenness, and to put on the Spirit of Christ; after speaking of the use of songs to one another and the Lord and thanksgiving, he then speaks of "submitting to one another out of reverence to Christ" (Eph 5:21). The following section of the letter expounds the various relationships within which a Christian might find themselves and how this Spirit enabled submission will look. After this, Paul addresses three spheres of submission, which are expanded upon in other parts of the Scriptures. Within marriage, Christ has structured a pattern of authority reflecting his own headship of the Church (Eph 5:22-33; Col 3:18-19; 1 Pet 3:1-7; Titus 2:5); between children and their parents, Spirit-empowered living also involves submission (Eph 6:1-4; Col 3:20-21; Luke 5:21); even between masters and slaves, the egalitarianism of undiscriminating union to Christ (Gal 3:28) does not negate the call to submit to those in a position of authority (Eph 6:5-9; Col 3:22-4:1; Titus 2:9), though elsewhere we see that the pattern of authority and submission expressed in this relationship of slaves and masters is transformed by Christ. Submission is still necessary, yet this is not worldly authority and worldly submission (1 Pet 2:18-25; Col 3:22-4:1). This submission to one another, as is fitting, is rooted in the submission of every member to Christ the Lord (Eph 5:24)—we are all under authority—and is itself a reflection of Christ's own submission to his Father (e.g. Matt 26:42; John 5:19-21; 7:14-19, 28-29; 8:28-29; 12:27, 49-50; 20:17; 1 Cor 10:2-3; 1 Cor 14:28).

In the congregation itself, this Spirit-empowered submission finds particular manifestation in each member's submission to the congregation's officers and the congregation as a whole, expressed in the appointment of officers and acts of church discipline. In Hebrews 13:17, the author commands, "obey your leaders and submit to them, for they are keeping watch over your souls, as those who will have to give an account" (ESV). This is echoed throughout the New Testament, where elders are commanded to express oversight and to shepherd the congregation (Act 20:28; 1 Pet 5:2), and to speak with authority (Titus 2:15, 1:13; 1 Tim 5:20). Therefore, each member is to submit to the authorities ordained over them, namely, the elders. In Matthew 18, Christ speaks of the power of the church to bind and loose (Matt 18:18), presumably to discipline those in error and extend Christ's forgiveness to those who repent (cf. 18:17, 19-20; 1 Cor 5:1-13). This has a concrete manifestation in the authority to exclude someone from the congregation and to welcome them, as seen with the sexually immoral man in Corinthians (1 Cor 5:1-13; 2 Cor 2:5-11; 2 Thess 3:6, 13-15). Thus, when the members of the church, in conjunction with their elders, ordain leaders, members ought to submit to this decision and honour these leaders; when a congregation acts to discipline a member, that decision ought to be submitted to, whether by those who must enact such a decision or by the one who receives such discipline (see Ch. III, V).

6. To Ensure the Health of the Local Congregation and the Salvation of Each Individual, a Congregation Is Obligated to Practice Discipline towards Members Found to Be in Continuing Sin.

We have already discussed discipline in the above section in terms of the congregation's submission to such decisions; in Chapter V, we will discuss discipline more thoroughly. However, we introduce it here one last time to highlight that discipline is both an obligation and a privilege (though today it seems odd to speak of it as such) for congregation members. Discipline is not an option; it is vital to the health of the local church and, by extension, the universal body of Christ. As such, it is both an obligation, something we must do, and a privilege, a pain that we benefit from. As the author of

Proverbs writes,

> My son, do not despise the LORD's discipline
> or be weary of his reproof,
> for the LORD reproves him whom he loves,
> as a father the son in whom he delights. (Prov 3:11-12)

Commenting on this passage, the author of Hebrews will write,

> It is for discipline that you have to endure. God is treating you as
> sons. For what son is there whom his father does not discipline? If
> you are left without discipline, in which all have participated, then
> you are illegitimate children and not sons. Besides this, we have
> had earthly fathers who disciplined us and we respected them. Shall
> we not much more be subject to the Father of spirits land live? For
> they disciplined us for a short time as it seemed best to them, but
> he disciplines us for our good, that we may share his holiness. For
> the moment all discipline seems painful rather than pleasant, but
> later it yields the peaceful fruit of righteousness to those who have
> been trained by it. (Heb 12:7-11)

Discipline is an act of love when expressed by God our Father or our earthly
parents, so also, discipline is an act of love when expressed by a congregation
acting for our good. We are privileged by our relationship to this
congregation to receive such care—painful as it may be.

To discipline someone, as a church, is not to treat them as an enemy but
as a brother (2 Thess 3:15). As indicated by the verse Paul quotes in 1
Corinthians 5, this ultimate act of Discipline, excommunication or *exairtion*
(to invent a neologism that avoids the unwelcome connotations of the first
term, transliterating the Greek verb used in 1 Corinthians 5 into an English
noun) is based on the Old Testament Law, which commanded the Israelites
to drive out the apostate and unbeliever for the sake of the community (e.g.
Deut 13:5): the community of God is to judge its members (1 Cor 5:12-13).
However, whereas in the Old Testament, this act was punitive, the New
Testament act is restorative: in the New Testament, *exairtion* is meant to see
the persons restored to right fellowship with the congregation and, ultimately,
Christ (1 Cor 5:4-5; 2 Cor 2:5-11; 2 Thess 3:14). Thus, whereas in the Old
Testament, *exairtion* was intended to purify the community and punish the
apostate, in the New Testament, it is meant to purify the community and

restore the one in sin.

A congregation is obligated to use its powers of discipline so that the person in question would not be lost forever. By committing themselves to a congregation, a member invites the Spirit-directed searching of the heart that identifies and addresses grave sin through individual members and the whole congregation. Woe to us who would ignore sin and thereby leave one of our members to drift from Christ who saved them (Heb 2:1-4; 3:13; 10:24-25).

III. OF ECCLESIASTICAL AUTHORITY AND CHURCH OFFICERS

Paul and Timothy, servants of Christ Jesus, To all the saints in Christ Jesus who are at Philippi, with the overseers and deacons: Grace to you and peace from God our Father and the Lord Jesus Christ. (Phil 1:1-2)

A. Concerning the Meaning of Authority
    1. What is meant by "authority" or "power" in an ecclesiastical context?
    2. That power Christ invests in the laity.
    3. That power Christ invests in the officers.
B. Of Church Offices
    1. Concerning apostles and evangelists.
    2. There is one office instituted for the rule, care, and instruction of the congregation. Office bearers are variously called elders, overseers ("bishops"), rulers, teachers, or shepherds ("pastors").
    3. There is one office instituted for the oversight of material matters in the church, the deaconate.
    4. Concerning women "ministers" or "pastors."
C. Concerning the Commission and Maintenance of Officers
    1. Election is an act of all members together.
    2. Ordination is an act of the ruling office.
    3. Ordination is local and, therefore, non-transferrable.

4. The church is responsible for the maintenance of its officers.

5. Elders are responsible to raise up elders.

It is certainly appropriate to speak of "authority" or "power" in the context of the church, for we have vast biblical warrant to do so (including the instances of submission language given above); however, we must tread carefully here. In many cultures, 21st-century Western culture being no exception, "power" and "authority" are loaded terms that cannot be readily transposed from a secular context to the church. Church officers wield power, but it is not the power of secular authorities, tyrants, or autocrats; the congregation holds power, but it is not that of the *demos*, the people granted power through social organisation and institutions. Power and authority in the context of the Church are simultaneously stronger than their contemporary analogues, being manifestations of the all-encompassing authority of God, the creator and sustainer of all things; gentler than these analogues, being directed towards the growth and well-being of those under authority; and subversive to worldly expressions of authority, being an authority expressed in sacrifice and selflessness. Before we discuss the actual powers given to the churches, we will first discuss the meaning of these key terms in their biblical context.

A. Concerning the Meaning of Authority

1. What Is Meant by "Authority" or "Power" in an Ecclesiastical Context.

Power in the contemporary West is associated with abusive self-aggrandization and manipulation; power is the attribute possessed by those who treat others as pawns in their plans, as disposable commodities to be used and discarded as it suits the one with "power." Power is characterised by the means and will to make things happen to one's own benefit. The term "power" is used to describe the posture and position of those who engage is the worst forms of physical and sexual abuse; it is also used for the politicians who twist the truth and neglect their responsibilities for the sake of their own gain. Absolute power corrupts absolutely, we are told. Yet this is not the way we learned of Christ and his lordship.

To the question of Pilate, "Are you the King of the Jews?" (John 18:33), Jesus responds that he is indeed a king, but one that breaks through the categories Pilate is using. Jesus is king, yet his kingdom is not furthered by violence and conquest (18:36); Jesus is king, and this means attesting to the truth, to the power and glory of God manifest in the death and resurrection of the Son of God that all who believe would have eternal life in his name (18:37). To his disciples, Jesus gives his own example as the paradigm for the sort of authority wielded by his people,

> A dispute also arose among them, as to which of them was to be regarded as the greatest. And he said to them, "The kings of the Gentiles exercise lordship over them, and those in authority over them are called benefactors. But not so with you. Rather, let the greatest among you become as the youngest, and the leader as one who serves. For who is the greater, one who reclines at table or one who serves? Is it not the one who reclines at table? But I am among you as the one who serves. (Luke 22:24-30)

Jesus follows this passage by speaking of a kingdom and thrones to be given to his disciples: he is not repudiating authority but redefining it. The leader leads as one who serves, as Jesus served his people unto death. We see this same redefinition of power—as compared to the rulers of the Gentiles—when we encounter those relationships of authority and submission discussed in the previous chapter. In Ephesians 5, wives are commanded to submit to their husbands, yet the authority of their husbands (correlated with Christ's headship of his Church) is described as self-sacrificing action for the sake of their wives. They are to lead unto death, caring for and providing for their wives as for their own bodies. We are not to read this as a repudiation of the authority invested in the husband's role; wives are commanded to submit to them (Eph 5:21-33). However, we are meant to see a redefinition of authority and power as witnessed in Luke 22:24-30: no longer are leaders to be associated with selfishness, pride, and abuse but with self-sacrificial service that seeks the good of those they lead. Parents are to be gentle with their children (Eph 6:4; Col 3:21). The masters of servants are to be just and fair to their servants (Col 4:1); their authority is not a license for abuse and exploitation (Eph 6:9). The leaders of the church, elders, are not to express their oversight with "domineering" but are to be examples to the flock (1 Pet 5:3), nor are they to seek their own gain (1 Pet 5:2).

When we speak of "authority" and "power" in the context of the local church, this is the sort of power we mean. It is authority to act decisively (Matt 18:17-20; 2 Thess 3:14-15; Titus 2:15; Heb 13:17) for the good of those who are under authority (Luke 22:24-30; 1 Cor 5:3-5; 2 Thess 3:14-15; 1 Pet 5:1-4).

2. The Power Christ Invests in the Laity.

The Congregational view of church polity or governance is often known for the power it invests in the laity, in contrast with Episcopalian or Presbyterian polities. On this point, on the powers invested in the laity, we must depart from the view set forth by our esteemed brethren in *The Cambridge Platform of Discipline*, or at least in part. *The Cambridge Platform of Discipline* presents two accounts of church power and responsibility based on an Aristotelian distinction between the being and well-being of the church (CPD Ch. VI.1-2). They argue that a church may be constituted by members alone, without ordained leadership; therefore, all the powers Christ invests in the local church may be exercised by the laity alone, including electing, ordaining, and deposing leaders, along with admitting new members and exercising discipline (e.g. CPD VIII-IX, X.1-2). I argue that we must depart from them on this point because the distinction between the being and well-being of the church, with the resulting account of the laity's authority, is not founded on Scripture. In other words, there is no Scriptural evidence that a church may be constituted by members alone, let alone that a church so constituted would have all the authority Christ invests in local congregations.

The text our brothers appealed to was Acts 14:23, which we discussed above (I.4). They depend too much on Aristotelian metaphysical and ethical categories as well as a reading of the passage that is not clear. Concerning this passage, we made the case from the context of Acts 14:23 that the verse does not mean churches predated appointing elders; indeed, we suggested that the text may very well imply that the groups of disciples mentioned previously became churches with the appointment of elders. In the case of the Aristotelian framework Mathers and others employed, this book does not afford the space to address it in full—and I have addressed it extensively elsewhere—but we can outline its role in their argument. I conclude that because this metaphysic is not taught in Scripture and their key verse does not imply that churches pre-existed elders, both arms of their argument fail.

In Aristotles' metaphysic, something is constituted as a thing—it has "being"—through the combination of form and matter; *The Cambridge Platform* argues that the matter of the church is its members (Ch. III) and that its form is the church covenant (Ch. IV). Therefore, according to their Aristotelian metaphysic, a church exists as such where there are members and a church covenant. The question is then raised, what is the elders' role if a church is constituted without them? For this purpose, they bring forth an important aspect of Aristotelian ethics. Something is constituted as what it is by the form-matter combination, yet things are teleologically oriented towards (they have an objective purpose aimed at) an ethical good. A bad person still has human being, but a good person has human well-being, the ethical end of their human being. A church with elders is, therefore, better off than one without them (it has well-being), yet a church without elders is still a church. If we accepted this framework, it still would not establish the point the Cambridge theologians intended, for they also import the Aristotelian view of language into the picture. They assume that where something is called a church, it must conform to the conditions given in Aristotle's metaphysic (in short, grammar maps onto ontology), but the biblical authors do not usually play by these linguistic rules. Therefore, I conclude that there is no biblical reason to accept the argument that churches have a simple being without elders and well-being with them.

The Cambridge Platform's analysis of the distribution of authority within a church possessing well-being—a church with elders—is different from that which they posit for a church that has a simple being. It is this distribution of authority that I believe is the unique insight of New England Congregationalism expressed in the Platform, one which aligns thoroughly with the biblical picture:

> This power of government in the elders does not any wise prejudice the power of privilege in the brotherhood, as neither the power of privilege in the brethren does prejudice the power of government in the elders. Instead, they may sweetly agree together, as we may see in the example of the Apostles furnished with the greatest church power, who took in the concurrence and consent of the brethren in church administrations (Acts 14:16, 23; 6:2; 1 Cor 5:4; 2 Cor 2:6-7). Also that Scripture, 2 Corinthians 2:9 and 10:6, do declare that what the churches were to act and do in these matters they were to do in a way of obedience, and that not only

to the direction of the Apostles but also of their ordinary Elders. (Heb 13:17)

11. From the premises, namely, that the ordinary power of government belongs only to the elders and that power of privilege remains with the brotherhood (as power of judgment in masters of censure, and power of liberty in matters of liberty), it follows that in an organic church and right administration, all church acts proceed after the manner of a mixed administration, so as no church act can be consummated or perfected without the consent of both. (CPD X.10-11)

In this mixed administration, the elders' power is to lead and initiate church action; the congregation's power is to accomplish that which the elders lead them in. In practice, the power Christ has invested in the laity is expressed through the choice of their leaders, the admission of new members, and acts of church discipline. Now, since elders are properly members of the church as well as its officers, the power invested in the laity includes the elders functioning in their capacity as church members: in Acts 1:15-26, the company of brothers and sisters whom Peter addresses includes the rest of the apostles, and neither his speech nor Luke's account of the election excuse Peter himself from the process. However, in Acts 6:1-7, the Twelve do give the choice into the hands of the congregation, seemingly excusing themselves.

a. Election

There is a consistent pattern in the appointment of church officials in the book of Acts. In the case of replacing Judas in the role of an apostle and the ordination of deacons, we read that congregations put forth candidates (Acts 1:23, 6:3; cf. Deut 1:13) who are then invested with the authority of office by those already in office. In his *Concerning the True Care of Souls*, Martin Bucer also suggests that the criteria "being above reproach" implicates the congregation in the choice of ministers, for they attest whether a candidate is appropriate for the role or not (1 Tim 3:2; Titus 1:6).[35] On the role of

---

[35] Bucer, *Concerning the True Care of Souls*, 63–64.

members in choosing their leaders, Bucer writes,

> It is necessary to have the consensus of the whole church, because ministers are not only to be blameless in the eyes of the Lord's people, but also trusted and loved by them. In the second place however, because it is only possible to receive the necessary testimony as to the suitability of ministers from the whole church, particularly if it is a large one, by the agency of a few who are particularly knowledgeable, the other elders and leaders are to conduct and direct the election and carry out the installation.[36]

From the precedence of Acts 1:23, 6:3, and Deuteronomy 1:13, we identify the choice of officers as a power invested in the laity.

b. Admission

I know of no passage in Scripture that explicitly addresses the process of admitting people into the church as members, though our discussion above showed that there is indeed a concept of "membership" in the New Testament. However, in the case of *readmitting* people who have been censured for unrepentant sin, Paul's command is addressed to the whole congregation: as they have acted together for discipline, so they are to act together to receive a brother or sister back. The eldership, therefore, will lead the congregation in admitting new members or readmitting censured members, yet the congregation itself follows through on this initiative by welcoming the brother or sister in full congregational communion. (Titus 3:10; Matt 18:17; 2 Cor 2:7-8)

c. Discipline

Though there are no passages explicitly addressing the admission of persons into church membership, there are verses explicating the discipline and excommunication of church members. In Matthew 18:15-20, the whole church (laity and leadership combined) has the power to excommunicate someone who refuses to listen to correction on disruptive sin. This is echoed in similar passages (1 Cor 5:3-5; 2 Cor 2:7-8; 2 Thess 3:13-15; Titus 3:10-11). If the church leader's role is to lead in acts of discipline, we can conclude that

---

[36] Bucer, 63.

the congregation's responsibility is to follow their lead in accomplishing the act. Thus, their power is expressed in the very act of obedience, accomplishing that in which the elder has the power only to lead.

3. The Power Christ Invests in the Officers.

As indicated above, the power granted by Christ to church officers is that of leaders or governors, not tyrants or monarchs. A church officer in themself has no power to perform an act proper to the church, though this does not disparage their role in every act proper to the church. Christ has invested them with the power to rule or lead the congregation in the expression of their authority, to ordain leaders through the laying on of hands, and to exercise prophetic authority.

a. Rule

As leaders, elders set the tone and direction for the congregation to use the authority invested in them by the risen Christ. The officers convene the congregation in its gatherings and direct it to important matters of business where necessary, including calling special gatherings exclusive to church members to deal with in-house business, such as church discipline. (Special gatherings are necessary when the participation of unbelievers and outsiders would be a hindrance.) The officers also lead in the election of leaders, overseeing the congregation as they express their authority. Elders then ratify that choice through the laying on of hands.

b. Ordination

The power of ordination is given by Christ explicitly to church officers to install other officers into their positions. The installation of new ordained leaders begins with the election by the members of a congregation but is consummated by the laying on of hands, prayers, and commission of the presbytery (Acts 6:6; 1 Tim 4:14, 5:22; 2 Tim 1:6; cf. Num 27:18, 23; Deut 34:9; Acts 8:17; 9:17; 19:6). The idea of "laying hands" appears frequently in the Old Testament in the context of sacrifice, but it is also used several times for the ordination of leaders over Israel.

In Numbers 8:9, the congregation lays their hands on the Levites, offering them as an offering to the Lord "that they may do the service of the Lord" (v. 11). Verse 14 indicates that in this way, the Levites are separated from the rest of the congregation for their specific service. In Numbers 27, Yahweh instructs Moses to lay hands on Joshua (v. 18). Verses 19-20 explain this further: Moses is to commission Joshua in the congregation's presence and invest him with some of his own authority. Verse 23 shows that laying hands is part of this commissioning process and investing authority. In Deuteronomy 34:9, we are told that Joshua "was full of the spirit of wisdom" because "Moses had laid hands on him" (ESV). In the New Testament, "laying on hands" is used for ordaining or commissioning persons (Acts 6:6; 13:3; 1 Tim 4:14, 5:22; 2 Tim 1:6) and for visibly communicating the power of the Spirit (Matt 9:18; 19:13, 15; Mark 5:23; 6:5; 7:32; 8:23; Luke 4:40; 13:13; Acts 8:17; 9:12, 17; 19:6; 28:8).

In the context of ordaining leaders, it would appear that God has entrusted to elders the power to install leaders into their posts by publicly commissioning them and to grant them visible and spiritual authority and power, both signified by laying on hands. By laying on hands before the congregation, authority that the congregation perceives to reside in the elder is transferred to the new leader, and the Spirit fills the leader with ministerial authority from Christ for the work they have been entrusted, along with the power to see it accomplished.

c. Ministerial Authority

In addition to leading the congregation in the admission and discipline of members, overseeing the election of and ordaining officers, and leading in other minor areas of business, the presbytery (that is, the group of elders, *presbyters*) is invested with special power from Christ for the care of his flock. These powers are often expressed in the context of leading the congregation in the accomplishment of church acts but are also expressed in one-on-one discipleship and corporate teaching.

This is the power of prophetic or ministerial authority. As those entrusted by Christ to care for his flock, the elder is tasked with teaching, exhorting, and rebuking with all authority. That is, their teaching, their encouraging, and their rebuking are accompanied by an authority unique to their office (Titus 1:9, 13; 2:15; 3:8; 1 Tim 4:11, 5:7, 20; 2 Tim 4:1-8; cf.1 Tim

2:12-3:7). This authority does not grant them inerrancy nor an unqualified presumption of innocence, much as parental authority does not mean parents will always be right and not make mistakes. Nevertheless, as parental authority implies that children should obey unless doing so would involve themselves in sin, the authority Christ invests in elders means that we should listen to our leaders *when they act within the sphere of their charge* unless doing so would violate our conscience. In the latter case, if an elder would counsel or invite one into sin, whether that be sexual sin or other behaviours contrary to God's commands, such as theft, a congregation member is not obligated to obey their elder; indeed, they are obligated to bring the sin to light (1 Tim 4:19-21; cf. Eph 5:13-14).

There are times when elders also speak beyond their charge, such as offering advice on buying stocks, financial management decisions, etc., which Scripture does not give clear insight into and for which they have not been given a clear prophetic word. Like all Christians, an elder *may* receive specific insight into someone's situation. Such insight must cohere with Scripture yet will demonstrate a level of insight into the appropriate course of action that can only be given by the Spirit, and where a prophecy is given, we ought to listen (cf. Ch. IV.E.3). However, in such cases, the prophet must tread carefully and verify that they are indeed speaking a word from the God (Deut 18:20-22); such cases are not expressions of the unique authority given to the elder but are unique expressions of God's authority mediated by any of his people whom he so chooses.

The pastor's sphere of authority is to administer the word of God by the power of the Spirit for the well-being of the flock he leads. When a pastor is so acting, our first reflex should be to submit to their leadership as ordained by God. However, every elder, though invested with immense authority, is still human and fallen, so sometimes they act authoritatively but do so in error. Once again, the reflex of the Christian should be to trust their pastor, but as the Bereans searched Scriptures to verify the words of Paul (Acts 17:11), we ought to measure all things by the Word of God. If we are compelled by Scripture to follow a different path than that counselled by our elders, the path of humility would be to sit down and express disagreement with their instruction, seeking the opportunity to learn if we are indeed in error and ought to be following even this command.

The power invested in the officers of a church—particularly the eldership—is immense, underscoring three significant points in the practical outworking of these principles. First, all care and diligence must be taken in the election and ordination of leaders: they must be shown to be competent and have the character laid forth by our Lord before they are granted his authority (1 Tim 5:22; 1 Tim 3:1-13; Titus 1:5-9; 1 Pet 5:1-5). Second, elders must keep "a close watch on [themselves] and on the teaching" (1 Tim 4:16). In doing so, they "will save both [themselves] and [their] hearers" (1 Tim 4:16, cf. Acts 20:28). They ought to be diligent to be seeking the Lord in his word before daring to exercise their authority over the flock. They must also watch themselves that they are not going beyond what is written or for which they have specific prophetic warrant: their role is not that of a counsellor or advisor to give advice on whatever is asked of them but to exhort, teach, and rebuke from God's Holy Scriptures, giving God's word through God's Spirit in Christ's power to all who come to them and all who sit under their teaching. They will give an account; they must lead as those who are themselves under authority (Heb 13:17). Third, the congregation must not take lightly their charge to obey their elders, for they are acting not on their own authority but with the very authority of Christ their Lord mediated through his chosen tools. As Paul writes of rulers of cities, nations, and empires, "whoever resists the authorities resists what God has appointed, and those who resist will incur judgment" (Rom 13:2; cf. Heb 13:17).

4. Responsibility Concomitant to these Powers.

The powers Christ has invested in his churches are immense, to bind and release sin, to offer the means of perseverance and growth in the faith or to withhold it, to speak with the very authority of the God reigning in heaven, and to together act as ambassadors of Christ's kingdom in a hostile world. It must be said that Christ has not invested this power to be used as a congregation wills; no, Christ has invested his power in local churches to see his kingdom come and his will be done. Terrible consequences await those who would abuse the power entrusted to them. "Many of you should not become teachers, my brothers and sisters," writes James, "for you know that we will receive greater scrutiny in judgment" (James 3:1, my translation). As Jesus puts it, "And for the person who causes one of these little ones who believe in me to sin, it would better for him if a donkey's millstone were strung around his neck and he were thrown into the sea" (Mark 9:42, my translation). For the congregation, they must exercise caution in the admission and expulsion of sinners from the congregation, as well as in the election of leaders, lest they partake of the sins of others (1 Tim 5:22). For leader's, they are to use their power for the good of those they serve (Eph. 4:1-16, cf. III.A.1 above). If a leader uses their power for their own selfish gain and so destroy the sheep for whom Christ died, they should expect to face severe judgment at the resurrection.

B. Of the Church Offices

1. Concerning Apostles and Evangelists.

In *The Cambridge Platform*, the brothers distinguish between ordinary and extraordinary Church offices. Of the ordinary offices, they distinguish between ruling and teaching elders and deacons, so a sort of 2.5-fold ministry: I will argue instead for a twofold ordinary ministry of pastor and deacon. This still leaves open the issue of the so-called extraordinary offices, which the Cambridge Platform says ended with the death of the office holders. These extraordinary offices are associated with those figures identified as "apostles" or "evangelists." Though it is not clear that an "evangelist" is an official role, apostleship has an official capacity. Apostles are commissioned by Christ or his churches, are ordained through the laying on of hands, and act in authoritative manners within local churches. However, the apostleship is characterised in contrast with the ordinary offices by its trans-locality: apostles do not seem to be connected with any specific church. More importantly, for congregational ecclesiology, Christ has not given us instructions on how this office is to be administered; in contrast, we would argue he has for the ordinary offices. Thus, from both its trans-locality and the ambiguity about the role and who ought to possess it, I think the New England Congregationalists rightly deduced that apostles are not an office Christ would have continued beyond those explicitly called thus in Scripture.

a. Evangelists

Concerning "Evangelists," we find the term mentioned three times in the New Testament. Philip, one of the Seven ordained in Acts, is called an "evangelist" in Acts 21:8. We are not told what qualifies him as an evangelist, but we do know from Acts 8 that Philip proclaimed Christ in Samaria after the Jerusalem church was scattered. He performed miracles and the power of the Spirit accompanied his preaching. The tile "evangelist" relates to the word we translate "Gospel," suggesting that an "evangelist" is someone who preaches the Gospel. Though ordained as one of the seven, Philip's role as an evangelist appears incidental to his ordination: it results from the Spirit's work while away from the local church where he was ordained. Someone may argue that Ephesians 4:11 places evangelists among other official roles in the church, such as apostles and teachers. However, notice how in this list, other than "apostles," none of the other roles are identified with the offices clearly delineated in the New Testament. Elder-overseers are described as pastoring but are not called "pastors"; they are also said to teach, but their role is not called "teachers." Moreover, "prophet" is evidently not an ordained role in the New Testament. Thus, I take it that his list describes certain functions that persons in Christ's church perform, not specific offices, as "pastor" and "teacher" are functions performed primarily by the elder-overseers.

The other reference we have to an "evangelist" is 1 Timothy 4:5, where Paul exhorts Timothy to "do the work of an evangelist." This is followed by the statement "fulfill your ministry" (ESV); however, this does not clearly equate "the work of an evangelist" with Timothy's ministry, both "doing the work of an evangelist" and "fulfill your ministry" being exhortations in a list of instructions (also "be sober-minded" and "endure suffering"). Therefore, I conclude that, as in the previous instances, an "evangelist" does not describe an office in Christ's churches but a function or role someone performs.

In all three cases, an evangelist is someone who presents the Gospel; though contemporary theologies of ministry rightly identify the Gospel as something relevant to all stages of the Christian life—so all ministry is, in some sense, preaching the Gospel—the Gospel in the New Testament is often associated with proclaiming the Good News of Christ to those who have not yet heard or received it. This is apt for Philip's role as an evangelist; thus, I surmise that Timothy was to fulfil his pastoral ministry of caring for the flock *and* bring the Gospel to unbelievers—to do the work of an "evangelist." I thus disagree with my esteemed congregational brethren that an "evangelist" describes an extraordinary, ordained role in Christ's churches. This leaves "apostles" as the only extraordinary ministry in the New Testament.

b. Apostles

The New Testament features several figures referred to as "apostles." We have reasons to distinguish between a technical and more general use of the term in the New Testament. In addition to the Twelve, James the brother of Jesus and Paul and Barnabas are referred to in the technical sense (Acts 14:14; Gal 1:19). However, without qualification (e.g. "the apostles Barnabas and Paul"), "the apostles" appears to refer to the Twelve (e.g. Acts 1:2; 4:33, 35, 36; 5:2, 12, 18, 29, 40; 8:1, etc.) and James, the brother of Jesus. The Twelve explicitly received their apostleship from Christ himself (Mark 3:14; Luke 6:13; Acts 1:2), with Matthias replacing Judas (Acts 1:26). When the disciples and apostles set out to choose a replacement for Judas, they specify that it must be someone who was among the disciples for Jesus' whole earthly ministry, from the baptism of John until Christ's ascension (Acts 1:22); they must be a witness to the resurrection. Paul counts James among the Apostles (Gal 1:19); though James was not there throughout Jesus' earthly ministry, as was Matthias, apparently he was a witness to the resurrection (1 Cor 15:7). Paul himself received his apostleship directly from Christ (e.g. Rom 1:1; 1 Cor 1:1; 1 Cor 15:7; 2 Cor 1:1; Gal 1:1), witnessing him on the road to Damascus (Acts 9:1-9; 1 Cor 9:1; 1 Cor 15:7). He considered himself to be the last and least of the apostles, specifically because he persecuted Christ's church (1 Cor 15:7-9).

Those who were apostles in the technical sense wielded immense authority from the Lord Jesus to plant and lead churches across the inhabited world, often functioning with authority over multiple congregations. As Apostles, they were also elders of the churches they led (1 Pet 5:1; 2 John 1; 3 John 1) while also being more than just regular elders. It is in this trans-local, global authority role granted by Christ himself that Apostles are regarded as first and foundations in Christ's Church. The distinctive elements of this apostleship suggest that it is an extraordinary office not meant to be continued in our churches today. First, in each case, these apostles were commissioned by Christ himself and had their apostleship attested by other apostles: their claim to be appointed by Christ could have been but was not disputed by others who were likewise appointed. Second, they were witnesses of the risen Christ, which Scripture does not indicate will be a continuing experience throughout history. Third, Paul at least seems to consider himself the last of this group (1 Cor 15:7-9).

Without a mandate to appoint further apostles (which would, according to the Biblical analogy, require an act of Christ himself along with the action of the other apostles), without a description of the range and limits of their authority, and without reason to believe that Christ will reveal himself personally as he did to Saul and the Twelve, it would seem that the office of apostle ended with the death of John, the last apostle. We can add to this that the role of an apostle is described as a foundation: the apostles laid the groundwork for the continuing work of the Church through the establishment of local churches, the appointment of elders, and the writing of the New Testament. So, though the "apostles" are credited with foundational roles in the establishment of Christ's church (1 Cor 12:28; Eph 2:20; Rev 21:14, see how Rev 21:14 has the *Twelve* as foundations), we don't find their number increasing with the growing church. Instead, few are designated as such.

There are other instances of the term ἀπόστολος (*apostolos*), but here it appears to be used in a non-technical sense. It is not clear whether Barnabas was qualified as an apostle in above ways. Acts 4:36 certainly sets him apart from the Twelve, but given his early participation in the church and familiarity with the apostles, it is certainly possible that he was (Acts 4:36-37; Acts 9:27; 11:22-26, 30; 12:25; 15:2, 25, 39). Paul includes his writing companions under the banner "apostle" when he writes of the rights available to him, such as bringing a wife on his journeys or receiving a wage from the churches. These include Apollos, Silvanus, and Timothy (1 Cor 4:1-13; 1 Cor 9:5-6; 1 Thess 1:1, 2:6). In their capacity as those sent by the apostles or from other churches, perhaps these could be translated something like "appointed messengers" or "church emissaries," to distinguish such as these from the closed group called "Apostles." In 2 Corinthians 8:23 and Philippians 2:25, the translation "messenger" or "emissary" seems appropriate. This role echoes other itinerant ministries in the New Testament, which we have discussed above (I.5.b.i.4); in this sense, there may be "apostles" today, but the term has unwelcome connotations and is best avoided.

2. There Is One Office Instituted for the Rule, Care, and Instruction of the Congregation. Office Bearers Are Variously Called Elders, Overseers ("Bishops"), Rulers, Teachers, or Shepherds ("Pastors").

In Church history, there have been several positions concerning the lead role(s) in the church. The most common positions distinguish between either ruling and teaching elders, which is found in many presbyterian or congregational churches and echoed in some episcopalian churches in the role of warden (called by some, "elders"), or between elders (presbyters or "priests") and bishops.[37] In the first case, two offices are maintained in the church, elders (πρεσβύτης) and deacons (διάκονος), but the former office is divided into two categories, ruling and teaching elders. On this model, all elders rule or lead, but only some elders teach. The ruling elders are often unpaid lay elders (a term used in Baptist churches) and the teaching elders pastors or paid staff.[38]

Episcopalian churches, such as Catholic churches, Eastern churches, Anglican churches, and many Pentecostal denominations, attribute the role of overseer or bishop (επισκόπος) to clergy who stand over several congregations. The term may also be used, as it was in the late 2nd century and later, for the "monarchical bishop," or the elder who led the team of elders (the presbytery, πρεσβυτέριον)—the first among equals (*primus inter pares*). In both cases, the bishop is both bishop and elder, though the elders are only elders. As the church grew out of persecution in the 3rd and 4th centuries, a hierarchy developed among the bishops, with provincial bishops

---

[37] Priest is an English term derived from "presbyter," which is transliterated from the Greek word translated "elder," but it fails to distinguish the two different roles that are designated "priest" when it is translated as such, the Old Testament cultic officers and the rulers of the congregations, elders. Thus, presbyter or elder is to be preferred to refer to the ruling role and "priest" to the cultic role, which echoes contemporary English usage.

[38] Though there are certainly differences between Strauch's work and the account given here, *Biblical Eldership* remains a great resource for thinking through the biblical account of elder-overseers. Alexander Strauch, *Biblical Eldership: An Urgent Call to Restore Biblical Church Leadership*, Rev. and expanded (Littleton, CO: Lewis and Roth Publishers, 1995).

(Archbishops) over local bishops.

We will argue that neither of these distinctions is correct. In the New Testament, overseers or bishops are identical to elders, and all elders are expected to teach. There is no evidence for a monarchical role of overseers among local congregations, nor the role of overseers across multiple churches (see Ch. I above), so according to the principles we laid forth in the introduction, we do not accept the episcopalian bishop as an ordained role in the church. It should be said that many episcopalians agree that this distinction is not founded in the Bible and develop a different approach to developing polity, one based on natural law, as we discussed in the introduction. I direct the reader to that discussion and the resources there for the reasons why we are pursuing a polity based on the Bible, not natural law.

a. Elders and Bishops are the Same

The reasons for holding that, in the Bible, elders and bishops are the same are two: nowhere are they distinguished clearly from one another, and they are frequently identified with one another. When Paul speaks to the Elders of Ephesus, he instructs them to watch themselves and their flock carefully; they have been made *overseers* of the flock (Acts 20:28). Here, the plural elders are also a plurality of overseers; there is not a single overseer among them. In Philippians 1:1, Paul speaks of "overseers and deacons"; again, there is a plurality of overseers, and they are in the same place we would expect "elders." 1 Timothy 3 similarly describes overseer as a role alongside deacon. In Titus 1, Paul begins describing the qualities of an elder, which are similar to the description he gives in 1 Timothy 3 (where he speaks of "overseers"), then he describes the reason an elder must be qualified in this way, "for an overseer, as God's steward, must be above reproach" (Titus 1:5-7). Finally, in 1 Peter 5, speaking to elders, Peter instructs them to "shepherd the flock of God that is among you, exercising oversight (ἐπίσκοπεω)"; here, he uses the verbal form of the noun translated overseer (ἐπισκόπος) to describe the role of an elder. Thus, we nowhere find the roles distinguished; their qualifications are described similarly (1 Tim 3:1-7; 2 Tim 2:1-2; Titus 1:5-9; 1 Pet 5:1-4); the terms are used interchangeably (e.g. Titus 1:5-7); and they both perform roles of pastoring, teaching, and oversight or rule. So I take the view that "elder" and "overseer" are two ways of describing the main leadership role in a local congregation.[39] The writings of so-called apostolic fathers are ambiguous on the role of bishop in relation to the elders. Writing in the 4th century, Jerome suggests that at a later time (relative to Paul's letters, apparently), "one presbyter was chosen to preside over the rest"; "this was done to remedy schism and to prevent each individual from rending the church of Christ by drawing it to himself." Jerome suggests this arose in Alexandria under Mark the Evangelist (i.e., the writer of the Gospel).[40]

Similarly, I see no reason to distinguish between ruling and teaching elders. All elders are expected to exercise oversight and to lead (1 Tim 3:1-7; Titus 1:5-9; Acts 20:28), and all of them are expected to teach (1 Tim 3:2; 2 Tim 2:1-2; Titus 1:9). In 1 Timothy 5:17, Paul indicates that elders who do their job well are worthy of a twofold honour, usually interpreted as honour and remuneration; he indicates that this is especially true for those who labour in preaching and teaching. Given that all elders are to be able to teach and that this is part of their rule and oversight, this should not be interpreted as indicating a subset of elders, ruling elders and ruling elders who teach. Instead, it suggests a division of labour; though all elders are to teach, it makes sense for some elders to specialise in this task. Because specialising in teaching and preaching is particularly time-consuming, the honour of remuneration seems particularly appropriate for these elders.

b. The Qualifications of an Elder

Having identified elders with overseers, we can draw on the passages that use either term to understand who is qualified to become an elder. We have already discussed election and ordination above, under the powers of the congregation, and will revisit them below, so here we will focus on who may be elected and ordained, not how this is to be done.

The primary qualifications for an elder are character, supplemented with

---

[39] This view is not modern; it is found in the Apostolic Fathers, and in the 4th century, Jerome makes this claim, citing Philippians 1:1, Acts 20:28, Titus 1:5-7, and 1 Peter 5:1-2, "For when the apostle clearly teaches that presbyters [i.e. elders] are the same as bishops..." Letter CXLVI, "To Evangelus," §1 (NPNF 2.6, pg. 288).

[40] Letter CXLVI, "To Evangelus," §1 (NPNF 2.6, pg. 288), cf. CXXV, "To Rusticus" §15 (NPNF 2.6, pg. 248)

several other important considerations. Elders are to be exemplary in character, above reproach (1 Tim 3:2; 1 Pet 5:3). Though no Christian is perfectly sinless (1 John 1:8), elders are to live repentant, humble lives characterised by obedience to Christ. Their behaviour is not the sort that will lead the flock astray or open the congregation to charges of immorality from either members or outsiders. They are to be well regarded by everyone, inside and outside the church (1 Tim 3:7). Though their obedience to Christ might earn them the world's condemnation, elders are to ensure that in every other way, they are faithful, humble citizens, walking in righteousness and obedient to God-ordained authorities (Rom 13:1-7). They must be sober, gentle, humble, devoted husbands (below we will argue that only men are permitted to be elders), good fathers, and slow to anger (1 Tim 3:1-7; Titus 1:5-9). They must not consider themselves better than those they lead but lead as servants (Matt 20:25-28; 1 Pet 5:1-4); they must not be greedy or quarrelsome (1 Tim 3:1-3; Titus 1:7; 1 Pet 5:2), and they must be eager to welcome strangers into their house, to care and provide for those who come along their path (1 Tim 3:2; Titus 1:8).

The expectations of an elder are so steep because Christ entrusts them with such great authority. When they fall, as we have seen far too often in recent history, Christ's redeeming work suffers greatly. Christians are terribly hurt and fall back into sin, Christ's name is shamed among unbelievers, and doors are closed for Gospel ministry. Paul instructs Timothy to appoint elders slowly, with great care, lest such consequences follow (1 Tim 5:22). Elders will not be perfect but must demonstrate humility and repentance, owning their sin proactively, not waiting for it to be revealed by others. They must continually grow in holiness; self-righteousness and spiritual pride are cancers that will destroy the leader, their families, and the churches they lead.

Because elders are imperfect and have great authority, the principle of plurality is important.[41] An elder is never a lone wolf; they always share their authority with equals to whom they are accountable for their ministry and

---

[41] Though he defends the principle of first among equals, David Harvey's account of the plurality of eldership is still helpful. Cf. David T. Harvey, *The Plurality Principle: How to Build and Maintain a Thriving Church Leadership Team* (Wheaton: Crossway, 2021). Cf. J. Alexander Rutherford, "Review of The Plurality Principle – Teleioteti Book Reviews," Teleioteti, 2021, https://www.teleioteti.ca/2021/07/06/review-of-the-plurality-principle/.

personal lives. They must keep a close watch on themselves and each other as much as they do the flock (Acts 20:28). This is also why we must not make a *primus inter pares*, a first among the elders. Christ is the head of the Church and each church; therefore, no man can stand above his co-elders (Eph 1:22; 4:15; 5:23). Each is equally accountable to one another and Christ, their head. As mentioned above, this does not mean there is no division of labour among a team of elders, but a division of labour cannot become a stratification of authority. We have no mandate for this from Christ, our Lord.

In addition to character qualifications, elders must be "able to teach" (1 Tim 3:2; 2 Tim 2:2; Titus 1:9). Other than the ability to manage one's household, and so the church (1 Tim 3:4-5), this is the only skill required of elders in the Bible. They don't even have to excel at teaching; they only need *to be able* to do so. This confronts the contemporary attitude towards church leadership, where only the best and brightest are sought, and they must demonstrate an extensive skill set before being ordained. The mere ability to teach aligns with Jesus' own choice of leaders for his church, fishermen and tax collectors—hardly an inspiring and excellent group. An elder must also not be a recent convert (1 Tim 3:6), though they do not necessarily need to be old (1 Tim 4:12; 2 Tim 2:22). Finally, an elder or overseer must be a male (1 Tim 2:8-15; 1 Tim 3:2); this has not been controversial for most of church history but has become so in recent years, so we will dwell on this point for a moment.

We believe it is right to stand with the church throughout its history in reserving the role of elder and overseer for qualified men for several reasons. However, we do believe that there are vital roles in the church that women are encouraged to occupy; we will discuss these shortly. First, in 1 Timothy 2:8-15, Paul forbids women from teaching or exercising authority. From the surrounding verses, it is often assumed that the context for this teaching and authoritative action is church activities rather than, say, in a "secular" context; that is, Paul's instructions do not immediately pertain to university positions or politics. This seems to be right. There has been debate over the extent of teaching, given that Priscilla and Aquila certainly teach Apollos in some sense (Acts 18:26). We do not need to resolve this issue here, for whatever the scope of teaching is, it is certainly associated primarily with the role of elder (e.g. 1 Tim 3:2; 2 Tim 2:2, 24; Titus 1:9); when coordinated with authority, Paul is clearly forbidding ordained eldership, whatever else he might also be excluding. This echoes other passages concerning the role of women in the gathered congregation (1 Tim 2:11; 1 Cor 14:26-35). In the following chapter of 1 Timothy, Paul describes an overseer as the "husband of one wife" (1 Tim 3:2; cf. 3:8, 5:9);[42] if married, an elder must be a faithful husband and not a polygamist (it goes beyond the scope of this book to address the question of remarriage). In 1 Timothy 3:4-5, Paul associates the ruling or leading role in the church with the leading or ruling role in the family, which is elsewhere attributed to men (1 Cor 11:3; Eph 5:24-6:4; Col 3:18-21; 1 Pet 3:1-7).

Second, every ordained elder or apostle in the biblical church is a male, though as we will see shortly, there is at least one example of a woman ordained as a deacon. The twelve apostles were males, as were all others identified as apostles. William Witt points out that as the New Covenant equivalent of the twelve patriarchs of Israel, maleness (and Jewishness) was essential to the typology of the Twelve. Yet, every other apostle is also male, so his valid point about the Twelve does not negate the argument made here.[43] Others have objected, arguing that Junia in Romans 16:7 is identified as an apostle, and this is a feminine name. However, the Greek construction here means "well known to the apostles" (e.g. ESV, NET) rather than well known "among the apostles."[44] Certainly, everyone named as an elder or overseer is a man. This follows the precedent of the Old Testament, where men exclusively held the role of elder. Therefore, based on the commands of God's apostles and the examples given in Scripture, we maintain that the role of elder or overseer is to be held exclusively by men.

However, this does not mean that women have no role in Christian, even ordained, ministry. In Christ, men and women alike are accorded with immense value; they are adopted "sons"—that is, heirs of the inheritance, male or female (Rom 8:18-25, compare vv. 19, 21, 23)—in Christ's family and are equally recipients of God's abundant grace and mercy. Women are also charged with a high calling, in marriage or singleness, to serve God

---

[42] On 3:8, see below under deacons.

[43] William G. Witt, *Icons of Christ: A Biblical and Systematic Theology for Women's Ordination* (Baylor University Press, 2021), 265.

[44] E.g. Michael H Burer and Daniel B Wallace, "Was Junia Really an Apostle?: A Re-Examination of Rom 16.7," *New Testament Studies* 47, no. 1 (January 2001): 76–91.

wholeheartedly and spread his kingdom (1 Cor 8:25-40). Though the role of elder-overseer is not open to women, many other avenues of ministry are open wide; in addition raising children and loving one's husband, which the Scriptures accord with great significance (1 Tim 5:14; Titus 2:4-5), the role of deaconess or ordained women is presented as a pathway for women, often single or widowed, to serve Christ's church in a formal sense (see below).

c. The Duties of an Elder

The duties of an elder may be gathered under three principal heads, to rule the church, to offer pastoral care, and to teach. On the other hand, ruling, caring, and teaching could all be seen as different aspects of the one duty, namely, to shepherd the flock over which they have been placed. Let us consider each of these in turn.

i. Ruling

In the Old Testament, elders primarily had the role of community leaders. In Numbers 11, God chooses 70 of the elders of the people, who are also "officials," to share the burden of leadership with Moses (11:16, 17). In Josh 7:6, the elders join Joshua in mourning. In the New Testament, the local church elders have an analogous role.

Paul attributes to the elders the role of ruling or leading (προΐστημι) the churches in 1 Timothy 3:4. We are not given many details into what this "rule" looks like, but it appears to include maintaining the orderly conduct of worship, leading the congregational gatherings, and ensuring the congregation is taken care of, growing in spiritual maturity (Eph 4:11-14; 1 Cor 14). They are also to lead the saints in the works of service, by example and equipping them to do this work (Eph 4:11-14; 1 Tim 1:1-4; 1 Pet 5:3). Perhaps we could also include within ruling ordaining other elders (1 Tim 4:14; 1 Tim 5:22).

The New Testament does not give much detail about what this ought to look like. However, we can surmise from the analogy Paul gives in 1 Timothy 3 that just as every family will need to be led uniquely so that its purpose is achieved before God, so every local church will also need to be led in such a way that its purpose is achieved. The elders are responsible for providing this rule. Using the analogy of a shepherd, the elders are to ensure that the entire flock is orderly and moving towards its goal, the growth of the kingdom and maturity in Christ.

ii. Offering pastoral care

If the elders' rule sets the path, ensuring appropriate organization and structural support for the growth and life of a congregation, pastoral care is the elders' specific leadership of the individual sheep entrusted to them. Elders are to pay close attention to their sheep in order that they might shepherd them (Acts 20:28). "Shepherd" is a rich metaphor used throughout Scripture, especially for God's care and provision for his sheep (Ezek 34:1-31). As under-shepherds of Christ the chief shepherd (1 Pet 5:3-4), elders are Christ's instruments to exercise his shepherding care for the Church.

As a shepherd provides for the health of his sheep and protects them, so the elders are concerned for the spiritual and physical health of their congregation. They use the tools of pastoral care and teaching to address the spiritual health of individual sheep while also using their authority in the church and their teaching to protect against false teachers who would destroy the sheep. The aim of their ministry "is love that issues from a pure heart and a good conscience and a sincere faith" (1 Tim 1:5). The image of a shepherd is not that of a cold, distant CEO who manages a complex bureaucracy but of intimate, relational care. Shepherds are "keeping watch over [our] souls, as those who will have to give an account" (Heb 13:17).

We see an example of this shepherding care in the lives of both Jesus and Paul, both of whom engage in meaningful relationships with those under their care, relate with them personally, and can speak firmly and lovingly into the different situations of their lives. Paul's letters are dripping with love for the congregations under his care, expressed in earnest prayer and joyful thanksgiving over them. To be a shepherd is to be personally invested in the sheep. Think of Paul's interaction with the different churches; take the Thessalonians as an example,

> But now that Timothy has come to us from you, and has brought us the good news of your faith and love and reported that you always remember us kindly and long to see us, as we long to see

you—for this reason, brothers, in all our distress and affliction we have been comforted about you through your faith. For now we live, if you are standing fast in the Lord. For what thanksgiving can we return to God for you, for all the joy that we feel for your sake before our God, as we pray most earnestly night and day that we may see you face to face and supply what is lacking in your faith? (1 Thess 3:6-10)

Paul rejoices in the churches' successes (e.g. Phil 4:10) and is burdened by their failures and suffering (e.g. 2 Cor 2:1-4; 11:28-29; 12:11-21).

As shepherds, elders are to minister God's word to the sheep with all patience and gentleness (1 Tim 6:11; 2 Tim 4:23-26), exemplifying Godly character in these relationships (1 Tim 4:12;.2 Pet 5:2-3). With authority given them by God (2 Cor 10:8, 13:10; Titus 2:15; Heb 13:17), elders provide specific instruction to those in need (e.g. 1 Cor 5:1-5; Philemon; Heb 2:1-4), adjudicate disputes (1 Cor 6:1-8; Phil 4:2-3; 1 Tim 5:19), rebuke and admonish those who are in sin (1 Tim 5:20; Titus 1:13-14), and encourage and restore those who are grieving and downtrodden (Gal 6:1-5; 1 Thess 2:11-12; 3:1-3; 2 Tim 3:16-4:5). As with anyone in the congregation, Elders may on occasion receive prophecies, authoritative words from God applying his Scriptures to the specific circumstances of a person's life, but their regular communication is invested with God's authority corresponding to their role, so they must be vigilant in their communication to speak appropriately and wisely in all circumstances. Though it is closely related to ruling and teaching, the aspects of shepherding I have discussed in this section are most often performed in private, with families, in small groups, or one-on-one. Teaching, on the other hand, is the elders' public, word-based ministry.

iii. Teaching and preaching

Several times in the New Testament, elder-overseers must be "able to teach." Teaching is thus an essential component of their ministry. So far as I can tell, διδάσκω (*didasko*), the word we translate as "teach," is slightly more restricted than our word "teach," at least when used in the context of Jesus and the Apostles' ministries. It nearly always refers to a public act of speaking, occasionally along with the word κηρύσσω, to speak publicly (Acts 28:31). The contrast between learning quietly and teaching in 1 Timothy 2:11-12 also suggests that "teaching" here is a public act, specifically in the gathered church (cf. 1 Cor 14:27-28, 33-35). Some instances are ambiguous, and Acts 20:20 distinguishes between Paul's teachings in public places and from house to house, but this may reflect a contrast between public places like the Areopagus or Hall of Tyrannus (Acts 17:16-34, 19:9) and the more intimate setting of house churches or small gatherings (Acts 12:12-17; 20:7-12).[45] Or this could reflect the more intimate ministry of the word we described as pastoral care, as John Calvin and Richard Baxter would have it.[46] However, in most instances, "teaching" is a public act of word ministry, explaining and applying the scriptures. This is what I intend when I say "teaching" is a duty of the elders. As we will consider below, "teaching" is often associated with the abiding authority of the elders (see §IV.E).

Teaching in this sense is a more specific form of public speaking, κηρύσσω. However, the elders won't only teach, but they will also publicly reprove, rebuke, and encourage in the public gatherings of the church. We could thus use the word "preaching" for the whole public ministry of the elders by which they explain and apply the Scriptures to God's people (2 Tim 4:1-5). However, the danger in doing so is that we might collapse this public ministry into contemporary Evangelical preaching or another culture's equivalent. The Bible does not give us details concerning what preaching must or will look like, only that it is a public act of speech invested with God's authority that is based on God's word (1 Tim 4:11, 13; 2 Tim 4:1-5; Titus 2:15). It is both explanation, making clear what is unclear, and application, offering timely conviction of sin, a rebuke, warning of judgment, or encouragement.

One component of this teaching function will be to equip the saints for the work of ministry (Eph 4:11-12). As elders address the congregation from Scripture, they will point them to the work God has entrusted to them. They must not only convict of sin and lead the saints to desire to do God's work

---

[45] Mikeal C. Parsons, *Acts*, Paideia Commentaries on The New Testament (Grand Rapids: Baker Academic, 2008), 291.

[46] Richard Baxter, *The Reformed Pastor: Updated and Abridged*, ed. Tim Cooper (Wheaton: Crossway, 2021); John Calvin, *Commentary upon the Acts of the Apostles*, trans. Henry Beveridge (Bellingham: Logos Bible Software, 2010), 2:244.

but also equip them to do that work.

3. There Is One Office Instituted for the Oversight of Material Matters in the Church, the Deaconate.

The elders' role is weighty; doing it all well will take much time and energy. There are many other things involved in the daily life of a congregation that need leadership and oversight, perhaps maintaining a property, making sure the needs of the congregation are met, balancing the books, etc. If a group of elders were to do all these things in addition to the duties Scripture entrusted to them, they would undoubtedly find the duties of care, teaching, and rule slipping—even if all they did was oversee the congregation's members in fulfilling these things. However, in God's foresight, he has provided another ordained office to support the elders and maintain the congregation, deacons.

When the Apostles found themselves stretched to the limit between teaching and making sure physical needs were met, they instructed the church in Jerusalem to choose men who would be able to take up the ministry to physical needs so the Apostles could focus on teaching (Acts 6:1-7). Though these are not explicitly called deacons, the problem they are called to address is "serving tables" (διακονεῖν τραπέζαις, *diakonein trapezais*), the verbal form corresponding to the noun "deacon" (διάκονος, *diakonos*), and their role fits well with what we are told about deacons elsewhere.

a. The Qualifications of a Deacon

As with elders, the primary qualifications for a deacon are character based. According to Acts 6, the Seven were chosen based on their good reputation and the evident presence of the Spirit working in them. In 1 Timothy 3:8-10, deacons are required to be mature in the faith and have a good reputation for godliness, specifically not being deceitful, drunkards, or greedy. Paul insists that they be tested first and only become deacons if they "prove themselves blameless." Male deacons must demonstrate themselves to be good leaders of their families, as with elders (1 Tim 3:12).

Unlike eldership, the role of deacon appears to be open to both men and women. Many would cite Romans 16:1, where Phoebe is identified as a "servant" or "deacon" of the church in Cenchreae. However, some have responded that she is, perhaps, just a "servant" given the less official use of this term throughout Paul's letters (Col 1:25, 4:7; 1 Tim 4:6). However, modified as it is by a specific congregation (cf. Phil 1:1), "deacon" seems probable.[47]

In Acts 6, when the Apostles ask the church to choose seven to become deacons, they specify "men" (ἄνδρας, *andras*). Paul also speaks about deacons with male-specific terminology and roles in 1 Timothy 3:12, yet the previous verse addresses "women." The ESV translates γυνή (*gunē*) in this verse as "their [that is, male deacons'] wives," yet I do not see a good reason for doing so. The word γυνή may mean a woman or a wife, as ἀνήρ (*anēr*) may mean a man or a husband, depending on context. However, nothing in the context connects these women with the deacons mentioned earlier; there is no possessive pronoun, "their," nor is there a definite article, which would be an appropriate way to indicate that these women were the spouses of the previously mentioned men. Furthermore, it would seem odd that Paul would outline the qualifications for a deacon's wife but not an elder's wife, given the weightier nature of the latter role. Thus, "women" would appear to indicate a subset of the broader role "deacon." 1 Timothy 3:12-13 returns to the men, so there does seem to be some distinction between the two. Perhaps, given the general reflection of male family leadership in the structuring of the church, referenced here in 1 Timothy 3:12, male deacons may have an element of leadership among the deacons that women do not (perhaps explaining the specification of men in Acts 6:1-6), but the matter is unclear. What is clear is that among the second ordained role in the local church, men and women both have a place. The role of women deacons may be reflected in Paul's obscure statement that widows are to be honoured and "put on the list" in 1 Timothy 4:9, for the language surrounding the qualifications for a "widow" are similar to those given for elders and deacons in 1 Timothy 3 (1 Tim 4:5, 9-10). However, providing care seems to be a priority in this passage (1 Tim 4:3, 16), so it is certainly possible that Paul describes who may qualify to be enrolled on a list for care (the usual interpretation of these verses).

---

[47] However, if someone could provide conclusive evidence that women are not to be deacons—evidence I don't believe exists—then the translation "servant" would be justified.

b. The Duties of a Deacon

We saw that with elders, God in Scripture has given a broad outline of their duties, which will need to be filled in in specific contexts; we are given even less for deacons. However, we can identify a broad sphere of responsibilities within which deacons function; the typical things a deacon will do within that sphere will be determined by many factors, including culture, the size of a congregation, the needs of the community, etc. In Acts 6:1-7, the Seven are appointed to handle the physical demands of the church community, "to serve tables," so that the Apostles can focus on word ministry. However, seven men would hardly be enough to manage the logistics of a church of thousands of people, and 1 Timothy 3:12 requires male deacons to demonstrate leadership skills in their homes before they may become deacons, so we could perhaps conclude that deacons are to manage the physical ministry of the church, not necessarily do all the labour themselves (depending on the size of a congregation). As Paul writes in Ephesians 4, God has given the various teaching functions of the church so that the congregation would be able to perform the work of ministry: ordained officers are not meant to do all the work necessary for a healthy, thriving congregation, but they are there to enable the congregation to do the work and make sure everyone is getting what they need (4:1-16). Therefore, under the rule of the elders, deacons are responsible for the broad administrative and logistical needs of a congregation so that the elders are freed to perform the ministry of the word and that all congregation members are taken care of.

4. Concerning Women "Ministers" or "Pastors."

It is a common practice in Evangelical churches that believe women cannot hold the office of elder to hire women staff members as "pastors" or "ministers." In the Sydney Anglican Diocese, those ordained as deacons, including women, are often "assistant ministers," who may do many of the same things as the senior ministers (presbyters = elders) except preaching or taking the primary leadership role in the church (some churches permit women to preach but not to be presbyters). Female deacons may offer pastoral care, administer the sacraments, participate in the planning and leadership of the church, lead services, and lead worship (though these roles differ from church to church). The position we have laid forth thus far in this book, and will expand upon in the following chapter, problematizes identifying an ordained women's role as "pastor" or "minister." However, I will suggest that there is undoubtedly a place for women on a church staff team.

We have argued that "deacon" is a role reserved for taking care of the broad administrative and logistical needs of the congregation, so titles should not be used for deacons that would confuse their position with the distinct role of elders, such as calling elders "ministers" and deacons "assistant ministers," or calling both "pastors" (a term used in Scripture for elders alone). Moreover, pastoral care is intimately caught up in the role of an elder: they alone are entrusted with the authority of Christ to lead the sheep in their church. They cannot outsource this role to those who are not ordained or ordainable to this role. So, entrusting pastoral care of women to women pastors introduces confusion, suggesting that the administration of care and censure by an elder can be separated from the authority invested in that role. Similarly, introducing a regular position where a deaconess preaches to women introduces confusion into the meaning of "preaching," which, as we will argue in the following chapter, refers to the authoritative ministry given to the elders in one crucial sense. There is another sense of the preaching permitted for unordained men and women alike, prophesying. However, prophecy is, by definition, intermittent, so hiring someone as a staff member to do so confuses prophesying with the teaching function of elders. Thus, appointing women as "assistant ministers" may introduce unnecessary ambiguity into the respective roles of elders, deacons, and unordained lay persons.

However, it would be wrong to leave this discussion on a negative note, for a criticism of a contemporary practice does not mean there is no alternative. Indeed, I suggest there is an alternative. Women are filled with the Spirit of God as much as men are, and they are to be equipped by the elder-overseers for the work of ministry, just as men are. It seems entirely appropriate for spiritually qualified women who desire to dedicate themselves to the service of Christ in the local church to receive remuneration for their labours. Hence, hiring women as church staff seems entirely appropriate. I will not delineate every possible role a woman could be employed for in a church—I don't think such a list could be created! Some examples would be counsellors in the sense that "pastoral care" is often used (at least here in

Sydney), namely, listening attentively to the other person. There is also a place for offering various forms of secular counselling that do not involve the authoritative application of Scripture to those being counselled, which is pastoral care associated with the role of elders. Perhaps a woman could be employed to minister to children (including youth) or "teach what is good, and so train younger women to love their husbands and children, to be self-controlled, pure, working at home, kind, and submissive to their own husbands" (Titus 2:3-5). A woman could also direct a music ministry. Indeed, given that the "teaching" is less to do with the communication of content but with the authority of Christ invested in elders for the application of the word of God (see Ch. IV), it would seem entirely appropriate for churches to hire gifted women to advise on theology or biblical exegesis, perhaps producing resources like commentaries and study guides for the elders and congregation. I have certainly benefitted from theological discussions with and books written by women. An issue only arises if such a role is equated with the authority God has invested in elders.

With an elder's authority, his public teaching is innocent until proven guilty, but with prophecy, it must be judged. Similarly, materials produced by women in this role would need to be evaluated as one would judge any book in the academic context; if the resources produced by a staff worker who is not an elder (male or female) were to be treated as the definitive position of the church, therefore bearing the authority of its leadership, this would be an error. So long as proper safeguards are in place to distinguish the work of unordained persons from the elders, such a role would be appropriate.

C. Concerning the Commission and Maintenance of Officers

1. Election Is the Act of All Members Together.

Section A of this chapter showed that Christ has charged the congregation with electing its own leaders. We are not given a pattern or program for doing this. Thus, there is flexibility under the leadership of the elders for the mechanics of this election.

2. Ordination Is an Act of the Ruling Office.

In Section A, we also showed that Christ has entrusted elders with the responsibility of installing leaders elected by the members. Election alone is insufficient to make one a leader; the elders lay hands on those elected and thereby commission new leaders and invest them with power and authority through the Spirit for the work they have been given.

3. Ordination Is Local and, therefore, Non-Transferrable.

Local congregations perform ordination by installing one of their own in a position of authority over this congregation. As a function of the local church for that local church, and without a mechanism to universalise this process (that is, ordination is a function of churches, and only congregations are churches, therefore trans-local entities cannot ordain), ordination is entirely a local matter. Therefore, ordination is non-transferable. One is not an officer for life or an officer in general, but an officer is always an officer of this or that congregation. If that officer leaves this congregation, they also leave behind their authority over that congregation. They are not thereby disqualified from office over that church or another, but they must once again be elected by the members and ordained by the elders.

4. The Church Is Responsible For the Maintenance of Its Officers.

A. Churches Have the Responsibility to See Their Officers Taken Care Of

Christ has commanded the congregation to maintain its officers through financial provision so far as they are able to do so. We see this primarily in the context of elders, yet if the work demands it, we may presume by analogy that a deacon would also be worthy of a wage for their labour. In 1 Timothy 5:17, Paul speaks of a dual honour to be given to elders who perform their duties well: the word "honour" may mean respect or remuneration; both senses seem to be what Paul intends here. In the following verse, Paul draws on Deuteronomy 25:4 and Jesus' teaching (Matt 10:10; Luke 10:7) to show that those who labour are worthy of earning a living from that labour. Thus, elders are worthy of a wage corresponding to the work they perform. Speaking of his apostleship, Paul argues that he and Barnabas deserve a wage for their labours (1 Cor 9:3-18). In Paul's ministry, we see that he at times received from churches (2 Cor 11:7-11), but he refrained from doing so when it would hinder a church (2 Cor 11:7-11; 12:13). He also laboured as a tentmaker to support his ministry (Acts 18:3). So, an officer does not have to receive a wage from a church if they have alternative means and it is in the best interest of a church to refrain from burdening it. However, the church is responsible for seeing its officers taken care of, so if someone needs a wage for their labour, the church ought to supply it.

Many considerations factor into how much a minister should receive: the Bible does not give us specifics in this matter, yet a minister is to be free from greed, and the New Testament consistently warns against material wealth, so a church ought to take seriously the dangers of offering too much to an officer. However, the New Testament does not mandate that officers live in poverty, so congregations should not expect that their leaders should live in significantly worse conditions than they do. Much wisdom will be needed to determine appropriate wages in a specific context, yet the passages above indicate that this wage should correspond to the labours an officer performs, so the elder who puts in the extra time to prepare a sermon every week ought to be remunerated more than one who spends less time labouring each week.

B. The Dangers of Professionalising Ministry

I hate to "beat a dead horse," as the adage has it, but certain issues seem to be reborn occasionally. Not too long ago, John Piper felt the need to address the "professionalisation" of ministry in his book *Brothers We Are Not Professionals*, yet the issue of treating pastoral ministry like a secular profession or vocation reemerges frequently.[48] The problems here could be discussed at length, but this would not suit the present context. Instead, I want to focus on one particular aspect of the professionalisation of ministry that should be considered concerning the maintenance and remuneration of elders. As discussed above, there are significant benefits to the proper remuneration of elders. However, real dangers emerge. Not only can an ill-considered wage foster greed or communicate the wrong message concerning the elder's role

---

[48] John Piper, *Brothers We Are Not Professionals A Plea to Pastors for Radical Ministry.*, Updated & Expanded (Nashville: B&H, 2013).

(as is the case when they are making more than the people in their congregation), but it also can affect the pastor's transparency. Imagine the pressure facing a pastor who relies on their ministry to provide for their family, perhaps to pay a mortgage or car loan: the requirements to be a minister of the Gospel are incredibly high, so the costs of sin have the potential to be severe. One can imagine the pressures facing a minister who faces the weight of being a man of God not only for the sake of the work God is doing in their life but also for their family's well-being. That is, if a pastor mucks things up, they may lose their ability to participate in professional ministry. However, given proper repentance and accountability, there is still much they can do in the church for Christ. However, if a pastor makes a severe mistake and ministry is their primary way to provide for their family, what is left for them if they lose "their" ministry?

A pastor once told me that one of the most important questions to ask a pastor in training was, "What would you do if you weren't able to do ministry?" That is, if or when God closes this door, what will you do? I did not quite understand this question at the time (I still wrestle with it as someone with no marketable skills outside of ministry!) yet it seems to capture the concern I seek to address here. Asking this question reveals several key issues that get to a minister's heart: 1) Will you continue to do ministry if you don't get paid for it? 2) Is ministry just a job for you? 3) Will you hide sin in the future over the fear that you will lose your "job" and, therefore, your ability to support your family?

Vocational ministry is a privilege, not a right. Ordained ministry is a noble aspiration, but there is much ministry to be done if someone cannot be ordained or get paid for ministry work. If someone is genuinely convicted by the centrality of Christ and the importance of his kingdom, they will do the work of ministry whether or not they are ordained or able to make a living doing so. The person who will only do ministry when they are recognised and paid is not the sort of person Christ is looking for to lead his church (see III.B.2). The attitude that corresponds to this is treating ministry as a job, where you fight for promotions, seek comfort in the work, see it as task-work or anything other than person-work. Finally, it is a dangerous place to be where you cannot envision another way to provide for yourself and your family other than ministry: if this is the case, what will you sacrifice to keep your livelihood? What corners will you cut to ensure people think you qualify for ministry? I do not mean to deny that God may call someone to the work of the ministry from a young age: nothing in the Bible says a minister must specialise in some backup skill before pursuing ministry, yet there is certainly wisdom in being prepared that the bar for ministry is high and there may be times when you need to step away from vocational ministry for a time, or perhaps forever, for the sake of being "above reproach," as Christ calls us to be.

C. The Virtues of Bivocational Ministry ("Tentmaking")

Having a skill that can be used to make money outside of ministry is not only valuable to avoid the pitfalls of professionalising ministry but also provides flexibility in ministry. We saw above that churches are responsible for taking care of the ministers as they have the means to do so, but the reality is that many churches cannot support an eldership team, perhaps even one full-time elder. This is true in poor countries and poor communities, but it is also true when a church is just growing, maybe a new church plant or a church re-pot. Without a secondary skill, potential pastors won't be able to commit to ministry in these churches, at least not without neglecting their duties to care for their families. Moreover, full-time ministry is more secure and, in some ways, easier than part-time ministry, so unless part-time ministry is encouraged and championed as a good and reasonable thing to pursue, up-and-coming ministers will seek the easier and more comfortable full-time positions in established churches.

Part-time ministry is often called "bi-vocational ministry" or tentmaking after the practice of the Apostle Paul. We are told that Paul was a tent maker by trade and supported his ministry by selling tents (Acts 18:2-3, 20:34; 2 Thess 3:8). Because of the flexibility tentmaking provides and the practical limitations many churches face in maintaining a full-time minister, it is wise to encourage young ministers to consider bi-vocational ministry as an important route for doing the Lord's work. As is appropriate for their life experience and aptitude, they should be encouraged to learn a marketable skill, not to distract them from the work of the Lord with "civilian pursuits" (2 Tim 2:4) but that they may have greater flexibility in doing the Lord's work so they can take up this difficult work without pay for the kingdom's sake.

5. Elders Are Responsible to Train Up Elders.

According to the common Evangelical practice, the training of elders is entrusted to scholars and academic institutions or bible colleges (which are somewhere between the church and academy). However, the Bible paints a different portrait: elders are called to train up elders.[49]

In 1 Timothy, we find a detailed account of the qualities that characterise an elder or overseer in the local church (1 Tim 3:1-7). As this letter is directed to Timothy, who functions as an elder (if he is not an elder himself), and this description is given in the context of considering those who would "aspire" to "the office of overseer" (1 Tim 3:1), it would seem that this was given so that Timothy and the Ephesian elders could identify future leaders. We saw above that elders are responsible for ordaining those whom the congregation elects. As elders are responsible for training the saints for the work of ministry and teaching them in the Scriptures, and elders will be the most knowledgeable about their role, it makes sense that they would be the ones to train future elders. This is especially so given that the essential qualifications for eldership are character, which is best discerned and grown in the context of relationships.

---

[49] Some helpful resources on this are, Colin Marshall and Tony Payne, *The Trellis and the Vine: The Ministry Mind-Shift That Changes Everything* (Sydney, NSW: Matthias Media, 2021); Colin Marshall and Tony Payne, *The Vine Project: Shaping Your Ministry Culture around Disciple-Making* (Sydney, NSW: Matthias Media, 2016); Cliff Clifton, *How to Start a Residency: Turning Members into Missional Leaders* (Alpharetta, GA: New Churches powered by Send Network, 2023).

IV. GATHERINGS, ORDINANCES, AND THE WORD OF GOD

Therefore, having put away falsehood, let each one of you speak the truth with his neighbor, for we are members one of another. – Ephesians 4:25 (ESV)

A. Concerning a Congregation's Gathering
  1. Regular Gatherings.
  2. Special Gatherings.
B. Concerning Baptism
  1. All who profess faith in Christ and seek to step out in obedience ought to be admitted for baptism.
  2. The Bible does not mandate that baptisms must be public, nor that only ordained officials may perform it.
  3. The mode of baptism given in the Bible and suitable to its symbolic significance is immersion.
  4. Baptism signifies the burial of one who is dead and their resurrection to new life in Christ Jesus.
C. Concerning the Lord's Supper
  1. That those who are reasonably considered believers may participate.
  2. The Bible does not specify who may officiate the Lords' Supper.
  3. That the Bible portrays the Lord's Supper as a symbolic meal involving bread and wine.

        4.   The Significance of the Lord's Supper.
    D. Concerning the Shared Life of Congregation
        1.   Congregations should regularly participate in life together apart from official gatherings.
        2.   Small Groups are not mandated but consistent with the Biblical instructions for community.
        3.   Congregations are obligated to take care of one another's physical needs, within appropriate limits.
    E. Concerning the Corporate Use of the Word of God
        1.   Scripture is to have a central place in the regular gatherings of a congregation.
        2.   Preaching is the application of the Word of God in the context of the church gathering.
        3.   Prophecy may be a specific mode of preaching.
        4.   Teaching is a specific mode of peaching.
        5.   Women may prophecy but not teach in the corporate gathering.

Thus far we have focused on what a congregation is, on its nature, members, and leaders. In the context of the authority entrusted by Christ to local churches, we have introduced many things congregations do. The rest of this book will consider the functions of a local congregation to greater depth. In this chapter, we will consider gatherings, ordinances, and the word of God in the context of the gathered church. In the following chapters, we will consider church discipline and the relationships of congregations with each other.

A. Concerning a Congregation's Gathering

1. Regular Gatherings.

Just as 1st century Jews would gather regularly in the synagogue (Matt 12:9-14, 13:54; Mark 1:21, 1:39, 3:1-6, 6:2; Luke 4:15-16, 4:44, 6:6-11, 13:10; John 6:59; Acts 13:13-16), so also Christians from the beginning of the New Covenant gathered regularly. We have references to Christians gathering (Acts 2:46), but more often than not, a gathering is presupposed by the New Testament epistles, as we discussed at Chapter I.4. Participation in the regular gatherings of a church is of great importance, as the author of Hebrews urges,

"And let us consider how to stir up one another to love and good works, not neglecting to meet together, as is the habit of some, but encouraging one another, and all the more as you see the Day drawing near" (Heb 10:24-25).

Though there are indications in the New Testament that Christians gathered on the first day of the week, Sunday (Acts 20:7; 1 Cor 16:2; Rev 1:10), and this quickly became the regular practice of churches throughout the world, Scripture does not ever say that a church must gather on Sunday— or even only once a week. I take this to be a freedom granted to us by the Lord. For Israel, Saturday was enshrined as a holy day in the rhythm of the nation. However, Christians in the New Testament are exiles and sojourners (1 Pet 1:1, 2:11; Heb 11:8-16, 39), without the expectation of a national rhythm conforming to their calendar. So, instead of being commanded to meet on a specific day, the Lord has seen fit to grant us freedom to choose a day to gather regularly that will fit the rhythm of the nations in which we sojourn.

When Christians gather, they are to sit under the word of God. This involves the reading of Scripture and its application through teaching and prophecy (Acts 2:42, 20:20; 1 Cor 11:2-15, 14:1-6, 14:22; 14:29-33 Col 3:16; 1 Tim 4:11, 4:13, 6:2; 2 Tim 4:1-5; Titus 2:3; Rev 1:3). Congregations also share in the Lord's Supper (1 Cor 11:17-34). The "breaking of bread" which congregations shared may refer to the Lord's Supper or to sharing a meal (Luke 22:19, 24:30; Acts 2:42, 46, 20:7, 20:11)—though these may not be mutually exclusive, as today's practice would imply (see be IV.C). Praying together and singing is entirely appropriate (Col 3:16). We are not given a detailed list of what should be done in the regular gathering of a church, but we are told that whatever is done must be done in ordered fashion, not haphazardly (1 Cor 14:1-25, 29-33). The leaders of the congregation are also to ensure that favouritism is not being shown to the rich and powerful over the poor (James 2:1-13). Agreeing with many streams of the Reformed Protestant tradition, the Word of God read and applied is at the heart of the regular gatherings of a church (Acts 2:42; 20:32; 1 Tim 4:11-16; 2 Tim 3:10-4:8). In addition to the texts where we are told that the Apostles taught in the gathering and that the leaders of churches were to devote themselves to reading and teaching the whole of Scripture, we also see the example of the Apostles and Jesus in the books of the New Testament: in what they wrote and the sermons they gave, even as under the Holy Spirit they gave the New

Testament, Christ and his apostles consistently taught from the Old Testament Scriptures. Paul, in 1 Corinthians 12-14, speaks of the importance and primacy of prophecy among the gifts of speech given by the Spirit; prophecy, as I will argue below, is an application of Scripture under the immediate authority of the Holy Spirit, so with the primacy of prophecy comes the primacy of the Scriptures (IV.E.3).

Regular gatherings are to be open to believers and unbelievers alike, which underscores the importance of having all things done in an orderly fashion so as not to expose the church to unnecessary criticism (1 Cor 14:24-25). Because regular gatherings are public affairs, certain functions of the church will require closed or special gatherings, which are not open to those who are not members.

2. Special Gatherings.

The Bible does not specifically address special gatherings, just as it does not explicitly address regular gatherings, but the need for these gatherings arises from the functions Scripture assigns to the church. On the analogy of the family, there are many family activities that may be performed in public, but others need to be done in private for the health and security of the family. In addition to public gatherings, we see the Apostles meeting with people from house to house (Acts 5:42, 20:20), and the Jerusalem council presents a special gathering convened to deal with specific church business (Acts 15).

If members of the church are responsible for voting on the leadership of the congregation, then a forum is needed whereby they and they alone can deliberate and make a decision. Similarly, the members of the church are responsible for weighing matters of discipline, which is not appropriate to magnify in the public sphere (outside of the legal requirements of the state). Also, Paul desires believers to settle matters of interpersonal "civil" disputes; a special gathering would seem to be appropriate for doing so (1 Cor 6:1-11). So, where the matter is "in house business" that requires the combined authority of the congregation, its members and leaders, a special gathering appears to be appropriate forum, rather than in the regular gathering (we will discuss discipline more in Chapter V).

B. Concerning Baptism

Among theologians, there is some debate over the term used to describe Baptism and the Lord's Supper. I avoid the terms "sacrament" or "means of grace" because I believe they are ambiguous and invite unbiblical speculation about what the baptism and the Lord's supper actually accomplish; following the Baptist tradition, I prefer the term "ordinance," referring to those things which the Lord Jesus Christ has specifically ordained for his church to do. In this section, we will consider Baptism; in the following, we will consider the Lord's Supper.

Before he ascended into heaven, Jesus commanded his disciples to bring his saving Gospel to all peoples of the world. They were to call people to repentance and faith and then teach them to obey Christ; part of this "discipleship" is "baptising them in the name of the Father, the Son, and the Holy Spirit" (Matt 28:16-20). We read of the disciple's response to this commission in the book of Acts; baptism was a regular practice they performed when someone believed in Jesus (Acts 2:38-41; 8:12, 14-16, 36-39; 9:18; 10:47-48; 16:15, 33; 18:8; 19:5). So, baptism became a regular practice in the life of the church. In this section, we will examine who should receive baptism, who should baptise, the mode of baptism, and its meaning.

1. All Who Profess Faith in Christ and Seek to Step out in Obedience Ought to Be Admitted for Baptism.

The "who" of baptism is closely tied up with its significance, so a partial answer now will be completed in §4 below. When Jesus commands his disciples to "baptise," the subjects are those whom they are discipling from all nations. The message of the Gospel is to repent and believe the good news, after which point those who have believed are taught obedience to Christ; Baptism seems to fall on the border of turning to Christ and walking in obedience. Indeed, in Acts, baptism seems to be the first step of obedience once someone has turned to Christ. Peter instructs those to whom he preaches that they need to be baptised when they believe (2:38-41), and when those in Samaria heard the good news and believed, they were then baptised (Acts 8:12). When the Ethiopian man responds to the Gospel in Acts 8, he asks to be baptised, and Philip grants the request immediately (8:26-39). When Paul encounters Jesus and believes, he is baptised (9:18). Again, in Acts

10, Cornelius and many gentiles with him respond to the preached word, receive the Holy Spirit, and are baptised (10:44-48). This pattern continues in the rest of Acts: those who respond to the Gospel with faith are baptised (16:15, 33; 18:8; 19:5). In each case, baptism is explicitly linked with the response of faith in those who hear the word of God. Once someone repents of their sins and believes in Jesus Christ, it is expected that they would be baptised.

Now, in none of these instances, nor in the passages we will consider shortly about the meaning of Baptism, is an age threshold introduced for when Baptism is to be administered. In many cases we have recounted, the person who believes asks to be baptised, and it appears that those preaching the Gospel call for baptism alongside faith in Jesus (e.g. Acts 2:38-41). The Bible never introduces or implies that there is an age when someone may be able to believe in Jesus, and in Jesus' ministry, many children are presumed to believe in him (Matt 18:1-14; 19:13-15; 21:12-17; Mark 10:13-16; Luke 1:39-45; 18:15-17). Because baptism is a response to belief in every instance where it comes up, which is also implied in Jesus' inclusion of baptism within discipleship, then baptism should be given to all who, in the judgment of charity, desire to be baptised after they have believed. Even Simon the magician is baptised after he believed (Acts 8:13), though later his faith turns out to be sham (8:14-24). This is consistent with the meaning of baptism, which we will consider shortly: baptism is a visible symbol of the inner work of the Spirit to put to death the old self and uniting the believer to Christ. The reality which baptism symbolises is closely tied up with belief, so it makes sense that baptism should be administered to those who believe. Now, because baptism is symbol of this reality, not a cause of it (as we will consider below), we do not need to fear for someone who dies unbaptised but claimed belief. The robber on the cross professes faith and Jesus promises him paradise even though he was not baptised (Luke 23:39-43). So, someone who believes is expected to be baptised, though if they are prevented by circumstances out of their control from being baptised, their salvation is not imperilled.

Thus far, I have argued that baptism is to be admitted to believers (judged so with a judgment of charity, cf. Ch. II.2), and that age should not be a barrier to their admission, so long as they have expressed their commitment to Christ. My rule of thumb, which I cannot prove from

Scripture but which seems prudent given what we have seen, is that if someone expresses their desire to obey Christ by being baptised and expresses commitment to Christ as he is taught in the Bible, they should be admitted. For example, I have no doubt my 4-year-old daughter knows who Jesus is and believes him, trusts him for salvation, and desires to follow him; she is also curious about baptism. As she asks questions, I will explain its significance and I am willing to baptise her as soon as she desires to obey Jesus by being baptised.

Some have argued that not only should those who believe be baptised, but so should their children, whether or not they express belief. This is often performed in infancy, before a child can express belief, (arguably) understand what belief means, and before they can express a desire for baptism. According to what I have shown thus far from Scripture, this practice is not biblical. However, proponents occasionally defend the practice by appealing to several passages in Acts, to the historical practice of the church, to biblical theology, and to a theology of the covenant. We will address the final category, what exactly Baptism does below: I will argue that Baptism does not signify mere entrance into the New Covenant but actual union with Christ, making it appropriate only for those who, in our best judgment, have actually been united to Christ through faith. However, we can address the other arguments here.

I do not place much weight on history, unless what is demonstrated in history is supported by Scripture. In this case, I do not believe the historical practice of infant baptism is rooted in Scripture, and I am not persuaded by the strength of the historical case. It is true that very quickly the majority of churches began to practice infant baptism; however, if this were the result of apostolic teaching, we would expect the churches to practice infant baptism from the earliest recorded period onward, but this is not what we find. Instead, we find infant baptism emerging in the late 2nd century. The first positive reference to infant baptism is found in Irenaeus (d. c. 202 AD), who accepts it (*Against Heresies* II.22.4);[50] the 2nd century author Justin Martyr identifies repentance and choice as the conditions of baptism (*First Apology*, LXI), and Tertullian writes against the practice of infant baptism (*On Baptism*,

---

[50] Notice that regeneration for Irenaeus is often argued to be tied to baptism, based on III.17.1.

XVIII), writing from the West in the 2nd century. The Didache assumes that the one being baptised is able to fast (7:1-4), which would seem to require older children or adults. In the following century, the Latin theologians Hippolytus and Cyprian write in favour of infant baptism, as will Origin at the end of that century. By the 4th century, it was the universal practice of the church. What this shows is that though infant baptism did become the catholic teaching, it did not begin as such; the 2nd century demonstrates a variety of views. Moreover, infant baptism as practiced early on is not infant baptism as practised by the Reformers and their heirs: for the early church, baptism was efficacious for the removal of sins (which is why some argued against infant baptism) and for regeneration. So, those who reject the removal of sins in baptism and baptismal regeneration do not find support for their version of infant baptism in the early church. Again, make what you will of this; the most important testimony to our practice is not what the early church practiced or believed but what Scriptures says and warrants.

The only explicit claims from Scripture made in favour of infant baptism come from several passages of the book of Acts, where we are told that heads of a house and their entire household were baptised (Acts 10:34-48; 16:15, 33; 18:8 [it is presumed the Crispus was among those baptised, also 1 Cor 1:14-15]). Two things may be said in response: first, this is an argument from silence; *infants* are not mentioned. Second, at best, this would be consistent with infant baptism but does not mandate it. That is, one must presume that these handful of households had infants in them; though a household was certainly a broader concept in the ancient world than it is today, it simply does not follow that though a household may have contained an infant, at least one of these households did. The Bible simply does not specify. If we could show that infant baptism was a practice warranted by Scripture, then the strongest claim we could make from these passages is that *if* infants were present in these households (for which we have no evidence), their baptism would be consistent with the testimony of Scripture elsewhere. This is hardly a rousing argument in favour of infant baptism. However, I would want to a make a stronger case in the opposite direction: given that every explicit mention of baptism has believers as their object, and no infants are mentioned in these passages as an exception, and since it is made clear that the *entire* household believed (Acts 10:44-48; 16:30-34; 18:8), then either 1) everyone in the household believed and was baptised, or 2) only those who were old enough to be believe where baptised and "entire household" is restricted in context to "the entire household, as many as were able to believe and be baptised." In the case of Lydia, we are not told that her household believed, but neither are we told that she believed—this is assumed (16:14-15). However, the weightier arguments for infant baptism are not made from these passages; instead, they come from biblical theology. However, these also fail on close examination.

The argument for infant baptism from the bigger picture of the Bible goes something like this: baptism marks one's entrance into the New Covenant community; thus, baptism is like circumcision in the Old Testament; as circumcision was extended to infants (males), and as the covenant community encompasses believers and their children, so baptism should be given to believers and their infant children, regardless whether the latter believe or able to express belief.[51] However, this argument breaks down upon closer examination. First, baptism is only indirectly connected with circumcision (and very indirectly at that): in the Old Testament, the inner work of the Spirit enabling belief is called the "circumcision of the heart." This circumcision of the heart was only experienced by a small portion of the population of Israel (Deut 10:16; 30:1-14); because baptism points to the same reality, the circumcision of the heart, Paul in Colossians speaks of baptism alongside the term "circumcision" (Col 2:6-15). However, the "circumcision" here that forms a background for the New Testament practice of baptism is *not* physical circumcision. Instead, it is the circumcision of the heart. Moreover, baptism is never spoken of as marking one's entrance into the New Covenant: it signifies one's death and resurrection into union with Christ, as we will see in a moment. Finally, if we were to admit that baptism was analogous to circumcision (which it isn't), and if we were to admit that baptism was marker of one's entrance into the covenant community, this still would not permit the practice of infant baptism.

We have talked about this somewhat in the earlier chapters (I-II), so we will only touch on the issue here. One of the biggest differences between the Old and New Covenants is that the New Covenant consists entirely of believers. For this reason, churches are never perfect representations of the

---

[51] E.g. Frame, *The Doctrine of the Christian Life*, 258–59; Michael Scott Horton, *The Christian Faith: A Systematic Theology for Pilgrims on the Way* (Grand Rapids, Mich.: Zondervan, 2011), 788–91.

invisible covenant community, for there will always be a mixture of false believers and genuine believers in the local church, until Christ returns. However, churches are to seek a pure community, disciplining members towards a holy community. Therefore, the practice of presuming children are part of the covenant community would go against the thrust of what makes the New Covenant properly new: it is a pure community (e.g. Deut 30:1-14 (Heb); Jer 31:33-34; Isa 54:13) (cf. Ch. II.1.d).[52] Thus, I believe that on the basis of Scripture's explicit teaching, without any biblical theological case prevailing against it, only those who profess faith are to be baptised.

2. The Bible Does not Mandate that Baptisms Must Be Public, nor that Only Ordained Officials May Perform It.

It is common practice in many churches today to practice baptisms before the gathered church. Other than prudence, that is, preserving the modesty and integrity of the men or women involved (taking cultural considerations into account), I see not clear Biblical argument against his practice. Moreover, done before the gathered church, baptism becomes not only a symbol of the believer's renewal in the Spirit but a reminder of God's work in each of us. However, despite is prevalence, I see no reason why baptism may not be performed in private or in small groups, though once again, prudence is necessary. Jesus does not indicate the appropriate setting for baptism when he gives the command to baptise in Matthew 28. Philip does not wait to gather the church before baptising the Ethiopian man (Acts 8:26-40). When households are converted and baptised, it seems that the new believers where baptised right away: there is no mention of gathering the church (Acts 10:44-48; 16:15; 16:33; 18:8). Therefore, we have no instruction or explicit example of baptism in the presence of the gathered church, at least one instance of individual baptism, and several where a group of believers baptise a group of new believers. Given the lack of clear direction, it is not more biblical to baptise in the presence of the gathered church than privately.

It is also a common practice among churches to insist that the ordained leadership perform baptism. Once again, we have no biblical precedent in this regard. Paul speaks of baptising very few personally in his ministry to the

---

[52] See further, Gentry and Wellum, *God's Kingdom through God's Covenants*; Gentry and Wellum, *Kingdom through Covenant (2nd Ed)*; Rutherford, *Prevenient Grace*.

Corinthians (1 Cor 1:10-17, cf. Acts 18:8), and Paul himself, along with the Ethiopian man, are baptised by men who are not officially ordained elders or apostles (to the best of our knowledge, Acts 8:26-40, Acts 9:17-19). The person baptising ought to be a believer, of course, but beyond that, Scripture does not specify who ought to baptise. Thus, we are free to take the appropriate course given the present circumstances when someone seeks baptism.

3. The Mode of Baptism Given in the Bible and Suitable to Its Symbolic Significance Is Immersion.

There has been much debate over the mode of baptism, whether it is appropriate to immerse someone in water or to merely sprinkle them. Some of this has involved assumptions concerning who may be baptised, another factor is the meaning of the word we translate "baptise," and there are also assumptions rooted in the tradition and the Old Testament background for the practices. For our purposes, it is worth noting that there are other words for "sprinkling," but "baptise" is particularly appropriate for immersion (e.g. Mark 7:4, Luke 12:50, 2 Kings 5:14, Isa 21:4; cf. Jdth 12:7; Sir 34:25); immersion is what was practiced in every account for which we have enough details to determine the mode. John baptises people in the Jordan river, and in case we are confused what this means, Jesus "comes up out of the water" when he is baptised (Mark 1:9-11). When the Ethiopian man is baptised, it is because they came across some water, which seems to suggest a body of water enough to be "baptised" with (Acts 8:36). Conversely, there is no instance where someone is explicitly sprinkled with water for baptism. When we consider the meaning of baptism, which we will do shortly, it becomes clear that immersion is entirely fitting and appropriate. That is, baptism symbolised the washing away of the filth of sin—like one would bathe to wash away mud and grime—and the death of our old self through burial and our resurrection to new life through union with Christ, who is alive and reigning in heaven. Sprinkling is hardly appropriate to convey the rich symbolism the Bible associates with baptism, symbolism to which we will now turn.

4. Baptism Signifies the Burial of One Who Is Dead and Their Resurrection to New Life in Christ Jesus.

When we consider the meaning of Christian Baptism, distinguished from the baptism John administered (though there are meaningful parallels), its significance is communicated in two ways. We are not given much detail on John's baptism, yet it is associated with repentance and the forgiveness of sins, as preparation for the arrival of the Messiah (Matt 3:1-6, 11-12; Mark 1:1-8; Luke 3:1-17). Paul recounts his own baptism with similar language: Ananias invited him to be baptised "and wash away your sins" (Acts 22:16). However, the rest of the New Testament focuses on the ideas of death and resurrection or new creation as the meaning of Christian baptism. In 1 Peter 3, Peter relates baptism to God's work to save Noah and his family in the midst of judgment. The Old Creation died in some sense at this time, with a small group being preserved in the midst of judgment to start creation anew. These themes of water, judgment, and salvation, or death and life through water, are familiar from Paul's accounts of baptism. Baptism is not an external washing but signifies internal renewal, it is "an appeal to God for a good conscience, through the resurrection of Jesus Christ" (1 Pet 3:21).

Paul speaks similarly, but with more detail, when he treats baptism in his letters. In 1 Corinthians, he draws a similar parallel between Christian baptism and the Old Testament as does Peter, this time with the Exodus. Crossing the Red Sea was, like the Flood, salvation through judgment. The same waters that moved aside to offer salvation to Israel, a way of escape, cascaded down upon the Egyptian army and destroyed them all (1 Cor 10:1-1-2). On the other side, Israel was severed from their earlier roots; their enemies were destroyed, and there was no way back. The whole wilderness experience, the water, the cloud, the manna and the water from the rock, constituted a recreation of Israel as one body (1 Cor 10:3-5). Christian baptism, we will see, is similarly a symbol of salvation through judgment, of death and resurrection. Through baptism, our union with Christ in the new humanity is vividly pictured (1 Cor 12:13).

Thus far, I have maintained a distance between the sign and what it signifies: I have indicated that baptism symbolises our union with Christ and our salvation but does not accomplish it. Peter will say that baptism saves us (1 Pet 3:21), and Paul that it unites us in one body (1 Cor 12:13). However, I believe we are justified in reading these passages as instances of synecdoche, where one aspect of a broader reality is substituted for the whole. As a part of our salvation, as the first act of obedience we undertake (given the opportunity) in response to faith, baptism is caught up with faith and repentance as the part of the Christian conversion experience, that decisive moment where we are transferred to Christ's kingdom and saved. For example, in 1 Corinthians 12:13, Paul speaks of being baptised "in one Spirit"; he brings the physical act of baptism up into a broader reality of the new creation and regeneration achieved by the Spirit. However, this reality as portrayed in Scripture begins to happen even before we believe, let alone are baptised; it is the perquisite for our entrance into the kingdom (John 3:1-15).[53] This will become more apparent as we turn to other passages which put forth the meaning of baptism.

Paul has one more thing to say in 1 Corinthians regarding baptism, which is perhaps one of the most controversial passages in the New Testament. The problem here is not how we translate the passage (though I will argue this is where the problem should lie) but on the meaning of the translation everyone assumes. In 1 Corinthians 15:29, Paul argues for a genuine, physical resurrection. After making this argument from the resurrection of Christ, Paul then appeals, on the usual reading, to the practices of the Corinthians themselves (or perhaps other churches), "Otherwise, what do people mean by being baptized on behalf of the dead? If the dead are not raised at all, why are people baptized on their behalf?" (1 Cor 15:29) The problem with this reading is that we have no other instance of people being baptised on behalf of the dead in the Bible. The usual argument goes like this, Paul is appealing to a practice known to the Corinthians that attests to their own belief in the resurrection, despite his general indifference (or perhaps disapproval) of the practice.[54] However, the problem with this argument is that Paul does not express disapproval of the supposed practice here in this passage or elsewhere, and his argument does not appeal to the Corinthians own beliefs but to the objective hope that those so baptised will be raised to new life. If this were the correct translation, I

---

[53] Cf. Rutherford, *Prevenient Grace.*

[54] See the discussion in Gordon D. Fee, *The First Epistle to the Corinthians, Revised Edition* (Eerdmans, 2014), 844–50.

believe we would have to wrestle with the implications of "baptising for the dead" in our theology of baptism. However, I think there is an easier solution, an interpretation of the passage that fits with the baptismal theology of the New Testament.

The Greek phrase τῶν νεκρῶν (*ton nekron*, "the dead") is usually translated and interpreted in the abstract, like the phrase "the place of the dead," referring to dead people in general. However, νεκρός may also refer to a dead body; given that the definite article can often convey the sense of possession communicated in English with possessive pronouns, we could translate this phrase, understood concretely in this way, as "their dead bodies." The preposition translated "on behalf of," ἐπί (epi), can mean "with reference to" or "in relation to," as I believe it does here. Translated so, the passage becomes less problematic,

> What, then, are they doing who are baptised with reference to their corpses? If corpses are not actually raised, why would they be baptised with reference to them? (1 Cor 15:29, my translation)

Baptism becomes an argument for the resurrection as does other important elements of the Christian faith to which Paul appeals in this chapter: why are we doing any "Christian" thing, Paul argues, if the resurrection will not happen? What's the point? In Baptism, our dead corpses are buried in a watery grave and then raised up with new life, a spiritual "first resurrection" anticipating the coming physical resurrection (cf. Rev 20:5-6).

In Romans 6, Paul speaks similarly,

> We were, therefore, buried with him through baptism into death, in order that, as Christ was raised from the dead through the gory of the Father, in the same way we also may walk in newness of life. For if we have been united with the likeness of his death, certainly we will also be with the likeness of the resurrection. (Rom 6:4-5, my translation)

So also in Colossians, Paul says that all those who were baptised were buried with Christ and raised with him to new life (Col 2:12). Echoing 1 Corinthians 12:13, Galatians 3:27 says that being baptised into Christ is putting on Christ.

From this, a uniform picture of baptism emerges. We are not told that baptism signifies "entrance into the covenant community," as is often claimed, nor that baptism is a public declaration of faith (though this is somewhat similar to my claim that baptism is often the first step of obedience in response to faith, which is based on the Acts accounts). Instead, we are told that baptism pictures us being plunged into death itself, buries the dead bodies associated with Adam and the old creation, and raises us up into Christ Jesus himself, as new creations united in the one body of Christ. This is a spiritual reality for now, a "first resurrection," where the hard, dead heart of sin is mortified and a new, spiritual heart is given (Rev 20:5-6). Through the Spirit, we are given new spiritual life (Eph 2:1-10, Col 2:11-15), anticipating the day when we will be made completely new (1 Cor 15:11-49). Baptism does not effect this reality but pictures it in a lived-out symbol, much as the Lord's Supper will also picture our participation in Christ's vicarious death.

Because the body which Christ has made under the New Covenant is holy and pure, dedicated to himself, then this symbol of resurrection life is only fitting for those who through faith, by the Spirit, have received Christ and have been united with him spiritually. That is, it is only fitting for those who have professed faith in the living Christ. For this reason, we do not consider infants who are unable to express faith or seek baptism as the proper objects of this ordinance. Moreover, given that it is a symbol that is not in itself efficacious but is a powerful display of an internal reality, a comfort and reminder to those who receive and witness it, offering baptism to an infant achieves nothing for them.[55]

C. Concerning the Lord's Supper

In addition to baptism, Jesus also instructed his disciples to remember him by breaking bread and drinking wine together, which Christians have variously called the Lord's Supper, Eucharist, or Mass (though these terms are not necessarily synonyms). For many in the Christian tradition, including contemporary Roman Catholicism and Eastern Orthodoxy, the Lord's

---

[55] On the power of this symbolism, see Tim Chester, *Truth We Can Touch: How Baptism and Communion Shape Our Lives* (Wheaton, Illinois: Crossway, 2020). Cf. Rutherford J. Alexander, "Review of Truth We Can Touch," *Teleioteti* (blog), April 27, 2020, https://teleioteti.ca/2020/04/27/review-of-truth-we-can-touch/.

Supper has been the centre of the church gathering. However, for the Reformed tradition, the reading and teaching of the Bible has replaced the Lord's Supper as the heart of the church gathering. As indicated already, we generally agree with the Reformed practice. As we will see in a moment, the Lord has instituted the breaking of bread and the drinking of wine to remember him, yet neither he nor the biblical authors give the Supper the significance many have sought to give it. As with our treatment of baptism, we will begin with who may participate in the Lord's Supper, we will then consider who may officiate it, the contents of the Supper, and finally its significance.

1. That Those Who Are Reasonably Considered Believers May Participate.

When Jesus first instituted the Supper, he did so with the Twelve. However, the example of the churches in Acts and Paul's instructions in 1 Corinthians indicate that this was taken to be something Jesus institute for all believers. Paul addresses a specific issue in the Corinthian church, that some were eating of the Supper in "an unworthy manner" (11:27). This resulted in judgment upon those who did so, sickness and even death (11:29-30). Paul instructs the Corinthians to judge themselves, "Let a person examine himself," "discerning the body" (11:28-29). Paul does not go into further detail what this looks like, but "discerning the body" is suggestive of the meaning of the Supper. Paul will go on to identify a specific problem that was incurring judgment, people eating without waiting for others and leaving nothing for the rest (11:17-22, 33-34). As we will see in a moment, the Lord's Supper declares the unity of Christians in one body, so the Corinthians were violating the meaning of the Supper with their practice. Thus, Paul calls the Corinthians to "discern the body" and to "judge" themselves: understanding that the supper declared their unity together in one body, they were to renounce practices that violated that unity. From this, I suggest, we can gather that the Supper is only for those who believe, that is, for those who are actually united together in one body.

This is important, for we want our practice to be consistent with the reality it symbolises. As with baptism, the Bible does not give an age threshold at which point a child is credited with faith and therefore part of Christ's body: we know from experience that children can express faith very young, and the Bible seems to affirm this (see IV.B.1). Therefore, I believe the same principle I applied to baptism is warranted here: if a child claims to follow Jesus and expresses the desire to partake of the Lord's Supper, it should not be withheld from them (though one should employ age-appropriate elements).

2. The Bible Does Not Specify Who May Officiate the Lord's Supper.

In many traditions, only the bishop or presbyter (priest) may officiate the Supper; Anglicans in Sydney, Australia, part from the general Anglican practice by also permitting deacons (which are assistant ministers in this system) to do so. In other traditions, pastors or elders will do so. However, the Bible does not place significance on the officiator's role in the Supper, does not prescribe such a role, and certainly does not restrict it to the clergy. It will certainly be appropriate for the elders to lead the congregation in the Supper, but I see no biblical reason why a lay person may not lead the church in the Lord's Supper.

3. That the Bible Portrays the Lord's Supper as a Symbolic Meal Involving Bread and Wine.

The Lord's Supper contains two elements in every biblical account (Matt 26:26-29; Mark 14:22-25; Luke 22:14-23; 1 Cor 11:12-26), bread and wine. These elements are closely tied to the significance of the Supper, the bread signifying both Christ's crucifixion as the bread is broken like Christ's body is broken and also the unity of Christ's people, one loaf representing one body. The red wine is a fitting symbol of Christ's blood that was shed. That these are both food items is also significant, for the apostles had gathered to participate in the Passover meal and the Supper itself looked forward to the great Wedding Feast of the Lamb when Christ returns. So, the bread and the wine are symbols of other realities, of Christ's physical body and spiritual body and of Christ's blood which effects a New Covenant.

As the elements are symbols, there is flexibility in what we use in our practice of the Supper, but our choice of elements ought to retain the symbolic significance of the elements Jesus used. Concerning the bread, I believe that a single loaf should be used, for the symbolism of the bread lies in its unity which is then divided, signifying Christ's diverse yet unified spiritual body. The wine symbolises the blood Jesus shed, but it also looks forward to the great wedding feast of the Lamb. Thus, the colour of the drink and that it is a drink associated with feasting are both parts of the symbolism of the wine. Some may want to stick to grape juice as a non-alcoholic substitute for red wine because they come from the same fruit, but it would seem that a dark red drink, appropriate for symbolising blood, which is or may be associated with feasting—so something someone would actually drink outside of Communion!—would be appropriate. There is a certain historical realism about using red wine, connecting with the actual institution of the Supper, and some may find similar connotations with dark grape juice, yet I don't see these as necessary to the Lord's Supper if there is a good reason to use a different drink for the element.

4. The Significance of the Lord's Supper

The meaning of the Lord's Supper has been debated throughout the history of the church, the most heated debates revolving around Jesus word's "this is my body." We will begin by investigating the symbolic significance of the Supper, what Jesus and Paul say is the meaning behind the recurring practice of the Supper, before investigating that question. The practice of the Supper according to Scripture has a three-fold significance. We are invited at the Supper to remember what Christ has done, reflect on and declare our present reality, and look forward to the future.

a. Remembrance

On the eve of his crucifixion, Jesus institutes the Supper, commanding the disciples to regularly commemorate the brutal events that are soon to occur. They are to do this "in remembrance of me" (Luke 22:19; 1 Cor 11:24): in the Supper we remember Christ. The bread points us to his body, "given" on our behalf. In light of his coming death, and perhaps even the physical breaking of the bread to distribute it, the meaning of "given for you" would seem to be, "given [over to death] for your sake." However, Mark and Matthew only say, "this is my body," without explaining its significance (Matt 26:26; Mark 14:22). Luke says that it is given "for you" or "on your behalf" (Luke 22:19), and Paul that it is "for you" (1 Cor 11:24). In the context of a Passover meal, which remembers the sacrifice of the lamb to preserve God's people, the sacrificial connotations of "given for your sake" are surely present.[56] This is clearer with reference to the cup, which is "poured out for you," both instituting the New Covenant and securing the "forgiveness of sins" (Matt 26:28; Mark 14:24; Luke 22:20; 1 Cor 11:25). So, when we participate in the Lord's Supper, we are called to remember Christ, what he has accomplished on our behalf.

b. Declaration

The Lord's Supper is not only remembrance, but also declaration. Through the New Covenant established in Christ's blood, Christians are made one in his body; so his body which he offered at the first Supper is us, all united through the Spirit as the earthly instantiation of the risen Christ. Paul draws attention to this aspect of the Supper when he calls out the hypocrisy of those who would violate the unity they shared in Christ while participating in a meal that so vividly declared that unity as they each partook of the one body of Christ in which they participate:

> The bread that we break, is it not a participation in the body of Christ? Because there is one bread, we who are many are one body, for we all partake of one bread. (1 Cor 10:16-17, cf. 11:17-22, 27-24).

Paul also tells us that we declare Christ's death until he returns (1 Cor 11:26).

c. Anticipation

By declaring Christ's death until he returns, we are those looking forward to his return as we partake of the Supper. Jesus tells his disciples that this would be the last time he would drink of "the fruit of the vine" until the day he would "drink it new in the kingdom of God" (Mark 14:25; cf. Matt 26:29). So, we eat of the elements in anticipation of the day when we will sit with Christ and feast together in the New Creation. Our participation in the Lord's

---

[56] Taking this position, for example, is D.A. Carson in his commentary on Matthew. D. A. Carson, "Matthew," in *The Expositor's Bible Commentary: Matthew–Mark (Revised Edition)*, ed. Tremper Longman III and David E. Garland, vol. 9 (Grand Rapids: Zondervan, 2010).

Supper signifies all of these at the same time, the past, present, and future.

d. "This is my body"

There has been intense theological speculation throughout the history of the church on the meaning of Christ's statement "this is my body." However, I must agree with D.A. Carson that on a purely exegetical basis, this speculation is anachronistic. None of the disciples would have believed that the bread had suddenly become Christ's body in the Aquinian sense, retaining the accidents of the bread but taking on the form of Christ's body (if that even makes metaphysical sense within Aquinas's system, for which I have my doubts). Luther famously divided with Zwingli and others over the meaning of the Supper, declaring that Christ's statement "this is my body" must be taken with some sense of literality—that it somehow, in some way, must be metaphysically associated with Christ's body. However, the word translated as "is" is far more flexible than Luther allowed it to be. It may indicate existence, God "is" (Heb 11:16), or identity (Rom 9:5); it may connect a subject with a predicate ("God is love," 1 John 4:8), with varying degrees of identity; it can also connect a symbol with its sign or indicate that one thing is a representation of another (Matt 9:13, 27:46; Mark 3:17, 7:2; Luke 15:26; Acts 17:20, 19:4; Rom 7:18, 9:8, 10:6, 8). There is much evidence that "is" (εἰμί) may indicate the connection between a symbol and what it symbolises, as I have suggested is the meaning of "this is my body." If we permit this as a possibility, it readily presents itself as the most likely interpretation. Instead of the complex metaphysical schemes developed to explain how the bread could actually be Jesus' body, we have the institution of a symbol.

How else would Jesus' disciples have interpreted it, when Jesus—a body—held the bread, something very different from himself at the moment? Moreover, Jesus then gives the bread and the cup symbolic significance, as we discussed above. One reason many are quick to reject the "symbolic" interpretation is because we tend to devalue symbols in the modern world—and the West has done so for centuries. However, the Bible shows far less reticence about symbolism. Throughout the Old Testament, God instituted lived symbols as a regular part of Israel's life: in addition to the Sabbath and Passover, there were numerous feasts and the sacrificial system. The Lord instituted the Supper on the night of the Passover, so his disciples would have readily connected the power of this new symbolism with that of the old. Symbols can and should be powerful things: if we are to practice the Lord's Supper well, we must remember this.

D. Concerning the Shared Life of Congregation

1. Congregations Should Regularly Participate in Life together Apart from Official Gatherings.

In the 20th century, there was a big push among churches to get out of the "Sunday-morning church" mindset, which (at least in practice) maintained that the gathered church was all that the church was. A slew of books addressed this issue, arguing that Christians must live as a Christians throughout the week and that churches must be active as churches beyond the Sunday morning gathering.[57] Some have argued that the "church" is properly a gathered entity, so it really does not exist outside of the gathering: Christians live Christianly outside of the gathering, but "churches" are not more than the gathering.[58] In my definition of the "church" above (Ch. I), I have indicated that my sympathies lie with the former group rather than the latter. There is simply nothing in Scripture that would indicate that a church only exists as it is gathered, and the sort of whole-life instructions concerning the life of the church given in the New Testament speaks volumes on this point. Could you imagine if Christians spoke the truth in love, turned the other cheek, laboured with their hands to give to the poor, sold everything for the sake of the local church, gathered money and distributed to the poor, gathered money and sent to other churches, hosted itinerant teachers, sang to one another, prayed together, and prophesied in the context of the local church gathering only? How long would such a gathering need to be—let alone the fact that it would be impossible to do all this in that context? Moreover, should Christian's judge one another's civil disputes only on Sunday morning—especially when unbelievers may be present (1 Cor 6:1-8, 14:22)? What about a pastor, should he only pastor on a Sunday morning?

---

[57] This was a topic of many Bible College lectures I experienced; my teachers were from this generation. E.g. Jerry Cook, *The Monday Morning Church* (West Monroe, LA: Howard Publishing Co., Inc., 2006).

[58] E.g. David VanDrunen, *Living in God's Two Kingdoms: A Biblical Vision for Christianity and Culture* (Crossway, 2010).

Paul certainly taught "from house to house" (Acts 20:20). There is no good reason to think that the church is confined to its gathering. So, though we are not given many details on what this should look like, local churches ought to participate in life together outside of the gathering of the church.

2. Small Groups Are Not Mandated but Consistent with the Biblical Instructions for Community.

One way churches have practiced this corporate life together beyond the Sunday gatherings is through small groups. As an expression of the corporate life of the church and so an opportunity to use the gifts of the Spirit in the service of one another, there is nothing in the Bible that would prohibit small groups. However, we also have nothing warranting the modern idea of small groups, so we should perhaps proceed with caution. Several dangers present themselves in the practice of small groups, dangers which churches need to be cognizant of and active in mitigating. I will mention three I have experienced (and read about), I am sure you can think of others.

a. Some Dangers with Small Groups

First, small groups easily become a platform for misguided theology and for bad hermeneutical practice. When an eager but unprepared or ill prepared leader takes up a small group, they are given a platform of limited but real authority; the theology they express in their leadership of the group will be taken with more authority than a random person's in church. Also, if the leader does not demonstrate sound principles of Bible reading, they risk inoculating group members in similar principles.

Second, small groups have often been used in the place of formal pastoral ministry. We have argued that a pastor's job is to shepherd the sheep; he cannot outsource this work to unqualified men or women. This issue is compounded when those who are entrusted with the role of pastoral care in a small group are not properly prepared to do so or to handle the load that comes with doing so.

Third, small groups often lack a purpose, or lose it very quickly. When those who lead a small group are not strong leaders, they easily let the group morph into an amorphous blob that does not really know why it gathers at all.

b. The Positive Use of Small Groups

I don't think these dangers (nor others) are fatal to the practice of small groups, but they ought to be a yellow light, call us to proceed with caution. Because they are not commanded or given on analogy by Scripture, small groups should not be treated as more important than Sunday gatherings or as necessary to spiritual development. However, what is unnecessary may still be helpful, and I think something like small groups could be encouraged in a helpful way. On the one hand, a church could encourage its members to meet regularly, throughout the week for fellowship, prayer, and the word. The same people may begin to meet, and that should not necessarily be discouraged, for regular communion can break down barriers and permit a greater level of trust, enabling the effective ministry of the word and prayer to one another. However, the leaders of the church should keep an eye on such groups to ensure that unhealthy ideas are not given a platform there.

There may also be room for small groups as a context for a different sort of pastoral care than could be offered in either the gathered church or one-to-one. If the eldership of the church undertakes to lead a small group, this would give them an additional context for teaching, a context which would enable them to contextualise the Scriptures for specific members of the congregation. It would also provide a context for modelling healthy principles of Scriptural interpretation. Small groups may also facilitate greater insight into the spiritual condition of the flock, for people will engage in a small group context in a different way than they will either on a Sunday morning or one-on-one. In the Bible, Christians are called to a corporate life, not individualism, so small groups could be seen as a more intimate context for discipleship that still retains the corporate nature of Christianity, rather than simple personal devotions or one-to-one discipleship.

In both uses of small groups I have offered here, a key element is the need for pastoral oversight of these groups. Because of the dangers that emerge if unqualified leaders are given authority over others, pastors must be diligent to implement strategies for oversight and accountability.

3. Congregations Are Obligated to Take Care of One Another's Physical Needs, within Appropriate Limits.

One final word on the shared life of the congregation is the Bible's mandate to take care of one another's needs. Because Christians are called to be a family, even a body, it is of the utmost importance that they take care of one another. The context Christ has given for this care is the local church. Under the oversight of church leaders and deacons, who are charged to make sure no one is neglected (Acts 6:1-7), the local church must ensure that its members are taken care of. In Acts, we are shown that believers went to great lengths to do this: they sold, land, houses, and other possessions, having "all things in common" (Acts 2:42-47; 4:32-37) Elsewhere, we read of care given to the widows (Acts 6:1-7; 1 Tim 5:1-17), and those who have need for unspecified reasons (Acts 2:45). Local churches will often show care for those who are not its members, consistent with God's own heart for the poor and needy: they are to do good to everyone, especially—but not exclusively—those who are of the household of faith (Gal 6:9-10). The primary emphasis in the New Testament is the way churches care for their own members and then for other churches (see §I.5.b.i.3)

However, Christian charity is not indiscriminate. We are shown this in the context of the local church, so I believe we may infer this for charity shown towards unbelievers as well. In 2 Thessalonians, Paul commands the Thessalonians not to enable idleness and sin through charity: "If anyone is not willing to work, let him not eat" (2 Thess 3:10). In the Bible, idleness is an easy pathway to sin (e.g. 1 Tim 5:13; 2 Thess 3:11); it is not just a sin in itself, but a gateway to a host of other sins, so it must not be tolerated. In 1 Timothy 5:4 and 8, Paul writes that the relatives of those who are in need, such as widows, should be the first to take care of them, lest the church be burdened. So, the church should not be quick to extend charity when believing family is neglecting their duties to provide; this would, instead, be an instance where exhortation and, if exhortation goes unheeded, discipline is needed. In the same chapter, Paul commands that charity should not be shown to believers who are morally corrupt, especially "self-indulgent" (1 Tim 5:6). So, churches have the responsibility to take care of their members, but they must be wise to do so in a way that does not enable sin.

E. Concerning the Corporate Use of the Word of God

1. Scripture Is to Have a Central Place in the Regular Gatherings of a Congregation.

In our discussion of the ordinances and church gatherings above, I indicated that I generally follow the Reformed tradition in making the word the centre of the gathered church, rather than the Eucharist, as in the Roman and Eastern traditions. However, I want to differ from many of my Reformed brethren in saying that the Scriptures are at the centre of the gathering, not exclusively preaching or the sermon. We can see this from several perspectives. First, Scripture is the authoritative foundation for all the shepherding word-actions the elders undertake, such as rebuking, teaching, correcting, and training in righteousness (2 Tim 3:16-17). In as much as these activities take place in the corporate setting, they are necessarily word-based. Second, Paul explicitly commends Timothy to be committed to the public reading of Scripture, as well as to teaching and preaching, public activities that are based on Scripture (1 Tim 4:13, 6:2; 2 Tim 4:1-51). Third, Paul commends the gift of prophecy highly, including in the gathered church; we will see shortly that prophecy is always, though to differing degrees, rooted in Scripture (1 Cor 14:1-40). Fourth, singing to one another is commended as an appropriate activity for the church, whether gathered or otherwise, and the Psalms were (and should be today) the basic songbook of God's people (Eph 5:19; Col 3:16). Fifth, the apostolic letters and Revelation were to be read in the congregations to which they were sent and others as well, setting a precedence for us to read them in our congregations (Eph 3:4; Col 4:16; 1 Thess 5:27; Rev 1:3). Paul instructs the Colossian church, "Let the word of Christ dwell in you richly, teaching and admonishing one another in all wisdom, singing psalms and hymns and spiritual songs, with thankfulness in your hearts to God" (Col 3:16).

Scripture does not show us what should go on in a local gathering—it gives extraordinary flexibility in this regard—yet it repeatedly points to Scripture as the central aspect of that gathering. This is suitable for the role of Scripture as God's abiding covenant testimony concerning himself, his people, and the way to live before him until Christ returns.[59]

The Evangelical tradition I have been learned places great emphasis on the preached word, and there is indeed great power in the word preached. But we often neglect the fact that God's word is itself powerful,

> For the word of God is living and active, sharper than any two-edged sword, piercing to the division of soul and of spirit, of joints and of marrow, and discerning the thoughts and intentions of the heart. And no creature is hidden from his sight, but all are naked and exposed to the eyes of him to whom we must give account. (Heb 4:12–13)

It is all too common that our emphasis on expository preaching—preaching whole books of the Bible—leads us to neglect *reading* whole books of the Bible. Brothers and sisters, we must not do this. Though I will argue shortly that the Word of God preached is God's Word, we must deliver to our congregations the whole counsel of God, our applications yes, but also the breadth of Scripture so that the Spirit may work in the lives of our congregations where our applications miss the mark. The Scriptures must be at the heart of our gatherings, taught yes, but first read and sung, even prayed. Many of people who gather on a Sunday, even in major Western cities, will not be literate, or at least will struggle to read the Bible for themselves. If we do not give them the whole word of God regularly, they may never learn it.

2. Preaching Is the Application of the Word of God in the Context of the Church Gathering.

In the contemporary church, at least in the English-speaking West, we use "preach" and "sermon" in a way that does not line up exactly with any one thing the Bible speaks of. The Greek words often rendered "preach" (κηρύσσω, *kērussō*) generally refers to a public act of speech, sometimes teaching (Matt 11:1), other times a call to action (Mark 1:15, 6:12). Like κηρύσσω, the English sermon is a public act of speech, yet it is a technically defined one. Sermons may be "topical," teaching on a specific issue or theological topic, though, in Evangelical churches, it is expected that such a

---

[59] Rutherford, *The Gift of Revelation: A Biblical Perspective on the Bible.*

sermon will still be demonstrably rooted in Scripture. An exegetical or expository sermon will, on the other hand, explain and (hopefully) apply a specific passage of Scripture. There are sermon-specific tropes and patterns that have been developed over the years, so sermons from various Evangelical churches will have great similarities. As we are attempting to develop and demonstrate a polity developed from the explicit teachings of Scripture and its case laws or examples (see Intro §B.2), we will need to reframe "preaching" for our discussion. Our discussion in this section will certainly have implications for Evangelical preaching more broadly, but the framing we have provided should be kept in mind.

By "preaching" in this section, I do not intend all the sorts of public speeches designated with κηρύσσω or its nominal equivalents. Instead, I intend specific, public acts of speech in the gathered congregation. As we have indicated thus far, we are not given a detailed account of liturgy in the New Testament: God has given us great freedom in the structure of our gatherings. Similarly, we have examples of Jesus' and the apostles' teaching, but we have no accounts of "sermons" or speeches given in the context of the gathered church (though, some of Jesus' teaching does take place in the synagogue). The closest things we have are the New Testament epistles, which were to be read in the context of the gathered church, especially Hebrews, which is more homiletical or sermonic than the other epistles. However, among the various activities described in the local church context, two stand out as related but (I will argue) different public acts, prophecy and teaching. Setting aside announcements, transitions, welcomes, and other materials that are not "teaching" in the common English use of the word, as well as the reading of Scripture, the other acts of speech that occur in the context of the local church, that is, all sermons, are either prophecy or teaching. This position is distinct from other views which hold that teaching and prophecy are identical, or which distinguish a prophecy from a sermon as a particularly miraculous demonstration of the Spirit's power.

Neither prophecy nor teaching, in the Bible, refer to the content of what is spoken, but instead refer to the manner of authority by which a speech is given. I will refer to this as the "mode" of a sermon, so a sermon may have two modes, prophecy or teaching. The actual content of a sermon may be many things, exhortation, instruction, rebuke, explanation, wisdom, insight into a particular circumstance, etc. However, a sermon in the gathered church will also be based on the Bible. The Bible provides the basic content of the sermon, but a sermon does not just repeat what the Bible says. No, a sermon applies the Bible to specific circumstances, unpacking it, communicating it, and using it to instruct, encourage, and admonish God's people. We could thus picture every sermon as a combination of three factors, a concrete circumstance or perhaps topic (for the circumstances I have in mind may not be an individual's crisis but could be, for example, a question concerning the nature of God), the Bible, and the person authorised to preach. In other words, a sermon is an application of the Bible to a circumstance or circumstances by an authorised person. What I have spoken of as the mode of authority describes one of two ways a person may be authorised to deliver a sermon.

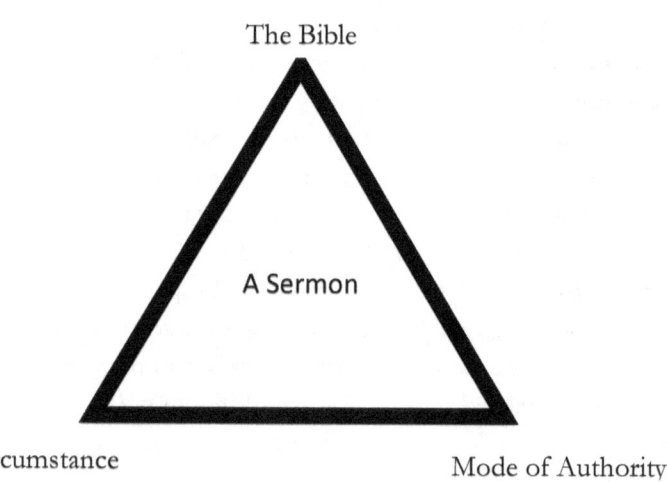

The Bible

A Sermon

A Circumstance   Mode of Authority

For many, it may be confusing to speak of "authority" apart from the biblical text, for of course, the Bible is God's very words, and so absolutely authoritative. This is true, and we feel this authority as we read the Bible. However, by what authority do we move from the Bible to an application? It's not by the Bible's own authority, for the Bible does not speak to the bridge between itself and the circumstance we are addressing. No, if someone is to "rebuke with all authority" (Titus 2:15), they need authority given to them by which they apply the authoritative Scriptures. This is what prophecy and teaching describe.

This means that sermons are not just an act of human communication but an act of divine communication through a human instrument: when preached accurately, with appropriate authority (prophetic or teaching), then the preaching of the Scriptures is the word of God. Now, my Reformed brethren—and many Evangelicals—will immediately raise their hands in objection—"hold on a second, sermons cannot replace nor equal God's word, the Scriptures!" To this I respond with a resounding "amen!" However, think about the prophetic ministry of Isaiah and Jeremiah, of Jonah: they spoke prophetically many times, yet only a portion of their prophetic speech was preserved by God to be part of the Bible (Jonah 1:1; 2 Kgs 14:25). Were the prophecies we do not have less the words of God than those we have? If we respond with a positive, then Isaiah and Jeremiah were false prophets, for they spoke for God without God's authorisation. This is, of course, false, so their lost words were as much God's words as what we find in the Bible. However, that does not put these words on the same level as Scripture, as abiding legislation for God's covenant. No, Scripture is a special and unique word from God that has global authority and abides until Christ's return; it is intended to legislate a people from every tribe, tongue, and nation. The preached word is God's word, just as Jeremiah and Isaiah's prophecies were God's word: they are authoritative communications from God to God's people. I address this with more detail in my book *The Gift of Revelation*, to which I direct the reader.[60]

However, because humans are imperfect, sometimes the preached word fails to live up to this standard. Sometimes a sermon is preached without appropriate authority; this is not a word from God (Deut 18:20-22). For example, if someone is not led by the Holy Spirit in prophecy, nor a rightly ordained teacher, then this is not a word from God. If someone has misread a circumstance, then this fails to be a word from God—in the case of a prophecy, this also shows that it was not from the Holy Spirit (Deut 18:22). If someone preaches a word that is not clearly rooted in the Scriptures, then this is likewise not a word from God (Deut 13:1-18; 1 Cor 14:29; 1 Thess 5:21; 1 John 4:1-6). Thus, our definition of a sermon presupposes that it is genuine, but it is possible to have a public act of speech in the gathered church that pretends to be a sermon but falls short in one of these three areas.

---

[60] *The Gift of Revelation*, 60-63.

We are told in Scripture to be discerning in what we hear, not to neglect or dismiss the preached word but to be certain that God himself is the one speaking through the preacher. This looks different for a prophecy or a teaching, so we will discuss these matters under each respective head.

3. Prophecy May Be a Specific Mode of Preaching.[61]

Prophecy has been much discussed in the recent years, especially with the emergence of Pentecostalism and Charismaticism in the 20th century, yet often it has been discussed without attention to the phenomenon as discussed in Scripture. For example, we often hear that New Testament prophecy is different from Old Testament prophecy, for the former was more authoritative or binding—as if one was a word of God and other not so much.[62] However, this distinction fails to pay attention to what Old Testament prophecy actually was: it was not all "thus saith the Lord" proclamations, nor was it all included in Scripture. We find throughout the Old Testament prophets and prophetesses whose words are not inscripturated, or at least only in part (e.g. 2 Kgs 14:25, 22:14-20; Isa 8:3), and even groups or schools of prophets (1 Sam 10:10, 19:20; 2 Kgs 2:6-8, 15). Moreover, not only are Isaiah, Jeremiah, and Ezekiel identified as prophets, with their clearly visionary and typically "prophetic" discourse, but so also the narrative of Jonah, which confronts the reader with Israel's failings through the story of its wayward prophets, or Samuel and Kings—"prophetic" books according to the Hebrew Bible—which provide an interpretation of God's work in history.[63] So, there is not a single "Old Testament" style prophecy to be contrasted with New Testament prophecy: the New Testament contains a "prophetic" book like Isaiah and Jeremiah, in Revelation (1:3), and also one like Samuel and Kings, in Acts. I see no basis from Scripture itself to draw a dichotomy between Old and New Testament prophecy, nor to say that the New Testament sort is less authoritative than the former.

---

[61] Cf. *The Gift of Revelation*, 60-63.

[62] E.g. D. A. Carson, *Showing the Spirit: A Theological Exposition of 1 Corinthians 12-14* (Grand Rapids: Baker, 1987), 97–98.

[63] On Samuel as prophecy, see Rutherford, *God's Kingdom*.

Someone may say that false prophecy was punishable by death in the Old Testament, but not so in the New (Deut 13:5; 18:20-22). This is true, but this does not mean the prophecies are of different weight under the different covenants. It is presumed in the Old Testament that false prophecy is accompanied by malicious intent; it is often associated with leading people astray. It is assumed that to speak in the name of the Lord when one has not received authorisation to do so is a terrible offence: this is a sinful presumption at its worst. Understood as such, then in a covenant that encompasses the whole of life, legislating government as much as cult and family life, such apostasy or presumption is met with death. That the New Testament does not treat false prophecy as an offense punishable by death is consistent with the change in dispensation by which the New Covenant community is not a civil body within which such civil punishments would be appropriate (see Chapter I). The New Testament does indeed take false prophecy seriously, and it is assumed that false prophets should be disciplined (Matt 24:11, 24; Mark 13:22; 1 Cor 12:10; 14:29; 1 John 4:1-3; 2 Pet 2:1).

False prophecy is such a big deal because prophecy is a big deal, just as it was in the Old Testament. Those who draw a firm distinction between Old and New Testament prophecy fail to identify the variegated nature of prophecy in the Old Testament. However, some have argued that New Testament prophecy is less authoritative because it may be vague and even, it is claimed, erroneous in the details. I am not convinced this is the case. As I have argued, true prophecy is a genuine word of God, whether it is in the New or Old Testament, and should be expected to come to pass. What, then, do we do with the supposedly erroneous prophecies in the New Testament? In Acts 21:4, we are told that certain disciples urged Paul not to go to Jerusalem "through the Holy Spirit" (ESV). The problem is that Paul was already certain the Spirit wanted him to go to Jerusalem (e.g. Acts 20:22-23). However, the typical interpretation is more problematic than is acknowledged: Luke himself attributes their words to be "through the Holy Spirit": whatever these disciples thought, would the God-inspired author of Scripture attribute mixed messages to the Spirit—saying "go" in one instance and "refrain" in another? Wayne Grudem suggests that New Testament prophecy is vague and suggestions that are not linked with concrete words, so these prophets perhaps misinterpreted a true word from the Spirit (notice how this is similar to how Moses describes *Old Testament* prophecy, Num

12:6-9).[64] However, *Luke* is the one who seems to juxtapose false testimony, if this is what the text is saying. But, perhaps, this is not what Luke is saying. Only once elsewhere does Luke use the phrase "through the Holy Spirit" (διὰ τοῦ πνεύματος, Acts 11:28); he does use the διά preposition with the genitive 47 times, with a range of senses. Like the rest of the New Testament authors, Luke prefers to use the preposition with the accusative for cause (with accusative, 26 times), however, Paul, who uses this preposition with the accusative often (34 times, excluding Hebrews), occasionally uses the preposition with the genitive for a causal sense (Rom 8:3; 2 Cor 9:13). Thus, if there is significant contextual warrant, then we could propose a causal sense for Acts 21:4, "They told Paul, because of the Holy Spirit, do not go into Jerusalem!" The sense may not be different than the more instrumental "through," but translating it causally opens a possibility that is less apparent when translated "through": Because of Spirit—perhaps the same prophecies Agabus had received—they urged him not to go. That is, because of what they knew the Spirit was saying—that Paul would face imprisonment and affliction—they didn't want him to go. It is not necessarily the case that the Spirit told them to say this; notice that Luke does not use prophecy language for this instance. So, it would be odd for Luke to write that the Spirit said one thing to Paul directly and another through the disciples, and I have offered an interpretation that avoids this. However, we are told that the prophecy of Agabus is more problematic.[65]

In Acts 21:10-14, we read that a prophet named Agabus (who we are told already was able to accurately predict the future, Acts 11:28) came down from Judea to meet Paul. He performed a sign-prophecy, taking Paul's belt, binding him, and then offering an interpretation, "Thus says the Holy Spirit, 'This is how the Jews at Jerusalem will bind the man who owns this belt and deliver him into the hands of the Gentiles'" (Acts 21:11). The problem, we are told, is that Agabus is wrong in the details. When Paul is arrested, we are not told *explicitly* that he was bound, and the mob first tries to kill him before the Romans intervene and take him—the Jews hardly "handed him over," it

---

[64] Wayne Grudem, *The Gift of Prophecy in the New Testament and Today*, Revised Edition (Crossway, 2000), 80–81.

[65] Carson, *Showing the Spirit*, 97–98; Grudem, *The Gift of Prophecy in the New Testament and Today*, 77–83.

is claimed. I honestly don't see the problems that Carson and Grudem see; let me show you why this isn't such a big issue. First, if Agabus made a mistake, this would be a problem, for he speaks as if his words are the Spirit's words: if what he said didn't come to pass, this would amount to a false prophecy based on presumption (Deut 18:20-22). Second, Grudem and Carson are both requiring more detail of Agabus prophecy than is evident.

Agabus acts out the prophecy and then interprets it. A sign prophecy is not a perfect image of what will happen (think of Ezekiel's signs, e.g. Ezekiel 4:1-17), so we need to focus on interpretation. In the interpretation, Agabus says that the 1) the Jews would bind Paul, and 2) the Jews would deliver him to the gentiles. Regarding the binding, we are told that Romans bound Paul; this was certainly caused by the actions of the Jews. Similarly, because of the Jews actions, Paul was handed over to the authority of the Romans. Grudem and Carson are certainly right that some prophecies exhibit more precision than this, yet this level of precision would be consistent with many prophecies in the Old Testament (e.g. Gen 49:10, 24; 1 Sam 8:10-18; 2 Sam 7:14; Isa 7:15-16). Prophecies are rightly called "riddles" (Num 12:6-9), for they use figures of speech and word pictures to convey a reality—they are symbolically rich. I would argue that each of the examples I have given above are fulfilled in a meaningful way, but reading too much into the symbolism used would lead to a misreading of the prophecy (such that the Messiah was to be a descendent of Joseph, that there would be no gaps in the rule of Judah's descendants, or that the Jesus would sin). That *some* Old Testament prophecies are quite specific does not mean that all are so: there are abundant examples that lack the sort of specificity Grudem and Carson expect. Prophecies in the Hebrew literature are known to be terse, so that Agabus attributes direct action to the Jews rather than including a means clause ("cause the Romans to bind Paul") or without clarifying intent ("unintentionally cause Paul to be handed over") is perfectly becoming of biblical prophecy: the consistent pattern in Acts is that the Jewish people in Jerusalem, occasionally more broadly, were directly responsible for the persecution of God's people and the Romans repeatedly exonerated the Christians, so the way Agabus' phrases his prophecy is theologically and rhetorically significant, and consistent with Luke's presentation of the early church. Often Old Testament prophecy (and narrative) will sacrifice the details for the theological purpose.[66] Thus, I maintain that these so-called problem passages present no issues for the view offered here.

Prophecy is a variegated phenomenon shared by the Old and New Covenant communities. But what is it? I propose that all prophecies that were not intended by God to be inscripturated (though I am not convinced Scriptural prophecy is any different, I just don't see the point of making this argument at this time) are an application of God's self-revelation (which is now definitively and entirely available to us in Scripture) to specific circumstances superintended by the Holy Spirit. That is, a "prophecy" does not derive its authority from the one speaking but from the Holy Spirit who immediately directs the person to speak. The Holy Spirit will not reveal something new about God or his covenant which has not been previously revealed, for the Scriptures are entirely sufficient and all prophecies are to be judged by Scripture (Acts 17:11; 1 Cor 14:29). Instead, whether the prophecy is a vision or didactic speech (a word from God, perhaps a sermon), it will only confirm what God has previously revealed. However, prophecies will not merely confirm or repeat what God has said but will apply God's Word to specific situations in the life of God's people.

I cannot think of a single verse that describes prophecy in this way, yet it is evident in every prophecy recorded in Scripture. Whether they speak of the past, present, or future, the prophecies of Isaiah, Jeremiah, and Ezekiel address the particular circumstances of the nation: they offer an indictment of past and present sin, they present God's present or future judgment, and they look forward to God's restoration of his people. Whatever events they describe, these prophecies were given to specific people and often told of specific events that warned or encouraged those people. Though the events or circumstances they speak of (past, present, or future) are often not based in earlier Scripture, what they say about them is rooted in the Torah. The evaluations of sin are rooted in the revelation of God's commands and character in the Torah; the judgments prophesied are based on the curses given in Deuteronomy; the restoration anticipated looks to Deuteronomy 31 and other passages (e.g. Deuteronomy 18), as well as God's character revealed there. So prophecy is an application of Scripture to specific

---

[66] Cf. V. Philips Long, *The Art of Biblical History*, Foundations of Contemporary Interpretation, v. 5 (Grand Rapids: Zondervan, 1994).

circumstances, whether present or a divinely revealed future; all prophecy is a product of the immediate action of the Holy Spirit, so a true prophecy is the Spirit's speaking (Acts 11:28, 21:11). However, though a prophecy comes from the immediate action of the Spirit, it is not uncontrolled or unmediated by the prophet. The prophecies recorded in Scripture evidence the distinctive styles of their human authors, so we should expect the same of non-Scriptural prophecy. Moreover, prophecies are to be given in an orderly fashion, so that receiving a prophecy does not mean it cannot wait (1 Cor 14:29-31), for "the spirits of prophets are subject to prophets" (1 Cor 14:32). Indeed, though all Scripture is prophetic in the sense of being the product of the Spirits' action in specific people, they also evidence careful thought and reflection. For this reason, I do not think the acknowledgement that all prophecy comes from the Spirit's direct action precludes human preparation; indeed, it is conceivable that the Spirit could use the prophet's preparations and mediations on Scripture to manifest a prophecy. Scripture does not give us a mechanism by which prophecy is formed and delivered, but it does tell us that when something is a true prophecy, it is the words of God through the Spirit.

Prophecy in this sense is broad, and it may be delivered in any number of settings. I am not suggesting that prophecy will always be a "sermon," yet there are times when a prophecy will involve public speech in the gathered church; as all prophecies are based on Scripture, this will thus be a sermon— however much or little preparation was involved or how much it conforms to the traditional model of a sermon. Indeed, teaching as discussed below is also "prophetic," for it will be a Spirit-attended application of Scripture to God's people; ministers of the Gospel rely on the Spirit's presence and power to do their work (e.g. 1 Cor 12:1-11; 2 Tim 1:6-7, 14). However, though a teacher is invested with the powers of prophecy (1 Tim 4:14), the authority for their teaching is not rooted in the immediate act of the Spirit by which they discern the appropriate thing to teach; no, their authority is rooted in the position to which they have been appointed. Christ has invested his authority in them (see III.A.3-4).

There are no restrictions on who may prophesy among church members in Scripture, a point we will consider in detail when we discuss prophecy and women in the New Testament (§5 below). However, false prophecy is associated with bad character, so character will be an important factor in the judging of prophecy (e.g. Acts 13:4-12; 2 Pet 2:1-3; 1 John 4:1-6). It needs to be asked, what relationship does the person prophesying have with the church, and how have they evidenced the fruit of the Spirit demonstrating his work in their lives? The last thing we will say about prophecy in this context is that it must be judged. John exhorts the churches to test the spirits by which a so-called prophet speaks: a genuine prophet will listen to Christ's apostles in Scripture and the churches he has established, but false prophets will deny important truths about Christ. Paul also expects that prophecies will be judged. A prophesy that has been spoken needs to be "weighed" (1 Cor 14:29); the Spirit seems to specially empower some people to discern by which spirit someone is speaking (1 Cor 12:10). This is consistent with the Old Testament attitude towards prophecy, which we touched on above. Thus, when someone claims to have a prophecy, this must be proven. A prophecy is not innocent until proven guilty: we must judge every prophecy to see if it is true or false. It appears that some people will be known to regularly speak true prophecies, so they may come to be known as a "prophet" (Acts 11:27-28), but what they say should still be weighed, for no one is foolproof.

In the church at Corinth, Paul instructs them to order their gatherings, to limit how many prophesy, and commands the whole congregation (excluding married women, see below) to judge prophecy. However, the Corinthian church was not a paradigm of the perfect church, and Paul is here correcting an overly chaotic gathering, so I don't believe that we need to take the exact manner Paul proposes for judging prophecy to be binding today. That is, if in the name of order, a small group of parishioners or elders (excluding married women, see below) were to vet prophecy before the gathering, this would seem as appropriate as mid-gathering judgment, so long as it is communicated to the congregation that prophecy is welcome and that there is careful judgment involved. The situation I envision is where God reveals something to a prophet, and that prophet spends time working on how to communicate it, then sends this to the team judging prophesy in order that it may be approved. It would be appropriate to still leave room open for discernment in the gathered church even if this practice is followed, in case the Spirit reveals something about that prophecy to someone listening.

4. Teaching Is a Specific Mode of Preaching.

The second "mode of authority" that justifies a sermon is that of teaching. Genuine Christian teaching is associated almost exclusively with the ordained leadership in the New Testament (there are some exceptions, e.g. Acts 15:1, 18:25). In addition to the teaching of Jesus and the apostles, Paul tells Timothy to "teach" and "preach the Word" (1 Tim 4:11, 13; 2 Tim 4:1-5) and describes the work of elders as doing so (see §III.B.2.c.iii).

As we discussed above, elders are invested with authority from Christ to command and urge God's people, expecting obedience. When this authority is expressed as public teaching in the gathered church, we call this preaching or teaching. Lionel Windsor describes what I am identifying as the teaching of congregational leaders as preaching, defined as the

> public component of the speech of a congregational leader to the congregation under his care, by which he ensures that the truth handed down in the Scriptures is learned and obeyed by that congregation, in light of the congregation's particular circumstances.[67]

Unlike prophecy, preaching in this sense does not rest in the immediate action of the Spirit, so it is not necessary to judge the preaching of an elder. Now, an elder may err, yet in this case, a sermon is presumed innocent until proven guilty; someone who will claim the elder is in error, that he is not speaking for the Spirit, must show this to be the case.

Think about how the Bible describes the teaching ministry of elders: they are to "command" and exhort "with all authority" (1 Tim 4:11, 6:1-3; Titus 2:15). We discussed the authority invested in elders in Chapter III, sections A and B.2. When the elders speak in the public gathering, they do so with the authority invested in them by Christ Jesus. They have the authority to "shepherd" their sheep, to speak from the Word directly into a person's life. With this authority comes incredible responsibility, as we

---

[67] Lionel Windsor, "Preachers and Leaders," in *Women, Sermons, and the Bible: Essays Interacting with John Dickson's Hearing Her Voice*, ed. Peter Bold and Tony Payne (Sydney: Matthias Media, 2014).

discussed above. This is why appointing elders is not to be done lightly.

5. Women May Prophesy but not Teach in the Corporate Gathering.

This brings us to, perhaps, the most difficult topic concerning "preaching" in contemporary discussion, whether or not women may preach in the gathered church. Our treatment of the questions has reframed the matter in a way that does not easily fit into the discussion as it has been held in recent years. Our analysis of the matter thus far has suggested that the wrong question is being asked: it is too broad.

We have argued in Chapter III that only men are permitted by Christ to be elders in his church: because the mode of preaching I have called "teaching" is associated with elders alone, women are not permitted by Christ to teach. We are not only dependent on such a deduction here, however, for Paul says this very thing in 1 Timothy 2, where he writes (with the authority of Christ) that he does not permit women "to teach or exercise authority over a man" (1 Tim 2:12). He says this in contrast with the attitude he would have from Christian women, learning in submission to the appropriate authorities. Notice how "submissiveness" is the converse of "exercise authority"; it is not an attitude expressed by women alone but by all who are under authority. Paul is not asking women to do anything more than the unordained men in the church, but he does indicate that women are not to be ordained to eldership, which is affirmed several verses later when he discusses the role of overseer (1 Tim 3:1-7). "Quiet" is thus in contrast with exercising authority and teaching: in contrast with these public, authoritative functions associate with elders and overseers, women are to learn, not teach, and submit, not lead in the local church.

To explain his reasoning, Paul appeals to the Fall narrative in a way that at first seems off-putting. It almost appears that Paul is saying women are more prone to deception than men, and therefore should not be given leadership. However, a closer reading shows that Paul is not making this point—nor is he trying to pin the responsibility of the fall on Eve, which is the opposite of the point Genesis makes. Instead, Paul is demonstrating a very close read of the Genesis narrative and the significant role-reversal demonstrated in Fall. In Genesis, God makes Adam first, and then Eve. God commissions Adam and creates Eve because Adam is insufficient for the task he has been given: he needs help (Gen 1:28, 2:15-18, 2:21-25). Adam is charged to lead, Eve to follow. Adam is charged to *guard* (שׁמר) the Garden, perhaps anticipating what is to come, and suggesting what his role should have been. We would expect that Adam would be the main player in the following narrative, but this is not so. No, the Serpent addresses Eve, and Adam—"who was with her" (3:6)—does nothing to stop him: he fails to keep the Garden. Adam failed to protect the Garden, to protect his wife. He failed to lead; instead, he was led. It is Adam who is held responsible when God enters the scene, as we would expect from God's ordering of Adam and Eve's relationship (Gen 3:9, 22-24; Rom 5:12-21; 1 Cor 15:22).

So, what is the significance that "Adam was not deceived, but the woman was deceived and became a transgressor"? The point is neither guilt nor gullibility—as if Adam is somehow off the hook for failing to guard the Garden and submitting to his wife without being directly addressed by the Serpent. No, Adam was made first, then Eve, so *Adam* should have led, not Eve—yet that is not what happened. Caught up in all complexity of that first sin is the disordered relationship between the first man and woman (cf. Gen 3:16, 4:7), which Paul now seeks to address: women are not to occupy that role which God originally entrusted to men within marriage, and to some men in eldership. Verse 15 makes sure that women readers would not be left on a negative note: yes, you are not to lead—to teach or have authority—but *"she,"* that is Eve, "will be saved through childbearing" (1 Tim 2:15). Lest we forget, God's promise amid the curse was that through the *woman*, not Adam, would come a son who would destroy the Serpent and bring salvation (Gen 3:15). Other women follow Eve, who was saved and saw the world saved through bearing children, by living Godly lives (1 Tim 2:15). Eve is not an example only of failure but also of sacrifice for the sake of the world, suffering in cursed childbearing to bring forth the one who undoes the curse. *She* "would be saved through childbearing" (cf. Gen 3:15), upon which God had pronounced a curse (Gen 3:16), thus setting an example for "them," "if they continue in faith and love and holiness, with self-control" (1 Tim 2:15).

So, women are not permitted to preach if by preaching we mean teaching. However, the question we need to ask is, does God permit women to prophesy? To this question, we must answer yes. In addition to the many prophetesses under the Old Covenant, we can add Philip's daughters "who prophesied" (Acts 21:9). The prophet Joel spoke of the coming of the Spirit of God, as fulfilled in the New Covenant, as a time "when your sons and your daughters shall prophesy" (Joel 2:28: see Acts 2:17). Paul corrects the Corinthians obsession with all things "spiritual" in 1 Corinthians, extolling the virtues of prophecy: in the process, he never forbids women from doing so, and actually presumes they will, arguing that it is dishonourable for a woman to "pray or prophesies" with her head uncovered (1 Cor 11:5).[68] This passage is even more important, because it assumes a gathered context for these activities, not only from the greater context (e.g. 1 Cor 11:17-34, 14:1-40), but also the reference to angels or messengers in verse 10. So women may preach if by preach we mean prophesy, and they may do so in the gathered church. This does not contradict 1 Timothy 2, for prophesying is not based on any authoritative role; no, it is based on the immediate activity of the Spirit and, therefore, his authority. The most problematic passage for this reading is 1 Corinthians 14:34.

Some manuscripts have verses 34-35 after verse 40, suggesting some scribes thought these verses were ill-suited for the context after verse 33, as in the majority of witnesses. Based on this variance, Gordon Fee has argued that these verses are not original but came from a floating tradition that scribes thought should be inserted but could not decide where.[69] Fee's suggestion has not been widely adopted and stands against the manuscript evidence, which unanimously attests to these verses. Instead, Metzger et al. are surely correct when they suggest that the manuscript tradition with these verses after verse 40 involve a scribal effort to find a more appropriate position for the verses that were received in their present position.[70] This is certainly understandable, for at first glance, these verses seem out of place: what in context would lead us to expect a prohibition on women speaking in the gathering? However, I believe we can make sense of these verses in their present context, and doing so does not contradict our argument thus far.

---

[68] Cf. J. Alexander Rutherford, "Is a Covering Long Hair or Veil? Interpreting 1 Corinthians 11:1-16," *Teleioteti* (blog), February 15, 2018, https://teleioteti.ca/2018/02/15/is-a-covering-long-hair-or-veil-interpreting-1-corinthians11/.

[69] Fee, *The First Epistle to the Corinthians, Revised Edition*, 780–92.

[70] Bruce Manning Metzger, *A Textual Commentary on the Greek New Testament*, 2nd Edition (London; New York, N.Y.: United Bible Societies, 1994), s.v.

First, it is probable that these verses address wives in particular, not women in general. It is well known that the same Greek word may mean "wife" or "women"; context determines which is intended. "Women" is perhaps the more common use, so it would make sense to assume that Paul speaks of "women" in general unless there is reason from context to think he speaks of "wives" in particular. Looking at the context, we find sufficient evidence to believe that this is indeed the case. For one, "women" (γυναῖκες) is accompanied with the article (αἱ): the article in Greek has a broad range of uses, but one common use is to indicate that the term in question is definite because of a specific relationship, which may often be accurately communicated in English with a possessive pronoun. This is why the KJV translates this as "your women." The ESV has "the women" (cf. NASB, NET), which is awkward in context: we would presume that there would be some indication in context which women are in view, yet there is nothing. The KJV is on the right track, but once specified with the article acting in this way, γυναῖκες (*gunaikes*) is better interpreted to mean "wives," so this phrase is probably to be understood as "your wives."

Second, we should note that "be silent" is not an absolute prohibition.[71] We have already seen that women are prophetesses and may prophecy in the gathered church—and surely they can sing! In verse 30, the same word is used for prophets refraining from speaking if another has a prophecy, and a nearly identical phrase is used in verse 27 for those who speak in tongues, commanding their silence if there is no interpreter. So, when we hear "be silent," we need to ask, "in regard to what?" Paul explains this, saying "it is not permissible for them to speak," which is contrasted with the positive instruction to "be in submission": submission expressed by not speaking is what "the law says" (v. 34). Notice the similarities to 1 Timothy 2:11-15 in this passage: both employ references to the Torah and a contrast between speaking and submission with silence. The sort of speaking that is not permitted is that which contrasts with "submission." In 1 Timothy 2, this sort of speech is associated with the abiding authority of an elder-overseer. It would make sense for the passage of the Law Paul speaks of here in 1 Corinthians 14 to be Genesis 1-3, to which he also appeals in 1 Corinthians

---

[71] The translation given throughout this paragraph are my own.

11:2-16. In that passage, as in 1 Timothy 2, the appeal to the creation narrative establishes a proper order between husbands and wives, with the former leading and the other following. Thus, the sort of speech that is not permitted is that which stands opposed to the proper ordering of male-female relationships ordained by God in the creation. However, verse 35 suggests that Paul is addressing something other than women teaching with the authority of the ordained ministry, which was his concern in 1 Timothy 2. Here, Paul says that if "they desire to learn anything," "let them ask their own husbands at home." This is odd, for in 1 Timothy 2:11, "submission" and "quiet" was the way women ought *to learn*. So, Paul is not saying wives should not learn in the gathered church, but that their learning must be characterised by "submission" and "silence" (1 Cor 14:34) or "quiet" (1 Tim 2:11). Their learning must not be associated with the specific form of "speaking" he addresses. That the issue is proper learning moves us away from viewing "speaking" as a prohibition against speaking in general, such as prophecy or tongues—which women are permitted to do. Perhaps Paul is anticipating women asking questions in the sort of "spiritually" charged public gathering the Corinthians were practising and Chapter 14 is attempting to reign in. However, the context suggests a more relevant issue, which works well with the argument we have been making.

Verses 29-33 had just dealt with the issue of order and prophecy. Prophets were to speak in an orderly manner so that all might learn and be encouraged. When the prophets speak, "the others" are to evaluate their prophecy. It is not clear whether "others" refers to "other [prophets]"—i.e. those beyond the two or three who speak—but it would seem to refer to the whole congregation ("the rest," οἱ λοιποί, being more appropriate if the rest of the prophets were in view).[72] Now, if an evaluation of the prophecy is revealed to another who is seated, they are to speak this revelation and it will then be evaluated ("if [the evaluation] is revealed to another seated, let the first one be silent").[73] Verses 32-33a give the principle for the ordering of

---

[72] Carson, *Showing the Spirit*, 120; Grudem, *The Gift of Prophecy in the New Testament and Today*, 60–62.

[73] ἀποκαλυφθῇ here is usually interpreted to mean "if a revelation is made" (e.g. ESV). However, I can find no comparable instance of the passive with the absolute meaning; that is, it expects a direct object. In the in active, the verb means

prophecy just commanded: prophets are not subject to ecstatic speech or uncontrollable necessity to speak. No, God is a God of order. Immediately following this point, we find our verses (introduced by a clause reminiscent of 1 Cor 11:16). The connection is asyndeton (without conjunction), so we must supply the relationship from context. I suggest that the connection between 33a and b is best expressed by the conjunction "now," indicating a qualifying statement or additional issue raised by that which precedes. If we translate as such, we can make sense of the connection:

> For God is not of disorder but of peace. [Now,] as in all the churches of the saints, your wives must be silent in the churches,[74] for it is not permissible for them to speak, but rather they are to be in submission, as the Law also says. And if they desire to learn anything, they must ask their own husbands at home, for it is shameful for a wife to speak in the church. (vv. 33-35, my trans.)

In the context of order and prophecy, where women may participate in prophecy, Paul insists that distinctions he has established elsewhere on the basis of the Law be maintained. Women must demonstrate their submission to God's ordering of relationships. The evaluation of a prophecy is a critical stage in the appropriate use of prophecy in the church: if "others"—that is, many—are to be involved in the evaluation, we can imagine that it should be a bit of deliberation. We can imagine statements and questions, both between those evaluating and towards the prophet. This process of evaluation is "learning" in that evaluation takes us deeper into the basis for and meaning of the prophecy, but it is also learning "something" about the prophecy. So, if a wife desires to "to learn anything [about the prophecy], she must ask her own husband at home." These verses are not so out of place after all but indicate that though women are permitted (and encouraged) to prophesy, married women are not to participate in the evaluation of prophecy. Paul

---

"to reveal something," (whether the something is direct or indirect content), so the passive would be expected to mean "something is revealed" (2 Thess 2:3). Thus, "if [something] is revealed to another seated." The question is, what is the object we are to imply from the context? As suggested above, the "discernment" or "evaluation" seems appropriate.

[74] The repetition of "churches" (plural) within a short space is awkward, yet it does not suggest that they have two different senses—as Verbrugge asserts. Instead, it suggests emphasis on the universality of this practice.

grounds this in the creation narrative ("the law says"), so we are to understand this prohibition as guarding the appropriate expression of ordered male-female relationships in the church when certain Spirit-led gifts could *appear* to contradict this order, though they do not do so. Thus, we conclude that the Bible commends women who prophesy and that prophecy will sometimes look like a contemporary Evangelical sermon. However, whether it is an unordained man or woman prophesying, there must be evidence that the sermon has been judged, whether by the entire congregation or its elders delivering their judgment to the congregation. Furthermore, by definition, prophecy as preaching will be intermittent. This contrasts with teaching, which does not need to be judged and will occur regularly.

V. DISCIPLINE

For though absent in body, I am present in spirit; and as if present, I have already pronounced judgment on the one who did such a thing. When you are assembled in the name of the Lord Jesus and my spirit is present, with the power of our Lord Jesus, you are to deliver this man to Satan for the destruction of the flesh, so that his spirit may be saved in the day of the Lord. – 1 Corinthians 5:3-5 (ESV)

1. That discipline is an act of the congregation directed towards one of its members for the benefit of that member and the congregation.
2. That Discipline is gradated.
3. Censure or discipline is proportionate to the sin.
4. In case of private sin, the offended party (where appropriate) ought to confront the offending party privately.
5. If an offending member does not respond to private rebuke, the offended party should bring another member.
6. If an offending member does not respond to the presence of another member with the offended party, the case is to be brought before the church.

7. The elders ought to investigate the matter and, where the breach has not been repaired, bring the case before a *special gathering*.

8. If the offending party does not respond to the public rebuke of the *special gathering*, further censure is to be prescribed, namely, the loss of the privileges of membership and disqualification from the Lord's Supper (Matt 18:17).

9. If the offending member does not respond to these censures, then they are to be put out of the congregation and considered a member of ill-standing ("*exairtion*").

10. "Extra-ordinary fellowship" forbidden to the member subject to *exairtion* is that fellowship unique to the church; ordinary fellowship of spouses and guardians is not restricted.

We now turn to one of the most controversial topics in ecclesiology today, church discipline. The controversy is not over whether or not the New Testament speaks of such things but how it may be implemented in our highly regulated and pluralistic society. There are clear examples of church discipline gone wrong among various cults, where excommunication is common. In more orthodox churches, church discipline has invited charges of spiritual abuse and authoritarianism. However, despite the present controversies and difficulties involved in implementing church discipline, this is an vital theme in New Testament ecclesiology and has featured prominently in the historical works on church life and Christian ministry, such as *The Cambridge Platform of Discipline, The Book of Pastoral Rule* of Gregory the Great, and *On the True Care of Souls* by Martin Bucer.[75]

Discipline in Christian practice incorporates something like excommunication as it is practised in non-Christian sects today, but I am using the neologism "*exairtion*" to distinguish the biblical and historical

---

[75] Gregory the Great, *The Book of Pastoral Rule*, St. Vladimir's Seminary Press "Popular Patristics" Series, no. 34 (Crestwood, N.Y: St. Vladimir's Seminary Press, 2007); Bucer, *Concerning the True Care of Souls*; Baxter, *The Reformed Pastor*.

practice from what goes by the name "excommunication" today. However, discipline is not just "excommunication" but also rebuke, public investigation and judication of disputes among congregation members, and the restriction of the rights of members (other traditions would also add "penance," or the imposition of external acts by which the genuinely repentant believer might demonstrate their repentance, e.g. *On the True Care of Souls*). In this section, I will attempt to lay forth the biblical contours of church discipline, leaving the churches with the much more difficult question of how to implement these practices in a way that is above reproach and legal in their context.

Another legal consideration is that when a member breaks the law, church discipline does not supersede or replace the authority Christ has given to the government. In civil matters, Paul instructs the churches to handle the matter themselves (1 Cor 6:1-11), but this is not the case for breaches of law: Christians are to submit to the ruling authorities (Rom 13:1-7; Titus 3:1; 1 Pet 2:13-17). Churches must not be a party to concealing unlawful behaviour. However, church discipline can and should run in conjunction with the enactment of the law: if someone is guilty of a crime and this issue is also a matter of church discipline, their prosecution in the criminal courts does not remove the need for discipline. Furthermore, the standards of guilt and innocence in the courts of the church may be different than those in civil courts: the church requires two or three witnesses—the principle of sufficient warrant—but the courts require evidence beyond a reasonable doubt.

1. That Discipline Is an Act of the Congregation Directed Towards One of Its Members for the Benefit of That Member and of the Congregation (Cf. CPD Ch. XIV).

The censures of the church are appointed by Christ for the preventing, removing, and healing of offences in the Church; for the reclaiming and gaining of offending brethren (Jude 23; 1 Cor 5:6); for the deterring of others from similar offences (Deut 13:11; 17:12-13; 1 Tim 5:20); for purging out the leaven which may infect the whole lump: for vindicating the honour of Christ, of his church, and the holy profession of the gospel (Rom 2:24); and for preventing of the wrath of God that may justly fall upon the church if they should suffer his covenant and the seals thereof to be profaned by notorious and obstinate offenders (Rev 2:14-16, 20). (CPD XIV.1)

> When church members see fellow Christians in the church doing what is patently wrong and then look elsewhere as if it were none of their business, then that church will soon be in a downward tailspin as far as true godliness and spirituality is concerned. Church discipline is the responsibility of the whole church. – Conrad Mbewe[76]

Discipline is an act of the entire congregation, not just its leadership or its members. In Matthew 18:15-20, a dispute may be escalated to the level of church discipline; when this happens, the dispute is brought before "the church." In 1 Corinthians 5:3-5, Paul commands the Corinthians, when gathered, to "deliver this man to Satan," which involves the removal ($\alpha\check{\iota}\rho\omega$, *airo*) or excommunication ($\dot{\epsilon}\xi\alpha\acute{\iota}\rho\omega$, *exairo*) of the sinner from the fellowship of the body (5:2, 11-13); this is the most severe act of discipline, what I am calling *exairtion*. In this passage, the congregation is to do this act when gathered; they do this with Paul present "in Spirit," "with the power of our Lord Jesus" (1 Cor 5:4). We have already seen that church acts are performed with the combined authority of the eldership and the congregation: though the elders and members are not distinguished here, we do find Paul acting with the congregation to do this. When the congregation acts this way, as in Matthew 18:20, they operate with the presence and authority of Christ.

Discipline is an act of the entire congregation towards *one of its members*. "Discipline" is not enacted towards unbelievers, for what have we "to do with judging outsiders?" (1 Cor 5:12) Nor is it directed to members of another church, for they are subject to that church's discipline and may only be accepted with hospitality or rejected by another church (2 John 9-11; 3 John 5-12). When performed correctly, that is, by a congregation towards its members, discipline has the aim of restoring the erring member, preserving the purity of the church, protecting the church and Christ from dishonour, and "deterring others from similar offences," as the *Cambridge Platform* has it (Deut 13:11; 17:12-13; 1 Tim 5:20).

a. Discipline Is Restorative

---

[76] Conrad Mbewe, *God's Design for the Church: A Guide for African Pastors and Ministry Leaders* (Wheaton: Crossway, 2020), 178.

In the first case, discipline is restorative, not retributive: it does not met out judgement proportionate to the sin committed but seeks to demonstrate the consequences of that sin so that the sinner would repent and be received in right fellowship. In 1 Corinthians 5:5, the man guilty of terrible sexual immorality is to be handed over to Satan, "so that his spirit may be saved in the day of the Lord" (ESV). Similarly, in 2 Thessalonians 3, they are to avoid relations with the disciplined believer that they may be "ashamed," warning him "as a brother," not treating him as an unbeliever. Both of these are instances of *exairtion*, but we presume the same is true for lesser acts of discipline. We find this, for example, in Matthew 18:15, where private rebuke or discussion of sin results in the restoration of the relationship. In Jude 23, Jude calls the church to "save others by snatching them out of the fire" (ESV).

b. Discipline Preserves the Purity of the Church

In the second case, discipline preserves the purity of the church. Called to be a holy community (e.g. Eph 5:27; 1 Pet 1:13-25), the presence of unrepentant sin among the congregation jeopardises the special calling of the local congregation. Left to run its course, the neglect of sin can (lead to the church's rejection by Christ). Jesus is patient, but in Revelation, he warns the Ephesian church that if they do not return to him, "I will come to you, and I will remove your lampstand from its place; I will do this if you do not repent" (Rev 2:5). As the temple in ancient Israel was rejected when it lost its purpose (Mark 11:15-33, 13:1-2), so also local churches can lose their place with Christ if they fail to seek the holiness to which he has called them. The "leaven" of sin can saturate the entire church and thus corrupt it (1 Cor 5:6-8).

c. Discipline Protects Christ and His Church from Dishonour

When churches fail to be holy as God is holy, they fail to shine as lights in the darkness: if the church is no brighter than the world, how will it be seen? (Matt 5:14-16; Luke 11:33-36.) Moreover, churches and their leaders are called to be above reproach (Col 1:21; 1 Tim 3:7): if the church permits sin to endure in its midst, people will attribute the corruption of the church to Christ whom the church calls Lord. We do not want it to be said of us as it was of ancient Israel, "The name of God is blasphemed among the Gentiles because of you" (Rom 2:24). When we walk in the ways of sin, and so do not deal with sin amid our churches, "the way of truth will be blasphemed" (2 Pet 2:2).

d. Discipline Deters Others from Similar Offences

Discipline is, finally, a vivid deterrent for others. When a church acts against sin, it communicates to each member that sin is grave and must not be tolerated. When an elder is rebuked for sin, this is to be done publicly "so that the rest may stand in fear" (1 Tim 5:20). This is a critical theme in Old Testament instances of judgment on the sin of insiders, of Israelites, but the passage in Timothy demonstrates that it remains a purpose for church discipline (e.g. Deut 13:11; 17:12-13). Thus, if a church fails to enact discipline, they not only withhold vital medicine from the one in sin but also from those in the congregation who would contemplate such sin. When the church enacts church discipline, it communicates to the world and the congregation that sin is truly sin; if we fail to do this, we fail to convey the wickedness of sin properly.

2. That Discipline Is Gradated.

Discipline is essential for a church's life, but we must be clear that discipline is not just *exairtion*. *Exairtion* is the most severe form of discipline, which we reserve only for those not remedied by the lesser forms. Discipline moves from the private rebuke through public address, terminating in *exairtion*. In Matthew 18:15-20, Jesus gives us a basic outline of the process of church discipline, pointing us to its gradated nature; from elsewhere in the New Testament, we may fill in several intermediate stages before *exairtion*. As we will discuss in the next section, public sin will immediately escalate to public censure, but private sin should begin with private action.

In the case of private sin, sin between one believer and another or a small group of believers, the offended parties will confront the offending party (where appropriate, see below). If reconciliation is not yet achieved, other brothers and sisters are brought forth to adjudicate the matter: they provide witness testimony against the offender so that he or she may be convicted of their offence.[77] If the offender does not respond to this private rebuke, the matter is treated as a public matter ("public" being defined not as public to the world but public to the church, the members or subjects of a special gathering). With some investigation, the matter is brought before the congregation in a special gathering (where members alone participate), and the public rebuke is delivered. If the member does not yet respond to this, then some of their rights as members may be stripped from them, culminating in their being barred from the Lord's supper. Finally, if they fail to respond to the loss of membership privileges, they are subject to full removal from membership in the church community, *exairtion*. We will treat each of these stages of discipline below.

3. Censure or Discipline Is Proportionate to Sin.

It must be said that discipline or censure is proportionate to the sin committed. A minor breach between members does not itself warrant *exairtion*, but if a member adds rebellion, pride, and divisiveness to the offence by resisting all efforts for reconciliation, then this new sin added to the former leads to the more severe acts of discipline. In this way, what is initially a private sin may escalate to a public matter. However, some sins begin as a public sin; in these cases, the matter should be treated as public from the start. Though the remedy for public sin may involve private rebuke, there must also be public rebuke so that censure may have its full effect (1 Tim 5:20). In our age, where abuses of authority are so prevalent, I suspect we get the need for this: if pastoral failings simply ended with private rebuke and private repentance, then the damage done to those in the congregation, the collateral damage of breaches of trust and second-hand exposure to the sinful behaviour, is not addressed. If Christ's honour in the church is to be upheld, public sin must receive proportionate censure.

4. In Case of Private Sin, the Offended Party (where Appropriate) Ought to Confront the Offending Party in Private.

Before a matter between believers who are part of a local church is brought before the church, it is ideal that it would be dealt with privately between the

---

[77] For help in the process of mediating such conflict, see Ken Sande, *The Peacemaker: A Biblical Guide to Resolving Personal Conflict* (Baker Books, 2004).

parties involved. Jesus instructs his disciples in this regard, "If your brother sins against you, go and tell him his fault, between you and him alone. If he listens to you, you have gained your brother" (Matt 18:15). If the dispute is not resolved in this manner, Jesus then instructs the offended party to bring along believers as witnesses in the matter, to seek a private resolution so far as it is possible (Matt 18:16). In this, we see that private resolution of disputes is to be preferred to public action, though as discussed above, public sin must be dealt with in a public manner. Only when private resolution fails is the matter to be brought before the church.

However, there is one broad area of exception to this rule of private and then public address of "private" sins, which I have signalled with the qualification "where appropriate." There are instances where a matter is the subject of church discipline and where it would be inappropriate for the offended party to confront the offender privately, certainly alone but maybe even in a small group. Sexual abuse would be one such instance, especially if the abuser is in a position of power over the abused (such as a pastor), but there are other instances. In any instance where it is reasonable to believe that private rebuke would endanger the offended party, whether physically, emotionally, or spiritually, the matter must be handled differently than the above process. If the matter is criminal in nature, it should be treated as a public sin, even if it occurred behind closed doors: it is public because the offence will be the subject of public spectacle. If it is not a criminal matter and not for another reason to be treated as a public matter, then it would seem appropriate for the offended party to lay their case before the elders with witnesses and for the elders and witnesses to then confront the (presumed to be) offending party on behalf of the offended. Great discernment is necessary in these matters.

5. If an Offending Member Does Not Respond to Private Rebuke, then the Offended Party Ought to Bring Another Member.

The ideal end of private confrontation is the restoration of fellowship between brothers and sisters. Jesus calls all Christians to engage in this sort of reconciliation, "if you are offering your gift at the altar and there remember that your brother has something against you, leave your gift there before the altar and go. First be reconciled to your brother, and then come and offer your gift" (Matt 5:23-24). However, the reality of the "already-not-yet" tension within which we live—that Christ has inaugurated the eschatological new creation but will not bring it in its fulness until he returns—means that what is ideal is not always present. Relationships break down, and even Christians are not always honest and open about their sin, ready to confess and repent when confronted. Because of this, it is sometimes necessary to bring forth evidence to demonstrate to the offender the reality of their sin, even if they deny it.

For this reason, Jesus instructs the offended brother or sister to bring other believers as witnesses to confront the unrepentant brother or sister. The principle for this confrontation is God's principle in the Old Testament for civil and criminal disputes, two or three witness. Two or three eyewitnesses are indubitably compelling evidence, but the principle goes beyond this: if more witnesses are necessary, this is certainly permissible. Furthermore, the nature of the sin shapes the nature of the evidence presented (e.g. Deut 22:22-27), so non-verbal "witnesses" are also acceptable evidence for bringing about genuine repentance in the offender.

When a member of the church brings others into the matter who are not themselves witnesses, these third parties are obliged to weigh both sides of the issue: they are not to presume the account of the offended is accurate (cf. Prov 18:17). Doing so is especially important in the case of a charge against an elder; Paul instructs Timothy in 1 Timothy 5:19 not to accept any accusation against an elder except on the evidence of "two or three witnesses." This is not to say that a lesser standard applies to those who are not elders but that extra caution needs to be taken in the case of elder-overseers because of the seriousness of their sin resulting from their authority and position (5:22; James 3:1) and also the greater chance that elder-overseers will be subject to false charges, for example, by those who would like to see a change in leadership or from Satan who would want to undermine Christ's churches by putting them to public shame.

We should be clear that the goal of private rebuke such as this is not to conceal sin or lessen its severity but to give the sinner the opportunity for repentance without further, more severe measures introduced. Once again, there are sins that are public and should be dealt with publicly; in such cases, to stop at a private rebuke without public address is to conceal the sin, which never ends well (1 Tim 5:24-25).

6. If an Offending Member Does Not Respond to the Presence of Another Member with the Offended Party, the Case Is to Be Brought before the Church.

If efforts have been made in private to bring a sinning brother or sister to repentance and repair a broken relationship, and these efforts have failed, the matter is escalated to the church's attention. As discussed above, "the church" means the entire congregation, its elders and its members, who, with their combined powers, are invested with authority from Christ to resolve matters. Paul writes to the Corinthians that Christians will have an eschatological role in judgment, so they should be capable of judging disputes between brothers and sisters. This passage is worth quoting in full,

> When one of you has a grievance against another, does he dare go to law before the unrighteous instead of the saints? Or do you not know that the saints will judge the world? And if the world is to be judged by you, are you incompetent to try trivial cases? Do you not know that we are to judge angels? How much more, then, matters pertaining to this life! So if you have such cases, why do you lay them before those who have no standing in the church? I say this to your shame. Can it be that there is no one among you wise enough to settle a dispute between the brothers, but brother goes to law against brother, and that before unbelievers? To have lawsuits at all with one another is already a defeat for you. Why not rather suffer wrong? Why not rather be defrauded? But you yourselves wrong and defraud—even your own brothers! (1 Cor 6:1-8)

The church has authority from Christ to enact the various levels of discipline discussed above: the members alone cannot do so, nor can the elders alone. Only with their combined authority—with the whole church acting—may discipline be enacted. If discipline is directed towards an elder, and no elders are able to enact the discipline (either being absent or disqualified by their own behaviour or investment in the issue), it is appropriate for the church to reach out to another local church with which they have good fellowship that this church may come alongside the first church in judgment, just as Paul came alongside the Corinthian church to deliver a sentence of censure upon the man who was guilty of sexual immorality.

7. The Elders Ought to Investigate the Matter and, Where the Breach Has Not Been Repaired, Bring the Case before a Special Gathering.

We are not given many insights into the mechanics of judging a dispute in the church, but drawing on the explicit biblical teaching and the reflection of Christians upon that teaching for the last 2000 years, we can tentatively offer some insights on the matter.

First, the appropriate place for adjudicating a dispute between brothers and sisters and determining the proper discipline to be delivered, if any, is not the public gathering of the church. As discussed above, believers and unbelievers alike are welcome to the public or regular gatherings of the church. Members and non-members are both able to participate. However, in the case of discipline, the matter is to be brought before "the church" (Matt 18:17), not the mixed multitude of the regular gathering. It is the saints who are charged with and capable of settling disputes (1 Cor 6:1-3), not those who have "no standing in the church" (1 Cor 6:4). Thus, this is a context where a special gathering (§IV.A.2) is necessary. In a special gathering, only members in good standing are welcome; in this context, they meet with the power of Christ to act decisively in such matters (Matt 18:18-20; 1 Cor 5:4-5).

Second, it is appropriate for the elders, in their function as rulers and shepherds of the congregation, to lead the proceedings of such special gatherings. This may involve conducting the events, determining the congregation's will, and presenting the facts for consideration. Paul instructs *Timothy* not to "admit a charge against an elder except on the evidence of two or three witnesses" (1 Tim 5:19).

So, the offended party may raise the issue with the elders for consideration by the church. The elders themselves do not have the authority to enact discipline, but they can investigate the matter, gather the data, make a preliminary judgment, call a special gathering, and then lead the rest of the congregation through the data to deliver the verdict. That the whole church is involved does not mean this must be a "democratic" vote. The elders may truly lead, but they cannot unilaterally make the decision themselves, so it is appropriate for them to persuade the congregation of the appropriateness of a judgment to which the congregation then assents.

8. If the Offending Party Does Not Respond to the Public Rebuke of the Special Gathering, further Censure Is to Be Prescribed, the Loss of Some Privileges of Membership and Disqualification from the Lord's Supper (Matt 18:17).

Further censure is required if the matter is brought before the church and the offending member does not respond to the church's rebuke. Before *exairtion* is decreed, the member is to be stripped of some membership privileges. In Matthew 18:17, Jesus instructs his disciples that the offender should be treated as a "gentile and tax collector." As in the case of an unbeliever, the offender may be barred from participation in the ordination of leaders or other matters where the congregation acts with their authority. This is a loss of some but not all privileges of membership. More significantly, a breach with a brother or sister and with the church disqualifies the offending member from participation in the Table of the Lord. The Lord's Supper is for believers alone, so treating the offender as an unbeliever means withholding their participation in the Table. This inference is confirmed in 1 Corinthians 11:27-34, where Paul argues that breaches in fellowship among the church members—even before church discipline is enacted—disqualify one from participating. How much more so when the breach is with the church? In the Supper, we declare our union one with another in the body of Christ: it is not fitting for one at odds with the body to participate.

9. If the Offending Member Does not Respond to These Censures, then They Are to Put out of the Congregation and Considered a Member of Ill-Standing (*"exairtion"*) (Matt 18:17; 1 Cor 5:1-13; 2 Thess 3:6-15).

By the mercy of God, the combination of the previous censures may be enough to bring the offender to repentance and lead to their restoration. However, if they still refuse to repent of their offence, the most severe censure remains. *Exairtion* describes excluding a church member from the extraordinary fellowship characterising the church. Paul describes this as handing them over to "Satan," that is, treating them as if they are in the sphere of Satan's rule, the World, not of Christ's kingdom (1 Cor 5:5). Jesus describes it as treating the offender as a gentile or tax collector (Matt 18:17). However, this is not a complete repudiation of their status in the church; it is temporary. We do not "regard him as an enemy," but "warn him as a brother" (2 Thess 3:15).

How does this cohere with Jesus' statement in Matthew 18:17? Treating the person as a tax collector or gentile describes withdrawing extraordinary fellowship. However, we do not do this to alienate or destroy them as we would an enemy; instead, this is a warning for a brother or sister. They are still a member, though one in ill-standing: the goal of *exairtion* is their restoration.

A member of ill-standing, the subject of *exairtion,* is barred from the Table and is not welcome to the extraordinary fellowship of the church. This most severe censure, *exairtion,* is not intended for the destruction of its subject but their healing through the destruction of the flesh, their sin and pride. Exclusion from the protection and love of the fellowship ought not to be resorted to lightly, yet it is necessary for the health of the church and of the offending individual.

It is not clear to me that *exairtion* requires its subject to be barred from the regular gatherings of the church, for even unbelievers are permitted to participate. However, the presence of one under censure may be discouraged. It will certainly make things awkward between that person and the church which has censured them, especially the one they have offended. This will probably prevent them from participating, as will withholding fellowship from them. In this way, *exairtion* will organically result in the offending member withdrawing from the regular gathering. However, if they insist on showing up, I do not think their presence necessarily nullifies the censure— a church does not have to hire a bouncer! However, there are certainly instances where the presence of the one under censure will harm the offended party. In these cases, it would be appropriate to take additional efforts to prevent the offending member from participating in the regular gathering. Wisdom will be needed in such cases.

10. "Extraordinary Fellowship" Forbidden to the Member Who is the Subject of *Exairtion* Is That Fellowship Unique to the Church; Ordinary Fellowship of Spouses and Guardians Is not Restricted (CPD XIV.5).

> While the offender remains excommunicate, the church is to refrain from all member-like communion with him in spiritual things, and also from all familiar communion with him in civil things, farther then the necessity of natural, domestical, or civil relations require, and are therefore to forbear to eat and drink with him, that he may be ashamed. (Matt 18:17; 1 Cor 5:11; 2 Thess 3:6, 14) (CPD XIV.5)

Participation in the local church is meant to create close, familial fellowship among its members. This fellowship is the basis for the mutual ministry of the body, as members care for and encourage each other in following Christ. To be excluded from this fellowship once enjoyed should be devastating. So severe is this that Paul likens it to once again being subjected to Satan (1 Cor 5:5; 1 Tim 1:20). Christians are to refrain from association with the censured brother or sister, even eating with them (1 Cor 5:11; 2 Thess 3:6, 14-15). However, the association they are to refrain from is that extraordinary familiar communion created by the church: the ordinary communion required of us by God is not to be cut off. This ordinary communion is not that of friends, which is included within the censure, but that of spouses or guardians, where cutting off association would violate God's commandments. If a son or daughter is under censure, the parents are not to withdraw from their familial responsibilities. If a spouse is subject to censure, their spouse is not to withdraw marital communion. It is similar if a parent is under censure. Culture will, to some extent, determine whether further family relationships are affected by the censure or not (in some cultures, grandparents share similar responsibilities to a parent, so they should not withdraw communion). In summary, spouses or guardians are not to separate from or deprive a censured spouse or dependent, so long as the censured person is willing to live with them (1 Cor 7:12-16).

VI. INTER-CHURCH RELATIONS

Now concerning the collection for the saints: as I directed the churches of Galatia, so you also are to do. On the first day of every week, each of you is to put something aside and store it up, as he may prosper, so that there will be no collecting when I come. And when I arrive, I will send those whom you accredit by letter to carry your gift to Jerusalem. If it seems advisable that I should go also, they will accompany me. – 1 Corinthians 16:1-4 (ESV)

1. The obligations of churches to one another.
2. The benefits of inter-church communion.
3. That synods or parachurch forms of fellowship have no ecclesiastical standing: they are not a "church."
4. The obligation of other churches in the ordination of ministers to a new presbytery.
5. Of synods.
6. The role of other churches in the deposition of a presbytery or mediating conflict between a presbytery and congregation.
7. Of the relationship between a congregation and non-congregational churches and denominations.
8. That we ought to seek a pure communion but express patience and charity.

Perhaps the sphere of practice and thought distinctive to historical Congregationalism is its understanding of inter-church communion. Unlike the "independents" or "separatists," from which Congregationalists distanced themselves, Congregationalism demands local churches be in communion with one another. There are obligations churches owe one to the other. However, unlike denominations, these obligations reside not in extra-congregational structures and authority but in each local congregation in relation to those congregations local to or known to it. Therefore, Congregationalism mandates intimate fellowship among churches but forbids any movement to institutionalise these relationships with any authority or functions Scripture gives to local congregations. In these sections, we will explore the obligations churches have to each other and delve into the outworking of these obligations in inter-church relations. We have discussed this to some extent in Chapter I.5.b, which the reader may consult in conjunction with this chapter.

1. The Obligations of Churches to One Another.

Together, Christians are the body of Christ. We have a universal communion even though we are locally found in church bodies or congregations. This universal communion has both individual and congregational dimensions, as discussed in Chapter I. In its congregational dimension, the universal communion of believers in the body of Christ is the foundation for the communion of local congregations. If we are all part of one body, we should seek to act on that unity. If every congregation shares the same purpose, that of Christ, then they should work together to achieve that purpose. This desire for unity does not override the discreet reality of the congregation but ought to drive local churches into active communion with one another.

Because of their union in Christ Jesus, every local church has obligations to other local churches within its sphere of fellowship. Every congregation cannot maintain a relationship with every other congregation, so seeking communion with the churches in one's geographical area should be the priority. However, it is also good to connect and support churches worldwide, though each congregation will be limited in the number of churches with which they can maintain communion. I have described this sphere of fellowship as those congregations "local or known to" a congregation.

A local congregation is obligated to support the work of other congregations through prayer, financial support, and accountability. We pray the Father's kingdom come and will would be done on earth; his will is accomplished through local congregations, so we have an interest in praying for these local congregations, that God would work in and through them for his glory. As a congregation, we must not labour under the delusion that we are the only embassy of Christ's kingdom in our area. We should labour to pray for and support the work of other churches around us.[78] We have many examples in Scripture of local churches giving financially to support other churches that are less provisioned than they are (e.g. 1 Cor 16:1-4). As congregations provide for their members so that no one is in need, they endeavour to use their resources to ensure other congregations that have less means are not in need. The principle, as with congregational support, is equality, that none would lack so that others may have abundance,

> For I do not mean that others should be eased and you burdened, but that as a matter of fairness your abundance at the present time should supply their need, so that their abundance may supply your need, that there may be fairness. As it is written, "Whoever gathered much had nothing left over, and whoever gathered little had no lack." (2 Cor 8:13-15)

If local churches are obligated to share in their possessions to support other churches and pray for God's work to prosper through them, how much more should they invest in the spiritual purity and health of these congregations? Congregations are obligated to hold one another to account for their behaviour. Congregations do not have authority over one another, so this practically will look like regular communion that speaks the truth in love (Eph 4:25), willing to address sin and error in the congregation or its leadership based on demonstrated love and trust. One congregation can exercise a sort of discipline over another, namely, withholding communion. This may mean withholding financial support, refusing to partner in local endeavours, or refusing to welcome members of the censured congregation

---

[78] I have printed the later congregationalist statement, "The Burial Hill Declaration" as the second appendix of this book, for I think it captures this impetus well.

to the Lord's Table or full communion with a congregation. I can think of no biblical example of this, but it appears to me to be valid by analogy with the practice of church discipline within a congregation, as discussed in the previous chapter, and the discussion in 2 John about welcoming those from other churches (2 John 9-11). If welcoming a believer in error is to participate in their wickedness, how much more so welcoming a church in similar error?

2. The Benefits of Inter-Church Communion.

The benefits of this communion ought to be evident. Churches in lower-income areas may receive resources to effectively reach their neighbours and care for their members through the generosity of churches with more resources. Sharing non-tangible resources like expertise and people can also help individual congregations effectively reach those around them. Close fellowship among congregations also facilitates the intercession of elders from one congregation in the discipline of a congregation's presbytery or sole elder and in the appointment of elders where a presbytery has yet to be established.

3. That Synods and Parachurch Forms of Fellowship Have No Ecclesiastical Standing: They Are Not a "Church."

As we covered in the first chapter of this book, the only entities that qualify as a "church," with its implications of authority and purpose, are local congregations. Though local congregations must seek fellowship with other congregations, this fellowship is not itself a "church." Thus, trans-local entities are neither rightly called churches, as in "The Church of England," nor are they permitted to function in the manner of churches, exercising the authority Christ has invested therein.

4. The Obligation of Other Churches in the Ordination of Ministers to a New Presbytery.

As we have discussed above, the authority to ordain elders or "presbyters," the leaders of local congregations, lies in the entire congregation, its members and elders together. Christ does not authorise Christians to appoint one of their number to be a leader over them: they may elect a leader, but they lack the power to ordain that man. Because a church is constituted by members led by overseers, no group of Christians may declare themselves a church apart from ordained leaders. Therefore, the birth of a new church requires the authority of those who have already been ordained as elders.

In the New Testament, the apostles invested authority in the first elders, creating churches. This authority of "laying on hands" has been invested now in elders, thus the office elder-overseer is self-replicating. So, in the case of a new congregation, it is requisite for another congregation's leadership to invest the authority of eldership in the members elected by the disciples who will become a church. They are to do this carefully, as discussed above in the context of regular ordination (where an existing presbytery appoints new elders). By investing authority in the new presbytery, the ordaining presbytery does not have direct authority over the new congregation: their authority derives from their own congregation, consisting of the elders with the members, and the new congregation has ecclesial authority invested in its new presbytery and members. However, because of the risks involved in ordination—namely, that the one ordaining is caught up in the sins of those they ordain (1 Tim 5:22-25)—it would seem best that the ordaining presbytery continue in relationship with the new church to offer counsel and accountability to the new presbytery. By doing so, they maintain a level of reputability with the new congregation and cognisance of its health so that if it becomes necessary to depose that new presbytery, the concerned members can turn to the elders of their sister church, once again drawing on their authority to perform the deposition.

5. Of Synods (Cf. CPD XVI).

From the time of the New Testament, Christians across the ages have found reason to convene synods or councils in order to address important issues. In church history, such councils have functioned as if they were churches, issuing depositions and adopting universalising edicts to bind individual congregations. Our argument thus far has demonstrated that synods may not function with such authority: they may not perform the functions Christ has given local congregations. As discussed in Chapter I, the Jerusalem Council is no exception to this rule (§I.5.b.i.2). Instead, the Jerusalem Council is an example of the advisory function for which synods are appropriate.

Synods may not perform the functions of a church, but they may advise local churches in the exercise of their powers. Thus, when a particular issue requires input beyond that available from a fellowship of local congregations, such a fellowship (a local church and the congregation(s) they have consulted) may summon a synod to draw on the broader wisdom of Christ's churches. When this happens, it is appropriate for delegations of non-ordained members and ordained members to be sent from each participating church to gather together and deliberate the issue (Acts 15:2-4, 15:6-23).

6. The Role of Other Churches in the Deposition of a Presbytery or Mediating Conflict between a Presbytery and Congregation.

Because Christ has invested his authority in churches, not its members or presbytery apart from the other, a house divided stands to halt the work of a church. If the elders and other members are in conflict, the church cannot exercise discipline, depose elders, elect new officers, or the like. Therefore, such a situation needs resolution quickly if Christ's work in that church is to prosper. For this purpose, Christ has provided local congregations who may come alongside the struggling church and provide counsel, mediation, and—if necessary—exercise discipline. It is best if such action is taken by a church with a history of fellowship with the struggling congregation. Churches should not wait until crisis strikes to forge meaningful relationships with nearby congregations; instead, they should actively seek to maintain such fellowships so that they may engage alongside one another in the work of the Lord and, if a crisis emerges, know to whom they may turn. Because local churches may be called on to mediate a conflict between the elders and the rest of the congregation, the pursuit of close relationships with local congregations should be a decision made by the entire congregation (members and elders together) to build trust among all parties.

In the case of a dispute, the struggling congregation may invite the counsel and action of another congregation in good fellowship. When they have done so, the elders and congregation of the healthy congregation should investigate the matter thoroughly before taking action. If discipline is appropriate, or peace may not be achieved without implementing discipline, the neighbouring congregation may act alongside the righteous party for discipline. That is, if the presbytery is guilty of disqualifying sin, then the elders of the neighbouring congregation may act with the church's members to depose their presbytery (they would then need to act to ordain a new presbytery). Or, if some in the congregation have disqualified themselves from membership, but the members refuse to act, the neighbouring church members may act in conjunction with the church's presbytery to enact discipline.

Though no one desires conflict, and peace is to be sought, sin must not be tolerated, so action must be taken. However, such drastic moves of discipline should be reserved for the occasions when peace is not achieved through the counsel of neighbouring churches and, perhaps, even a local synod.

7. Of the Relationship between a Congregation and Non-Congregational Churches and Denominations (Cf. *The Burial Hill Declaration*).

Though we have argued in this document that only congregations are properly churches and may act with the authority of a church, we know that many brothers and sisters worldwide disagree with us. We have included the historical Congregationalist document *The Burial Hill Declaration* below (Appendix 2), despite its nationalistic inclinations, because it accurately demonstrates congregationalism's freedom for expressing ecumenicism.

> Affirming now our belief that those who thus hold 'one faith, one Lord, one baptism,' together constitute the on Catholic Church, the several households of which, though called by different names, are the one body of Christ; and that these members of his body are sacredly bound to keep 'the unity of the spirit in the bond of peace,' we declare that we will cooperate with all who hold these truths. With them we will carry the gospel into every part of this land, and with them we will go into all the world, and 'preach the gospel to every creature.' May He to whom 'all power is given in heaven and earth' fulfill the promise which is all our hope: 'Lo, I am with you always, even to the end of the world.' Amen. (*The Burial Hill Declaration*)

Having declared that denominations are not "churches," congregations do not thereby disavow partnership with local congregations that participate in denominations. No, following the biblical example, we insist on forging relationships with all local congregations with which we can hold fellowship in good conscience. It is conceivable that even congregations in completely abhorrent denominations could be held in good fellowship if their leaders and members professed the right faith in word and deed. Local churches ought to seek fellowship with all local congregations with which they can fellowship in good conscience. They ought not to rely on denominational adherence to determine what churches to engage with but gain an understanding of each church through good faith communion. Thus, congregationalism urges us to engage with other churches despite our differences, evaluating what is consistent with our conscience on a case-by-case basis.

8. That We Ought to Seek a Pure Communion but Express Patience and Charity.

In Chapter I, we identified the global communion of local congregations as a genuine expression of the global church. However, we also saw that this is not an indiscriminate unity: it is a unity centred on the reality of the Church's invisible being. In practice, the global church will be (like the local church) a mixed entity: it will have believing and apostate churches working together and believing individuals alongside unbelieving individuals. However, though it is mixed now, the ideal remains that of the invisible church, the pure, unmixed community. Towards this end, hospitality and the sharing of resources are to be done with discernment: local churches and individuals ought to support those who confess the truth so that they might become our fellow works in the truth (3 John 8), yet we must be careful not to welcome the false teacher, lest we "[take] part in his wicked works" (2 John 11). The promised New Covenant has come, and its purity exists in the ideal reality of the elect believers known only to God, but until the consummation of the age, we live with an imperfect fulfilment of the covenant—an already-not-yet experience of God's promises.

We strive for the ideal of the perfect, invisible church, but the Church in its global interactions will make mistakes, so it will be mixed. Jesus is patient with his churches: in Revelation 1-3, we read six out of seven churches receiving stern words from their Saviour, yet despite the rebuke they receive, his Spirit and presence still abide with them. He has not abandoned his people nor the imperfect churches they form. There comes a time when

Christ will remove his presence; he brings a strong word against the apostate church: "I will come to you and remove your lampstand from its place, unless you repent" (Rev 2:5). The church of Ephesus had abandoned their first love (2:4), yet Jesus desires their repentance. There will be no perfect church in this age, and our understanding of the global church should reflect Christ's own patience in calling those who claim his name to repentance.

VII. THE RELATIONSHIP OF CONGREGATIONS AS CONGREGATIONS TO THE STATE

Let every person be subject to the governing authorities. For there is no authority except from God, and those that exist have been instituted by God. Therefore whoever resists the authorities resists what God has appointed, and those who resist will incur judgment. – Romans 13:1-2 (ESV)

Do not be unequally yoked with unbelievers. For what partnership has righteousness with lawlessness? Or what fellowship has light with darkness? What accord has Christ with Belial? Or what portion does a believer share with an unbeliever? – 2 Corinthians 6:14-15 (ESV)

Honor everyone. Love the brotherhood. Fear God. Honor the emperor. – 1 Peter 2:17 (ESV)

1. God has ordained civil magistrates for the public good.
2. God's people are to be subject to civil magistrates and to pray for them.

3. A congregation is not to be partial to any state and, therefore, not accept any state investment that would prejudice its exilic nature.
4. A congregation should submit to all requirements of the state except where doing so would prejudice its nature and calling.

Infant baptism excepted, the single area of most significant divergence between the congregationalism expressed in this document and that of the *Cambridge Platform of Discipline* is its account of the relationship between the church and the "state," or the civil magistrate. For guidance in these matters, we have drawn on the 2nd London Baptist Confession (1689). As discussed in the introduction, we have chosen to follow the historical stream of Congregationalism rather than the Baptists in this document because of important ecclesiological distinctives of the former. However, the two are rather close in many matters, and our repudiation of infant baptism and the traditional Reformed understanding of civil magistrates brings us close to the Baptists. However, once again, our emphasis lies on ontology (what we are) rather than a principle of autonomy (our supposed rights). We insist on the separation of the church from the state not on the basis of a church's freedom from civil authority nor the state's freedom from ecclesial influence, but rather on the basis of what the church *is*.

The state is an entity of this world; the Church is not. The state is in the hands of the Devil; the Church is in Christ's hands. The state aims at temporal order; the church at eternal peace. However, the fact that the church is an otherworldly entity does not free it from the state's authority. No, as with its members, churches are bound to obey the civil magistrates. Nevertheless, as an embassy of an alien kingdom, churches must not make themselves at home with any one of the nations on this earth.

1. God Has Ordained Civil Magistrates for the Public Good.

> God, the supreme Lord and King of all the world, has ordained civil magistrates to be under him, over the people, for his own glory and the public good; and to this end has armed them with the power of the sword, for defence and encouragement of them that do good, and for the punishment of evil doers. (Rom 13:1-4) - London Baptist Confession 1689

In the eyes of God, the state is a good thing. The social ordering of human society under civil authorities is God's good design. From early in Scripture, we find the social ordering of human societies into families and kingdoms. In Romans 13, we are told that God has established civil authorities to preserve the public good. Indeed, we are told that Christ has given them authority to do so (Rom 13:1-2).

2. Though Ordained by God, States Are Under the Sphere of Satan's Authority.

No matter how cruel or unjust they may be, states are nevertheless tools in God's hands. In the Old Testament, God moves the nations as he wills, to tear down or build up. He wields the Babylonians to judge the wicked of Judah while saving the righteous (Habakkuk 1-3) as he had used the Assyrians to judge Israel (2 Kings 17:6), though he deposed Sennacherib, their king, for his blaspheme (Isaiah 36-37). Under the reign of the horrid emperors of Rome, Nero in particular, God told his people to be subject to civil authorities whom he had appointed. Therefore, our submission to civil authorities is not contingent on the righteousness of their rule: God even uses the wicked as his tools to exercise his authority, so we must submit to them.

Indeed, a careful reading of the biblical narrative demonstrates that civil magistrates, though given their authority from God, are aligned with the kingdom of Satan.[79] That is, all humans are under the authority of Satan, the god of this world and ruler of the powers of the air, unless they are redeemed by Christ and made partakers of his kingdom (John 8:39-47; Eph 2:1-10; 2 Cor 4:4). Therefore, as humans under Christ's rule form an institution with Christ as its head, the church, so humans under Satan's power form institutions under his headship, states. Throughout the Bible, particularly in Daniel and Revelation, nations are portrayed as satanic beasts with Satan, the ancient serpent and dragon, at their helm. Such imagery occurs elsewhere (e.g. Isa 27:1, Isa 51:9; Ezek 29:1-6; Psalm 74). The state should, therefore, be interpreted as tools in the hands of Satan, as he stands at the helm of his erstwhile kingdom of humanity set up in opposition to Christ's kingdom. Nevertheless, the association of civil magistrates with Satan does not negate the authority God has invested in them, so churches must be submissive to

---

[79] See J. Alexander Rutherford, "Towards a Biblical Theology of Satan's Kingdom," *Teleioteti Journal for Christian Ministry* 01, no. 01 (June 15, 2023): 42–52.

the governing authorities.

3. God's People Are to Be Subject to Civil Magistrates and to Pray for Them.

> Civil magistrates being set up by God for the ends aforesaid; subjection, in all lawful things commanded by them, ought to be yielded by us in the Lord, not only for wrath, but for conscience' sake (Rom 13:5-7; 1 Pet 2:17); and we ought to make supplications and prayers for kings and all that are in authority, that under them we may live a quiet and peaceable life, in all godliness and honesty. (1 Tim 2:1-2) - London Baptist Confession 1689

Because the state derives its authority from God, God's people owe allegiance to the civil magistrates (Rom 13:5-7). This is not to be a begrudging submission, but Christians must show genuine honour to those over them (1 Pet 2:17). In word and deed, churches ought to recognise the legitimacy of earthly rulers under Christ. They ought to pay their taxes and go through the administrative loops often required by contemporary nations. Because civil magistrates have genuine authority from Christ in their proper sphere, Churches ought to submit to these authorities. Thus, the proper exercise of the church's authority in discipline is not a substitute for the proper exercise of the state's authority. Instead, Christ expresses his authority through the state and the church to achieve respective goods, namely the public good and the good of the church members, concurrently. Therefore, someone may simultaneously be subject to church and civil discipline: church discipline should not be treated as a substitute for civil discipline, nor vice versa.

Because civil authorities are ordained for good, we ought to pray for them that they would exercise their authority for that end (1 Tim 2:1-2). Part of the Christian calling to do good to everyone is interceding for their nations before God the Father, asking that peace would be established and justice would flourish (Gal 6:10).

4. A Congregation Is not to Express Partiality to Any State and, therefore, not Accept Any State Investment That Would Prejudice Its Exilic Nature.

Because congregations are exilic embassies, present instantiations of an eschatological kingdom, they must not engage in relationships with states that would jeopardize their otherworldly identity. Indeed, because states are under Satan's authority, churches must be wary of their associations with the civil magistrate, lest they become "unequally yoked" or engage in a partnership that drags them off the narrow path to which Christ has called them (2 Cor 6:14-7:1).

In Western countries, governing authorities often offer grants to community and religious organisations; churches often take advantage of these resources. Danger emerges when accepting such resources requires the church to align itself with the state or bind itself to the state. For example, nothing about a church as described in Scripture requires it to be registered as a charity in a Western nation. Churches often register as such because they are thus able to access many resources the government provides to charities and religious organisations. However, if doing so would cause a church to compromise its mission in any way, then this should be avoided. Perhaps the demands of registering as such would require a larger staff team than the church can employ, requiring them to go beyond their means or shift resources from those tasks that are proper to their calling. This would be an instance where seeking the resources offered by the state may compromise a church's primary calling. I sense a minefield here, though I struggle to identify concrete issues. The principle should be clear, however: if accepting state support requires a church to structure itself in a way that does not support its primary calling, then the church should pursue Christ's call; if accepting state support requires the church to align itself with the agenda of the state, perhaps for social or community-oriented objectives, the church should proceed with caution, for "what accord has Christ with Belial?" (2 Cor 6:15).

There is an issue here that I suspect will occur more frequently than the issue of accepting government grants, that is, the question of partiality. If churches are genuinely embassies of Christ's eschatological kingdom, then no one nation is their home, even though they live within a specific nation. Churches must resist the urge to align themselves with the nation that is their temporary home. For example, if accepting government support requires advertising, branding, or communication that sends the message that the church supports or is an entity of that government, however mistaken that message may be on paper, churches must not do so. How will they welcome all nations if they say, on the one hand, all are welcome while presenting themselves, on the other hand, as allies of a nation that is, perhaps, responsible for atrocities in someone's home country or more generally? Here in Sydney, it is common for historic churches to have a war memorial, a record of all the church members who fought in the World Wars. There is often a tribute to these soldiers incorporated into the commemorative plaque. Once a year, churches often participate in ANZAC celebrations, remembering those who died fighting these wars. Consider what message these memorials communicate to our neighbours. For one, they communicate that the church is aligned with the military objectives of the State. Those objectives may be righteous—God has ordained the State for the public good—yet the church is to avoid aligning themselves with Satan, with whom states are aligned, so no matter how righteous, churches must not communicate their investment in the state's battles. Imagine the message these memorials communicate to a Japanese family that decides to visit a church, perhaps who lost many family members in the war? More recently, what will an Afghani or Iraqi family who suffered severely under the recent wars feel when the church communicates their support of the Australian Army?

Whether individual church members should participate in warfare or express their support is a matter that lies outside the scope of this book; here, we are merely dealing with the church's actions. Because of the exilic and eschatological nature of the Church, and the state's allegiance with Satan, churches should avoid committing to or communicating partiality for any earthly kingdom.

5. A Congregation Should Submit to All Requirements of the State Except where Doing So Would Prejudice Its Nature and Calling.

Finally, a congregation must submit to and honour governing authorities except in those cases where doing so would comprise its unique nature. Congregations are not to express partiality for any state, so if the government mandates that they display pro-government symbols and deliver government propaganda (as I understand is the case in the official church in China), congregations must not obey. If the civil magistrates restrict the reading of the Word, or require prescribed or censured sermons, the church must not submit in these matters, for the church is obedient to Christ above all else. Where submission to earthly authority would compromise obedience to

Christ, obedience to Christ must prevail. However, this exception must not be taken as a license to dishonour and disregard the civil authorities as the congregation sees fit. No matter the local government, churches owe them their prayers and honour.

Given that God ultimately presides over all civil authority, churches should err on the side of submission unless it is clear that doing so would be disobedience to Christ. In other words, the burden of proof lies on the church to substantiate its disobedience: they owe obedience; disobedience must be the exception, not the rule. As Peter writes in the context of servants suffering under unjust masters,

> For this is a gracious thing, when, mindful of God, one endures sorrows while suffering unjustly. For what credit is it if, when you sin and are beaten for it, you endure? But if when you do good and suffer for it you endure, this is a gracious thing in the sight of God. (1 Pet 2:19-20, 3:13-17)

Also,

> But let none of you suffer as a murderer or a thief or an evildoer or as a meddler. Yet if anyone suffers as a Christian, let him not be ashamed, but let him glorify God in that name. For it is time for judgment to begin at the household of God; and if it begins with us, what will be the outcome for those who do not obey the gospel of God? (1 Pet 4:15-17)

CONCLUSION

In the preceding chapters, I have attempted to commend a vision of congregational polity that builds upon historical Congregationalism but is willing to depart from this tradition where it is found to conflict with God's revelation in Scripture. I have not attempted to offer an exhaustive account of biblical polity sufficient for any church. Instead, I have only sought to provide a skeleton of the biblical teaching that churches may use to develop an account of polity appropriate for their circumstances.

I have attempted to show you from Scripture that only local congregations are "churches," yet this does not mean that a congregation is independent or autonomous from the rest of Christ's body. No, every church is part of Christ's body and is obligated to engage in fellowship with other churches to achieve Christ's purpose on earth and maintain accountability. I have also argued that congregations ought to strive for a pure communion of members, employing discipline where necessary to achieve this end. Because local congregations are to be pure communions, they ought to practice credo or believers' baptism. Local congregations must also seek purity in their fellowship with other local churches, lest they become complicit in the wicked deeds of false brothers and sisters. However, in discerning this pure fellowship, congregations must show patience and charity as Christ demonstrates towards his churches in Revelation 1-3. We also argued that the authority in the local church resides neither in the elders nor members alone but in both elders and members so that only by working together can the church perform the duties which Christ has entrusted to it.

I pray that this revived congregational polity—neo-congregationalism as I have called it—will provoke you to think clearly and biblically about the choices you make in structuring or being involved in a local church and in engaging with other local churches. Soli Deo Gloria in all God's churches, forever and ever, amen.

APPENDIX 1: THE CAMBRIDGE PLATFORM OF DISCIPLINE (1649), IN MODERNISED ENGLISH

Many things can and have been said about New England Congregationalism and English Puritanism. Many today direct us to the riches of the doctrinal confessions produced by the Puritans, particularly the Westminster Confession (adopted with some alterations as the Savoy Declaration by Congregationalists). Others address the steep decline in the health of New England churches following the 17th century. It is hard to ignore the fruit of Congregationalism even as we try to appreciate it. The fruit of which I speak are the various liberal denominations it spawned, such as the Unitarian Universalist Church and, in part, the United or Uniting Church (depending on the country). Some may argue the drift towards liberal theology was not a direct result of Congregational principles but perhaps a result of inconsistency in the practice of those principles, such as the so-called halfway covenant (which permitted children of baptised, unbelieving parents [or at least, parents who had no conversion experience] to be baptised and accepted as members of a church).[80]

---

[80] Walker quotes from Increase Mathers' *First Principles of New England* (1675, pp. 3-4), "Though the Child be unclean where both the Parents are Pagans and Infidels, yet *we may not account such Parents for Pagans and Infidels, who are themselves baptised, and profess their belief of the Fundimental Articles of the Christian Faith, and live without notorious Scandalous Crime, though they give not clear evidence of their regenerate estate*, nor are convinced of the necessity of Church Covenant. ... *We do therefore profess it to be the judgment of our* [Boston] *Church ... that the Grand-Father a member of the Church, may claim the privilege of*

The distinguished Congregationalist scholar Williston Walker would give a more positive spin on developments within Congregationalism through the 19th century, but it is hard to deny that from an Evangelical perspective, something went wrong.[81] The decline of New England Congregationalism and its role in the development of distinctive American ideals which don't sit well with many non-American Evangelicals (such as Christian nationalism and radical individualism) makes it easy to neglect and dismiss the positive contributions Puritan Congregationalism offers to our understanding of God's word and his world.

Like their Presbyterian brothers, the Congregationalists were convinced that Scripture has something to say about church polity, about the way we structure church gatherings and organise authority and responsibilities among a congregation and its leadership. However, in contrast with their Presbyterian brothers, the Congregationalists developed a different understanding of the role of churches in relation to one another and the division of authority within a local congregation. They stressed that in the Bible, Christ's Church exists as churches—local bodies of organised believers—not as trans-local entities, such as synods or denominations. They also explicated, though perhaps not consistently, the proper division of authority between the elders and the congregation.

The Cambridge Platform of Discipline, produced by Richard Mather and adopted in substance by the Cambridge Synod (1646-1648), printed in 1649, is a thorough account of Congregational polity, succinctly laying forth an understanding of the local church, its organisation, and the relationship between local churches. Because of its enduring value as a testimony to the Bible's teaching concerning church polity, I have chosen to offer a stylistically edited version that conforms better to contemporary standards in the hope that others will read and be challenged by it. In conjunction with the Platform, I have also printed a similarly edited version of the Burial Hill Declaration, produced several generations later. I find this Declaration valuable in its explicit articulation of the implications of congregational polity

---

Baptisme to his Grand-Child, though his next Seed the Parents of the Child be not received themselves into Church Covenant." Quoted in Walker, *The Creeds and Platforms of Congregationalism*, 251.

[81] See the narrative of Walker, *The Creeds and Platforms of Congregationalism*.

for the relationship between congregational churches and non-congregationalist churches. I have taken digitised versions from the early editions of these documents and edited them in light of the versions printed in *The Creeds and Platforms of Congregationalism*; I have then corrected typographical errors in line with modern (Australian) conventions. Finally, I have adjusted the grammar, syntax, and (occasionally) word usage to align it with contemporary English style. My aim has not been to make these documents feel as though they could have been written by our contemporaries but to maintain their historical style while overcoming potential barriers this style presents to understanding. One area of difficulty is the document's free use of italics; I have tried to retain instances where the appropriate emphasis will be conveyed.

I pray that you would read these documents in light of Scripture and benefit from the fruitful dialogue that will ensue. I pray that in doing so, Christ's Church would be strengthened. Soli Deo Gloria, Amen.

J. Alexander Rutherford

A PLATFORM OF CHURCH DISCIPLINE GATHERED OUT OF THE WORD OF GOD AND AGREED UPON BY THE ELDERS AND MESSENGERS OF THE CHURCHES ASSEMBLED IN THE SYNOD OF CAMBRIDGE IN NEW ENGLAND

To be presented to the churches and general court for their consideration and acceptance, in the Lord.

The eight month of the year 1649

Psalm 84:1.
How lovely are your Tabernacles, O Lord of Hosts?

Psalm 26:8.
Lord, I have loved the habitation of your house and the place where your honour dwells.

Psalm 27:4.
One thing have I desired of the Lord that will I seek after, that I may dwell in the house of the Lord all the days of my life to behold the Beauty of the Lord and to inquire in his Temple.

Chapter I: Of the Form of Church-Government and That It Is One, Immutable, and Prescribed in the Word of God.

1. Ecclesiastical polity or church government, or discipline is nothing else but that form and order that is to be observed in the Church of Christ upon earth, both for the constitution of it and all the administrations that are to be performed therein. (Ezek. 43:11; Col 2:5; 1 Tim 3:15)

2. Church-government is considered in a double respect either in regard of the parts of government themselves or necessary circumstances thereof. The parts of government are prescribed in the word, for the Lord Jesus Christ, the King and Law-Giver of his Church, is no less faithful in the house of God than was Moses, who from the Lord delivered a form and pattern of government to the Children of Israel in the Old Testament, and the holy scriptures are now also so perfect as they are able to make the man of God perfect and thoroughly furnished unto every good work and, therefore, doubtless to the well-ordering of the house of God. (Hebrews 3:5-6; Exodus 25:40; 2 Timothy 3:16)

3. The parts of church government are all of them exactly described in the word of God, being parts or means of instituted worship according to the second commandment. Therefore, they are to continue one and the same unto the appearing of our Lord Jesus Christ, as a kingdom that cannot be shaken until he shall deliver it up unto God, even the Father, so that it is not left in the power of men, officers, churches, or any state in the world to add, or diminish, or alter anything in the least measure therein. (1 Tim 3:15; 1 Chron 15:13; Exod 20:4; 1 Tim 6:13, 16; Heb 12:27, 28; 1 Cor 15:22)

4. The necessary circumstances (as time and place etc.) belonging unto order and decency are not so left unto men as that under pretence of them, they may thrust their own inventions upon the churches Instead, they are circumscribed in the word with many general limitations. Where they are determined in respect of the matter to be neither worship itself nor circumstances separable from worship in respect of their end, they must be done unto edification. In respect of the manner, they are to be done decently and in order, according to the nature of the things themselves and civil and church custom. Does not even nature itself teach you? Yea, they are in some sort determined particularly, namely that they be done in such a manner, as all circumstances considered, is most expedient for edification; so, if people do not err concerning their determination, the determining of them is to be accounted as if it were divine. (1 Kings 12:28, 29; Isa 29:13; Col 2:22, 23; Acts 15:28; Matt 15:9; 1 Cor 11:23, 8:34; 1 Cor 14:26, 40; 11:14, 16; 14:12, 19; Acts 15:28)

Chapter II: Of the Nature of the Catholic Church in General, and in Special, of a Particular Visible Church.

1. The Catholic Church is the whole company of those that are elected, redeemed, and (in time) effectually called from the state of sin and death unto a state of grace and salvation in Jesus Christ. (Eph 1:22, 23; 5:25, 26, 30; Heb 12:23)

2. This church is either triumphant or militant. As triumphant, it is the number of them who are glorified in heaven; as militant, it is the number of them who are conflicting with their enemies upon earth. (Rom 8:17; 2 Tim 2:12, 4:8: Eph 6:12-13)

3. This militant church is to be considered as invisible and visible. It is invisible in respect of their relation wherein they stand to Christ, as a body unto the head, being united unto him by the spirit of God and faith in their hearts. It is visible, in respect of the profession of their faith, in their persons and in particular Churches. So, there may be acknowledged a universal visible Church. (2 Tim 2:19; Rev 2:17; 1 Cor 6:17; Eph 3:17; Rom 1:8; 1 Thess 1:8; Isa 2:2; 1 Tim 6:12)

4. The members of the militant visible church are to be considered either as not yet in church-order or as walking according to the church-order of the Gospel. In order, and so besides the spiritual union and communion common to all believers, they enjoy more over a union and communion ecclesiastical-political: so, we deny a universal visible church.[82] (Acts 19:1; Col 2:5; Matt 18:17; 1 Cor 5:12)

5. The state of the members of the militant visible church walking in order was either before the law, economical, that is in families; or under the law, national; or, since the coming of Christ, only congregational (the term Independent, we approve not): therefore, the state of those walking in church-order is neither national, provincial, nor classical. (Gen 18:19; Exod

---

[82] The difference in capitalisation between this and the former paragraph is original. In §3, the platform recognises that all believers are truly united by their common profession, yet §4 acknowledges that this true union is expressed in the association of local congregations, not corporate structures.

19:6)

6. A congregational church is, by the institution of Christ, a part of the militant visible church consisting of a company of saints by calling united into one body by a holy covenant for the public worship of God and the mutual edification one of another in the fellowship of the Lord Jesus. (1 Cor 14:23, 36; 1:2; Exod 19:5-6; Deut 29:1, 9-15; Acts 2:42; 1 Cor 14:26)

Chapter III: Of the Matter of the Visible Church Both in Respect of Quality and Quantity.

1. The matter of a visible church are Saints by calling. (1 Cor 1:2; Eph 1:1; Heb 6:1; 1 Cor 1:6; Rom 15:14; Psalm 50:16-17; Acts 8:37; Matt 3:6; Rom 6:17)[83]

2. By Saints, we understand,

i. Such as have not only attained the knowledge of the principles of religion, and are free from gross and open scandals, but also do together with the profession of their faith and repentance walk in blameless obedience to the word, so that in charitable discretion they may be accounted saints by calling (though perhaps some or more of them be unsound, and hypocrites inwardly), for the members of such particular churches are commonly by the holy ghost called saints and faithful brethren in Christ (1 Cor 1:2; Phil 1:1; Col 1:2) and sundry churches have been reproved for receiving and suffering such persons to continue in fellowship amongst them as have been offensive and scandalous: the name of God also by this means is blasphemed, the holy things of God defiled and profaned, the hearts of the godly grieved, and the wicked themselves hardened and helped forward to damnation. The example of such does endanger the sanctity of others; a little leaven leavens the whole lump. (Eph 1:1; 1 Cor 5:2, 13; Rev 1:14-15, 20; Ezek 44:7, 9, 23:38-39; Num

---

[83] "Matter" here is based on the Aristotelian/Scholastic metaphysic, known as hylomorphism. Every being is, in this paradigm, composed of matter and form, as a table is made from wood defined by the form of tableness. The brothers here will identify the saints as the matter and the covenant as the form constituting the simple being of the church, with the eldership necessary for the church to possess wellbeing, that is, for it to be oriented to what is good.

20, 29; Hag 2:13-14; 1 Cor 11:27, 29; Ps 37:21; 1 Cor 5:6)

ii. The children of such, who are also holy. (1 Cor 7:14)

3. The members of churches though orderly constituted may in time degenerate and grow corrupt and scandalous, which though they ought not to be tolerated in the church, yet their continuance therein through the defect of the execution of discipline and just censures does not immediately dissolve the being of the church, as appears in the church of Israel, and the churches of Galatia, Corinth, Pergamum, and Thyatira. (Jer 2:21; 1 Cor 5:12; Jer 14; Gal 5:4; 2 Cor 12:21; Rev 2:14-15, 21:21)

4. The matter of the Church in respect of its quantity ought not to be of greater number then may ordinarily meet together conveniently in one place, nor ordinarily fewer than may conveniently carry on Church-work (1 Cor 14:21). Hence when the holy scripture makes mention of the saints combined into a church-estate, in a town or city, where there was but one congregation, it usually calls those saints the church in the singular number, as the church of the Thessalonians, the church of Smyrna, Philadelphia, and the like (Rom 16:1; 1 Thess 1:1; Rev 2:8; 3:7). But when it speaks of the saints in a nation or province wherein there were sundry congregations, it frequently and usually calls them by the name of churches, in the plural number, as the churches of Asia, Galatia, Macedonia, and the like (1 Cor 16:1, 19; Gal 1:2; 2 Cor 8:1; 1 Thess 2:14). This is further confirmed by what is written of sundry of those churches in particular, how they were assembled and met together the whole church in one place, as the church at Jerusalem, the church at Antioch, the church at Corinth, and Cenchrea, though it were more near to Corinth, it being the port thereof, and answerable to a village, yet being a distinct congregation from Corinth, it had a church of its own as well as Corinth had. (Acts 2:46; 5:12, 6:2; Acts 14:27; 15:38; 1 Cor 5:4; 14:23; Rom 16:1)

5. Nor can it with reason be thought but that every church appointed and ordained by Christ had a ministry ordained and appointed for the same, and yet it is evident that there were no ordinary officers appointed by Christ for any other then congregational churches: elders being appointed to feed not all flocks but the particular flock of God over which the Holy Spirit had made them the overseers, and that flock they must attend, even the whole

flock (Acts 20:28), and one congregation being as much as any ordinary elder can attend, therefore there is no greater church then a congregation, which may ordinarily meet in one place.

Chapter IV: Of the Form of a Visible Church and of Church Government.

1. Saints by calling must have a visible political union amongst themselves or else they are not yet a particular church as those similitudes hold forth which Scripture uses to shew the nature of particular churches: as a body, a building, or house, hands, eyes, feet, and other members must be united or else, remaining separate, are not a body. Stones and timber, though squared, hewn, and polished, are not a house until they are compacted and united, so saints or believers in the judgment of charity are not a church unless orderly knit together. (1 Cor 12:27; 1 Tim 3:15; Eph 2:22; 1 Cor 12:15; 16:17)

2. Particular churches cannot be distinguished one from another but by their forms. Ephesus is not Smyrna, and Pergamum Thyatira (Rev 1), but each one a distinct society of itself, having officers of their own, which have not the charge of others: virtues of their own, for which others are not praised; [and] corruptions of their own, for which others are not blamed.

3. This form is the visible covenant, agreement, or consent whereby they give up themselves unto the Lord (Exod 19:5, 8; Deut 29:12-13) to the observing of the ordinances of Christ together in the same society, which is usually called the church-covenant, for we see not otherwise how members can have church-power one over another mutually. (Zech 11:14, 9:11)

The comparing of each particular church unto a city and unto a spouse seems to conclude not only that there is a form but that that form is by way of a covenant. (Eph 2:19; 2 Cor 11:2)

The covenant as it was that which made the family of Abraham and children of Israel to be a church and people unto God, so it is that which now makes the several societies of Gentile believers to be churches in these days. (Gen 17:7; Deut 29:12-13; Eph 2:12, 19)

4. This voluntary agreement, consent, or covenant (for all these are here taken for the same)—although the more express and plain it is, the more fully it puts us in mind of our mutual duty, stirs us up to it, and leaves less room for the questioning of the truth of the church-estate of a company of professors and the truth of membership of particular persons: yet we conceive, the substance of it is kept where there is real agreement and consent of a company of faithful persons to meet constantly together in one Congregation for the public worship of God and their mutual edification. This sort of real agreement and consent they do express by their constant practice of coming together for the public worship of God and by their religious subjection unto the ordinances of God there. This is supported if we do consider how Scripture covenants have been entered into, not only expressly by word of mouth, but by sacrifice; by handwriting, and seal; and also sometimes by silent consent, without any writing, or expression of words at all. (Exod 19:5-8, 24:3, 17; Josh 24:18-24; Ps 50:5; Neh 9:38, 10:1; Gen 17; Deut 29)

5. This form then being by mutual covenant, it follows, it is not faith in the heart, the profession of that faith, cohabitation, nor baptism that constitutes a church: i. not faith in the heart? because that is invisible; ii. not a bare profession because that declares them no more to be members of one church than of another; iii. not cohabitation, for atheists or infidels may dwell together with believers; iv. not baptism because it presupposes a church estate, as circumcision in the Old Testament, which gave no being unto the church, the church being before it and in the wilderness without it. Seals presuppose a covenant already in being. One person is a complete subject of baptism, but one person is incapable of being a church.

6. All believers ought, as God gives them opportunity there unto, to endeavour to join themselves to a particular church, doing so in respect of the honour of Jesus Christ, in his example and institution, by the professed acknowledgment of and subjection unto the order and ordinances of the Gospel (Acts 2:47, 9:26; Matt 3:13-15; 28:19-20; Ps 133:2, 3, 87:7; Matt 18:20; 1 Jo 1:3). They do so as also in respect of their good communion founded upon their visible union and contained in the promises of Christ's special presence in the church, whence they have fellowship with him and, in him, one with another; also for the keeping of them in the way of Gods commandments and recovering of them in case of wandering (which all

Christs sheep are subject to in this life), being unable to return of themselves; together with the benefit of their mutual edification and of their posterity, that they may not be cut off from the privileges of the covenant; otherwise, if a believer offends, he remains destitute of the remedy provided in that behalf. Should all believers neglect this duty of joining to all particular congregations, it might follow thereupon that should have no visible political churches upon earth.

Chapter V: Of the First Subject of Church Power or, to Whom Church Power Does First Belong.

1. The first subject of church power is either supreme or subordinate and ministerial. The supreme (by way of gift from the Father) is the Lord Jesus Christ; the ministerial, is either extraordinary, as the apostles, prophets, and evangelists, or ordinary, as every particular congregational church.

2. Ordinary church power is either the power of office, that is such as is proper to the eldership, or power of privilege, such as belongs to the brotherhood. The latter is in the brethren formally and immediately from Christ, that is, so as it may according to order be acted or exercised immediately by themselves. The former is not in them formally or immediately and therefore cannot be acted or exercised immediately by them but is said to be in them in that they design the persons unto office, who only are to act or to exercise this power.

Chapter VI: Of the Officers of the Church, and especially of Pastors and Teachers.

1. A Church being a company of people combined together by covenant for the worship of God, it appears thereby that there may be the essence and being of a church without any officers, seeing there is both the form and matter of a church, which is implied when it is said, the Apostles ordained elders in every church (Acts 14:23).

2. Nevertheless, though officers be not absolutely necessary to the simple being of churches when they be called, yet ordinarily they are necessary to their calling and to their well-being. Therefore, the Lord Jesus out of his tender compassion has appointed and ordained officers, which he

would not have done if they had not been useful and needful for the church. Yea, being ascended into heaven, he received gifts for men and gave gifts to men (Eph 4:12-13), whereof officers for the church are justly accounted no small parts, they being to continue to the end of the world and for the perfecting of all the Saints (Rom 10:17; Jer 3:15; 1 Cor 12:28; Eph 4:11; Ps. 68:18; Eph 4:8, 11).

3. These officers were either extraordinary or ordinary: extraordinary as apostles, prophets, and evangelists; ordinary as elders and deacons.

The apostles, prophets, and evangelists, as they were called extraordinarily by Christ, so their office ended with themselves, whence it is that Paul directing Timothy how to carry along church-administrations gives no direction about the choice or course of apostles, prophets, or evangelists but only of elders and deacons. And when Paul was to take his last leave of the church of Ephesus, he committed the care of feeding the church to no other but unto the elders of that church. The like charge does Peter commit to the elders. (1 Cor 12:28; Eph 4:11; Galatians 1; Act 8:6, 19, 26; 11:28; Rom 11:7-8; 1 Cor 4:9; 1 Tim 3:1-2, 8-13; Titus 1:5; Acts 20:17, 28; 1 Pet 5:1-3; 1 Tim 3:1; Phil 1:1; Acts 20:17, 28; 1 Tim 5:17)

4. Of elders (who are also in Scripture called bishops), some attend chiefly to the ministry of the word, as the pastors and teachers. Others attend especially unto rule, who are therefore called ruling elders. (Eph 4:11; Rom 12:7-8; 1 Cor 12:8)

5. The offices of pastor and teacher appears to be distinct. The pastor's special work is to attend to exhortation and therein to administer a word of wisdom; the teacher is to attend to doctrine and therein to administer a word of knowledge. It is the work of either of them to administer the seals of that covenant unto the dispensation whereof they are alike called, as also to execute the censure, being but a kind of application of the word, the preaching of which (together with the application thereof) they are alike charged with. (2 Tim 4:1-2; Titus 1:9; Eph 4:11-12, 1:22-23)

6. And for as much as both pastors and teachers are given by Christ for the perfecting of the saints and edifying of his body, which saints and body of Christ is his church, therefore, we account pastors and teachers to be both

of them church officers. We do not say that the pastor is for the church and the teacher only for the schools—though this we gladly acknowledge, that schools are both lawful, profitable, and necessary for the training up of such in good literature, or learning, as may afterwards be called forth unto office of pastor or teacher in the church.

Chapter VII: Of Ruling Elders and Deacons.

1. The ruling elder's office is distinct from the office of pastor and teacher. The ruling elders are not so called to exclude the pastors and teachers from ruling, for ruling and governing are common to these with the other, whereas attending to teach and preach the word is peculiar unto the former.

2. The ruling elder's work is to join with the pastor and teacher in those acts of spiritual rule which are distinct from the ministry of the word and Sacraments committed to them. Of which sort these be as follows: 1) to open and shut the doors of Gods house by the admission of members approved by the church, by ordination of officers chosen by the church, by excommunication of notorious and obstinate offenders renounced by the church, and by restoring of penitents forgiven by the church (2 Chron 23:19; Rev 21:12; 1 Tim 4:14; Matt 18:17; 2 Cor 2:7-8; Acts 2:6); 2) to call the church together when there is occasion, and seasonably to dismiss them again (Acts 21:18, 22-23); 3) to prepare matters in private, that in public they may be carried an end with less trouble and more speedy dispatch; 4) to moderate the carriage of all matters, in the church assembled, as to propound matters to the church, to order the season of speech and silence, and to pronounce sentence according to the mind of Christ, with the consent of the church (Acts 6:2-3, 13:15; 2 Cor 8:10); 5) to be guides and leaders to the church in all matters whatsoever pertaining to church administrations and actions (Heb 13:7, 17); 6) to see that none in the church live inordinately out of rank and place, without a calling or idly in their calling (2 Thess 2:10-12 [sic 3:10-12]); 7) To prevent and heal such offences in life or in doctrine as might corrupt the church (Acts 20:28, 32); 8) to feed the flock of God with a word of admonition (1 Thess 5:12); 9) as they shall be sent for, to visit and to pray over their sick brethren (James 5:14; Acts 20:20); 10) and at other times as opportunity shall serve thereunto.

3. The office of a deacon is instituted in the church by the Lord Jesus.

Sometimes they are called helps. (Acts 6:3, 6; Phil 1:1; 1 Tim 3:8; 1 Cor 12:28)

The Scripture tells us how they should be qualified: grave, not double tongued, not given to much wine, not greedy for dishonest gain. They must first be proved and then use the office of a deacon, being found blameless. (1 Tim 3:8-9)

The office and work of the deacons is to receive the offerings of the church, gifts given to the church, and to keep the treasury of the church; and therewith to serve the tables which the church is to provide for: as the Lord's table, the table of the ministers, and of such as are in necessity, to whom they are to distribute in simplicity. (Acts 4:36, 6:2-3; Rom 12:8)

4. The office therefore being limited unto the care of the temporal good things of the church, it extends not unto the attendance upon and administration of the spiritual things thereof, as the word, and Sacraments, or the like.

5. The ordinance of the Apostle, and practice of the church, commends the Lord's Day as a fit time for the contributions of the Saints (1 Cor 16:1-3).

6. The instituting of all these officers in the church is the work of God himself, of the Lord Jesus Christ, of the Holy Spirit. Therefore, such officers he has not appointed are altogether unlawful either to be placed in the church or to be retained therein and are to be looked at as human creatures, mere inventions and appointments of humans, to the great dishonour of Christ Jesus, the Lord of his house, the King of his church—whether they be popes, patriarchs, cardinals, archbishops, lordbishops, archdeacons, officials, commissaries, and the like. These and the rest of that hierarchy and retinue, not being plants of the Lord's planting, shall all certainly be rooted out and cast forth. (1 Cor 12:28; Eph 4:8, 11; Acts 20:8; Matt 15:13)

7. The Lord hath appointed ancient widows (where they may be had) to minister in the church, in giving attendance to the sick, and to give succour unto them, and others, in the like necessities. (1 Tim 5:9-10)

Chapter VIII: Of the Election of Church Officers.

1. No man may take the honour of a church officer unto himself but he that was called of God, as was Aaron. (Heb 5:4)

2. Calling unto office is either immediate, by Christ himself (such was the call of the apostles, and prophets); this manner of calling ended with them, as hath been said. Or it is mediate, by the church. (Num 8:10; Acts 6:5-6, 13:2-3)

3. It is fitting that before any be ordained or chosen officers, they should first be tried and proved, for hands are not suddenly to be laid upon any, and both elders and deacons must be of honest and good report. (1 Tim 5:22, 7:10; Acts 16:2, 6:3)

4. The things in respect of which they are to be tried are those gifts and virtues which the Scripture require in men that are to be elected to such places, viz. that elders must be blameless, sober, apt to teach, and endued with such other qualifications as are laid down, 1 Tim 2 and 3, Titus 1:6-9. Deacons are to be fitted, as is directed, Acts 6:3 and 1 Tim 3:8-11.

5. Officers are to be called by such churches whereunto they are to minister. Of such moment is the preservation of this power that the churches exercised it in the presence of the Apostles. (Acts 14:23, 1:23, 6:3-5)

6. A church being free cannot become subject to any but by a free election; Yet when such a people do choose any to be over them in the Lord, then do they become subject and most willingly submit to their ministry in the Lord, whom they have so chosen. (Gal 5:13; Heb 13:17)

7. And if the church has power to choose their officers and ministers, then in case of manifest unworthiness, and delinquency they have power also to depose them. For to open and shut: to choose and refuse; to constitute in office and remove from office are acts belonging unto the same power. (Rom 16:17)

8. We judge it much conducing to the well-being and communion of churches, that where it may conveniently be done, neighbouring churches be sought for advice and their help made use of in the trial of church officers,

in order to their choice. (Song 8:8-9)

9. The choice of such church officers belongs not to the civil-magistrates, as such, or diocesan-bishops, or patrons: for of these or any such like, the Scripture is wholly silent, as having any power therein.

Chapter IX: Of Ordination, and Imposition of hands.

1. Church officers are not only to be chosen by the church but also to be ordained by imposition of hands and prayer, with which at the ordination of elders, fasting also is to be joined. (Acts 13:3; 14:23; 1 Tim 5:22)

2. This ordination we account nothing else but the solemn putting of a man into his place and office in the Church where-unto he had right before by election, being like the installing of a magistrate in the commonwealth. (Numb 8:10; Acts 6:5-6; 13:2-3)

Ordination therefore is not to go before but to follow election. The essence and substance of the outward calling of an ordinary officer in the Church does not consist in his ordination but in his voluntary and free election by the Church and in his accepting of that election, whereupon is founded the relation between pastor and flock, between such a minister and such a people. (Acts 6:5-6, 14:23)

Ordination doth not constitute an officer, nor give him the essentials of his office. The apostles were elders without imposition of hands by men: Paul and Barnabas were officers before that imposition of hands, Acts 13:3. The posterity of Levi were Priests and Levites before hands were laid on them by the Children of Israel.

3. In such churches where there are elders, imposition of hands in ordination is to be performed by those elders. (1 Tim 4:14; Acts 13:3; 1 Tim 5:22)

4. In such churches where there are no Elders, imposition of hands may be performed by some of the brethren orderly chosen by the church thereunto. For if the people may elect officers which is the greater, and wherein the substance of the office consists, they may much more (occasion and need so requiring) impose hands in ordination, which is the less, and but

the accomplishment of the other. (Num 8:10)

5. Nevertheless in such churches where there are no elders, and the church so desire, we see not why imposition of hands may not be performed by the elders of other churches. Ordinary officers laid hands upon the officers of many churches: the presbytery of Ephesus laid hands upon Timothy, an evangelist. The presbytery of Antioch laid hands upon Paul and Barnabas. (1 Tim 4:14; Acts 13:3)

6. Church officers are officers to one church, even that particular church over which the Holy Spirit has made them overseers, insomuch as elders are commanded to feed not all flocks but that flock committed to their faith and trust and which depends upon them. Nor can constant residence at one congregation be necessary for a minister, nor yet lawful, if he be not a minister to one congregation only but to the church universal, for he may not attend on part only of the church, whereto he is a minister, but he is called to attend unto all the flock. (Acts 20:28)

7. He that is clearly loosed from his office-relation unto that church whereof he was a minister cannot be looked at as an officer, nor perform any act of office in any other church, unless he be again orderly called unto office, which when it shall be, we know nothing to hinder but imposition of hands also in his ordination ought to be used towards him again. For so Paul the Apostle received the imposition of hands twice of least, from Ananias. Acts 9:17 and Acts 13:3.

Chapter X: Of the Power of the Church and Its Presbytery.

1. Supreme and lordly power over all the churches upon earth belongs only unto Jesus Christ, who is the king of the church, and the head thereof. He has the government upon his shoulders and has all power given to him, both on heaven and earth. (Ps 2:6; Eph 1:21-22; Isa 9:6; Matt 28:18)

2. A company of professed believers ecclesiastically confederate, as they are a church before they have officers and without them; so even in that estate, subordinate church-power under Christ delegated to them by him does belong to them in such a manner as is before expressed (Ch. 5 S. 2) and as flowing from the very nature and essence of a church: it being natural to

all bodies and so unto a church body to be furnished with sufficient power for its own preservation and subsistence. (Acts 1:23; 14:23; 6:3-4; Matt 18:17; 1 Cor 5:4-5)

3. This government of the church is a mixed government (and so has been acknowledged long before the term independency was heard of): in respect of Christ, the head and king of the church, and the sovereign power residing in him, and exercised by him, it is a monarchy; in respect of the body, or brotherhood of the church, and power from Christ granted unto them, it resembles a democracy; in respect of the Presbytery and power committed to them, it is an aristocracy. (Rev 3:7; 1 Cor 5:12; 1 Tim 5:17)

4. The sovereign power, which is peculiar unto Christ, is exercised I) in calling the church out of the world unto holy fellowship with himself; II) in instituting the ordinances of his worship and appointing his ministers and officers for the dispensing of them; III) in giving laws for the ordering of all our ways, and the ways of his house: IV) in giving power and life to all his institutions, and to his people by them; V) in protecting and delivering his church against and from all the enemies of their peace.

5. The power granted by Christ unto the body of the church and the brotherhood is a prerogative or privilege which the church does exercise: I) in choosing their own officers, whether elders or deacons; II) in admission of their own members and, therefore, there is great reason they should have power to remove any from their fellowship again (Act 6:3,5; 14:23; 9:26). Hence, in the case of offence any one brother has power to convince and admonish an offending brother; and in the case of not hearing him, to take one or two more to set on the admonition, and in the case of not hearing them, to proceed to tell the church (Matt 18:15; 16:17); and as his offence may require, the whole church has power to proceed to the public censure of him, whether by admonition or excommunication, and upon his repentance to restore him again unto his former communion. (Titus 3:10; Col 4:17; Matt 18:17; 2 Cor 2:7-8)

6. In case an elder offend incorrigibly, the matter so requiring, as the church had power to call him to office, so they have power according to order (the counsel of other churches, where it may be had, directing thereto) to remove him from his office. Being now but a member, in case he adds

contumacy to his sin, the church that had power to receive him into their fellowship has also the same power to cast him out that they have concerning any other member. (Col 4:17; Rom 16:17; Matt 18:17)

7. Church-government, or rule, is placed by Christ in the officers of the church, who are therefore called rulers, while they rule with God (1 Tim 5:17; Heb 13:17; 1 Thess 5:12): yet in case of maladministration, they are subject to the power of the church, according as has been said before. The Holy Spirit frequently, yea always, where it mentions church-rule and church-government, ascribes it to elders, whereas the work and duty of the people is expressed in the phrase of obeying their elders and submitting themselves unto them in the Lord. Thus, it is manifest that an organic or complete church is a body politick, consisting of some that are governors, and some that are governed, in the Lord. (Rom 12:8; 1 Tim 5:17; 1 Cor 12:28-29; Heb 13:7, 17)

8. The power which Christ hath committed to the elders is to feed and rule the church of God, and accordingly to call the church together upon any weighty occasion. When the elders do so, the members so called may not refuse to come without just cause. When they come, they may not depart before they are dismissed. Nor may they speak in the church before they have leave from the elders, nor may they continue so doing when they require silence. Nor may they oppose or contradict the judgment or sentence of the Elders without sufficient and weighty cause because such practices are manifestly contrary unto order and government, are in-lets of disturbance, and tend to confusion. (Acts 20:28, 6:2; Num 16:12; Ezek 46:10; Acts 13:15)

9. It belongs also unto the elders to examine any officers or members before they be received of the church (Rev 2:2; 1 Tim 5:19; Acts 21:18, 22-23), to receive the accusations brought to the church, and to prepare them for the church's hearing (1 Cor 5:4-5). In handling of offences and other matters before the church they have power to declare and publish the counsel and will of God touching the same, and to pronounce sentence with consent of the church. Lastly, they have power, when they dismiss the people, to bless them in the name of the Lord. (Num 6:23-26)

10. This power of government in the elders does not any wise prejudice the power of privilege in the brotherhood, as neither the power of privilege

in the brethren does prejudice the power of government in the elders. Instead, they may sweetly agree together, as we may see in the example of the Apostles furnished with the greatest church-power, who took in the concurrence and consent of the brethren in church-administrations (Acts 14:16, 23; 6:2; 1 Cor 5:4; 2 Cor 2:6-7). Also that Scripture, 2 Corinthians 2:9 and 10:6, do declare that what the churches were to act and do in these matters they were to do in a way of obedience, and that not only to the direction of the Apostles but also of their ordinary Elders. (Heb 13:17)

11. From the premises, namely, that the ordinary power of government belonging only to the elders and that power of privilege remains with the brotherhood (as power of judgment in masters of censure, and power of liberty, in matters of liberty), it follows that in an organic church and right administration, all church acts proceed after the manner of a mixed administration, so as no church act can be consummated or perfected without the consent of both.

Chapter XI: Of the Maintenance of Church Officers.

1. The Apostle concludes that necessary and sufficient maintenance is due unto the ministers of the word: from the law of nature and nations, from the law of Moses, the equity thereof, as also the rule of common reason (1 Cor 9:9, 15; Matt 9:28; 10:10; 1 Tim 5:18). Moreover, the scripture not only call elders labourers and workmen, but also speaking of them does say that the labourer is worthy of his hire and requires that he who is taught in the word should share with him all good things; it mentions it as an ordinance of the Lord, that they which preach the Gospel should live of the Gospel; and it forbids the muzzling of the mouth of the ox that treads out the corn. (Gal 6:6; 1 Cor 9:9, 14; 1 Tim 5:18)

2. The Scriptures having been shown to require this maintenance as a bound duty and due debt, not as a matter of almes and free gift, therefore, people are not at liberty to do or not to do what and when they please in this matter, no more than in any other commanded duty and ordinance of the Lord. Instead, they ought of duty to minister of their carnal things to them that labour amongst them in the word and doctrine, as well as they ought to pay any other work men their wages, to discharge and satisfy their other debts, or to submit themselves to observe any other ordinance of the Lord.

(Rom 15:27; 1 Cor 9:14)

3. The apostle, enjoining that he who is taught share with him that teaches all good things (Gal 6:6), does not leave it arbitrary what or how much a man shall give, or in what proportion, but even the later, as well as the former, is prescribed and appointed by the Lord. (1 Cor 16:2)

4. Not only members of churches, but all that are taught in the word, are to contribute unto him that teaches, in all good things. In case that congregations are defective in their contributions, the deacons are to call upon them to do their duty (Acts 6:3-4). If their call suffices not, the church by her power is to require it of their members, and where church-power through the corruption of men, does not or cannot attain the end, the Magistrate is to see that the ministry be duly provided for, as appears from the commended example of Nehemiah (Neh 13:11). The Magistrates are nursing fathers and nursing mothers and stand charged with the custody of both tables of the Law because it is better to prevent a scandal, that it may not come and easier also then to remove it when it is given (Isa 49:23). Its most suitable to rule that by the churches care, each man should know his proportion according to rule, what he should do before he do it, that in this way his judgment and heart may be satisfied in what he does and just offence prevented in what is done. (2 Cor 8:13-14)

Chapter XII: Of Admission of Members into the Church.

1. The doors of the churches of Christ upon earth, do not by God's appointment stand so wide open that all sorts of people good or bad may freely enter therein at their pleasure. Instead, such as are admitted thereto as members ought to be examined and tried first, whether they be fit and meet to be received into church-society or not (2 Chron 23:19; Matt 13:25; 22:12). The Eunuch of Ethiopia, before his admission, was examined by Philip, whether he did believe on Jesus Christ with all his heart. The angel of the church at Ephesus is commended for trying such as said they were apostles and were not (Acts 8:27; Rev 2:2; Acts 9:26). There is like reason for trying of them that profess themselves to be believers.

The officers are charged with the keeping of the doors of the Church and, therefore, are in a special manner to make trial of the fitness of such who enter. Twelve angels are set at the gates of the temple, lest such as were ceremonially unclean should enter thereinto. (Rev 21:12; 2 Chr 23:19)

2. The things which are requisite to be found in all church members are repentance from sin and faith in Jesus Christ (Acts 2:38-42; 8:37). Therefore, these are the things whereof men and women are to be examined at their admission into the church, and which then they must profess and hold forth in such sort as may satisfy rational charity that the things are there indeed. John Baptist admitted people to baptism, confessing and bewailing their sins: and of other it is said that they came, confessed, and shewed their deeds (Matt 3:6; Acts 19:18).

3. The weakest measure of faith is to be accepted in those that desire to be admitted into the church because weak Christians, if sincere, have the substance of that faith, repentance, and holiness which is required in church members and such have most need of the ordinances for their confirmation and growth in grace (Rom 14:1). The Lord Jesus would not quench the smoking flax, nor break the bruised reed, but gather the tender lambs in his arms and carry them gently in his bosom. Such charity and tenderness are to be used as the weakest Christian, if sincere, may not be excluded nor discouraged. Severity of examination is to be avoided. (Matt 12:20; Isa 40:11)

4. In case any through excessive fear, or other infirmity, be unable to make their personal relation of their spiritual estate in public, it is sufficient that the elders having received private satisfaction, make relation thereof in public before the church, thereby testifying their assents thereunto. This seems to be the way that tends most to edification. But whereas persons are of better abilities, there it is most expedient that they make their relations and confessions personally with their own mouth, as David professes of himself (Psalm 66:16).

5. A personal and public confession and declaring of God's manner of working upon the soul is lawful, expedient, and useful in sundry respects and upon sundry grounds. Those three thousand (Acts 2:37, 41) before they were admitted by the Apostles, did manifest that they were pricked in their hearts at Peter's sermon, together with earnest desire to be delivered from their sins, which now wounded their consciences, and their ready receiving of the word of promise and exhortation. We are to be ready to render a reason of the

hope that is in us to everyone that asks us (1 Pet 3:15): therefore we must be able and ready upon any occasion to declare and shew our repentance for sin, faith unfeigned, and effectual calling, because these are the reason of a well-grounded hope (Heb 11:1; Eph 1:18). "I have not hidden your righteousness from the great congregation," Psalm 40:10.

6. This profession of faith and repentance, as it must be made by such at their admission that were never in church-society before, so nothing hinders but the same way also be performed by such as have formerly been members of some other church. The church to which they now join themselves as members, may lawfully require the same. Those three thousand that made their confession (Acts 2) were members of the church of the Jews before, so were they that were baptised by John. Churches may err in their admission, and persons regularly admitted may fall into offence (Matt 3:5-6; Gal 2:4; 1 Tim 5:24). Otherwise, if Churches might obtrude their members, or if church-members might obtrude themselves upon other churches without due trial, the matter so requiring, both the liberty of churches would hereby be infringed in that they might not examine those concerning whose fitness for communion they were unsatisfied. Furthermore, besides the infringing of their liberty, the churches themselves would unavoidably be corrupted and the ordinances defiled whilst they might not refuse but must receive the unworthy, which is contrary unto the Scripture, teaching as it does that all churches are sisters and therefore equal (Song 8:8).

7. The like trial is to be required from such members of the church as were born in the same or received their membership and were baptised in their infancy or minority by virtue of the covenant of their parents, when being grown up unto years of discretion they shall desire to be made partakers of the Lord's Supper. Towards these, because holy things must not be given to the unworthy, therefore it is requisite that these as well as others should come to their trial and examination and manifest their faith and repentance by an open profession thereof before they are received to the Lord's Supper and otherwise not to be admitted to the table. (Matt 7:6; 1 Cor 11:27)

Yet these Church-members that were so born or received in their childhood before they are capable of being made partakes of full communion have many privileges which others (not church-members) have not: they are in covenant with God; they have the seal thereof upon them, viz. baptism;

so, if not regenerated, yet they are in a more hopeful way of attaining regenerating grace and all the spiritual blessings both of the covenant and seal; and they are also under church-watch and consequently subject to the reprehensions, admonitions, and censures thereof, for their healing and amendment, as need should require.

Chapter XIII: Of Church-Members Their Removal from One Church to Another, and of Letters of Recommendation, and Dismission.

1. Church-members may not remove or depart from the church, and so one from another as they please, nor without just and weighty cause but ought to live and dwell together, for as much as they are commanded not to forsake the assembling of themselves together (Heb 10:25). Such departure tends to the dissolution and ruin of the body, as the pulling of stones and pieces of timber from the building, and of members from the natural body, tend to the destruction of the whole.

2. It is therefore the duty of Church-members, in such times and places when counsel may be had, to consult with the Church whereof they are members about their removal that accordingly they, having their approbation, may be encouraged or otherwise desist. They who are joined with consent should not depart without consent, except forced thereunto. (Prov 11:16)

3. If a member's departure be manifestly unsafe and sinful, the church may not consent thereunto, for in so doing they should not act in faith and should partake with him in his sin. If the case be doubtful and the person not to be persuaded, it seems best to leave the matter unto God and not forcibly to detain him. (Rom 14:23; 1 Tim 5:22; Acts 21:14)

4. Just reasons for a member's removal of himself from the church are, I) if a person cannot continue without partaking in sin; II) in case of personal persecution, so Paul departed from the disciples at Damascus, also, in case of general persecution, when all are scattered; III) in case of real, and not only pretended, want of competent subsistence, a door being opened for better

supply in another place, together with the means of spiritual edification. In these, or like cases, a member may lawfully remove, and the church cannot lawfully detain him.

5. To separate from a Church, either out of contempt of their holy fellowship, out of covetousness, or for greater enlargements with just grief to the church (1 Tim 4:10); out of schism or want of love (Rom 16:17); and out of a spirit of contention in respect of some unkindness or some evil only conceived (Jude 19), or indeed, in the church which might and should be tolerated and healed with a spirit of meekness (Eph 4:2-3), and of which evil the church is not yet convinced (though perhaps himself be) nor admonished (Col 3:13; Gal 6:1-2): for these or like reasons to withdraw from public communion in word, or seals, or censures, is unlawful and sinful.

6. Such members as have orderly removed their habitation ought to join themselves unto the church in order where they do inhabit if it may be. Otherwise, they can neither perform the duties nor receive the privileges of members (Isa 56:8; Acts 9:26). Such an example tolerated in some is apt to corrupt others, which if many should follow, would threaten the dissolution and confusion of churches, contrary to the Scripture (1 Cor 14:33).

7. Order requires that a member thus removing have letters of testimony and of dismission from the church whereof he yet is (Acts 18:27) unto the church whereunto he desires to be joined, lest the church should be deluded, that the church may receive him in faith, and that it would not be corrupted by receiving deceivers and false brethren. Until the person dismissed be received into another church, he does not cease by his letters of dismission to be a member of the church whereof he was. The church cannot make a member not a member but by excommunication.

8. If a member be called to remove only for a time, where a church is, letters of recommendation are requisite and sufficient for communion with that church, in the ordinance and in their watch: as Phoebe, a servant of the church at Cenchrea, had letters written for her to the church of Rome, that she might be received, as is becoming of saints. (Rom 16:1-2; 2 Cor 3:1)

9. Such letters of recommendation and dismission were written for Apollos; for Marcus to the Colossians; for Phoebe to the Romans; and for

sundry others to other churches. The apostle tells us that some persons, not sufficiently known otherwise, have special need of such letters, though he for his part had no need thereof (Acts 18:27; Col 4:10; Rom 16:1; 2 Cor 3:1). The use of them is to be a benefit and help to the party for whom they are written, and for furthering of his receiving amongst the Saints in the place where he goes and the due satisfaction of them in their receiving of him.

Chapter XIV: Of Excommunication and Other Censures.

1. The censures of the church are appointed by Christ for the preventing, removing, and healing of offences in the Church; for the reclaiming and gaining of offending brethren (Jude 23; 1 Cor 5:6);[84] for the deterring of others from similar offences (Deut 13:11; 17:12-13; 1 Tim 5:20); for purging out the leaven which may infect the whole lump: for vindicating the honour of Christ, of his church, and the holy profession of the gospel (Rom 2:24); and for preventing of the wrath of God that may justly fall upon the church if they should suffer his covenant and the seals thereof to be profaned by notorious and obstinate offenders (Rev 2:14-16, 20).

2. If an offence be private (one brother offending another), the offender is to go and acknowledge his repentance for it unto his offended brother, who is then to forgive him, but if the offender neglects or refuses to do it, the brother offended is to go convince and admonish him of it between themselves privately (Matt 5:23-24; Luke 17:3-4). If thereupon the offender be brought to repent of his offence, the admonisher has won his brother (Matt 18:15), but if the offender does not hear his brother, the brother offended is to take with him one or two more, that in the mouth of two or three witnesses, every word may be established (Matt 18:16), (whether the word of admonition if the offender receive it, or the word of complaint, if he refuse it:) for if he refuse it, the offended brother is by the mouth of the elders to tell the church (Matt 18:17). And if he hears the church and declares the same by penitent confession, he is recovered and gained. And if the church discern him to be willing to hear, yet not fully convinced of his offence, as in case of heresy (Titus 3:10), they are to dispense to him a public admonition, which declaring the offender to lie under the public offence of

---

[84] The original has "Jude 29"; following Walker, I have assumed the intended reference is v. 23.

the church, does thereby withhold or suspend him from the holy fellowship of the Lord's Supper until his offence be removed by penitent confession (Matt 18:17). If he still continues obstinate, they are to call him out by excommunication.

3. But if the offence be more public at first, and of a more heinous and criminal nature, to wit, such as are condemned by the light of nature (1 Cor 5:4, 5), then the church, without such gradual proceeding, is to cast out the offender from their holy communion for the further mortifying of his sin and the healing of his soul in the day of the Lord Jesus.

4. In dealing with an offender, great care is to be taken that we be neither overstrict or rigorous, nor too indulgent or remiss. Our proceeding herein ought to be with a spirit of meekness, considering ourselves lest we also be tempted (Gal 6:1) and that the best of us have need of much forgiveness from the Lord. Yet the wining and healing of the offender's soul, being the end of these endeavours, we must not daub with untempered mortar, nor heal the wounds of our brethren slightly: on some have compassion, others save with fear. (Matt 18:34, 35; 6:14, 15; Ezek 13:10; Jer 6:14)

5. While the offender remains excommunicate, the church is to refrain from all member-like communion with him in spiritual things, and also from all familiar communion with him in civil things, farther then the necessity of natural, domestical, or civil relations require, and are therefore to forbear to eat and drink with him, that he may be ashamed. (Matt 18:17; 1 Cor 5:11; 2 Thess 3:6, 14)

6. Excommunication being a spiritual punishment, it doth not prejudice the excommunicate in nor deprive him of his civil rights, and therefore does not touch princes or other magistrates in point of their civil dignity or authority. And the excommunicate being but as a publican and a heathen, heathens being lawfully permitted to come to hear the word in church assemblies, we acknowledge therefore the same liberty of hearing the word permitted to the heathen may be permitted to excommunicated persons. And because we are not without hope of his recovery, we are not to account him as an enemy but to admonish him as a brother. (1 Cor 14:24-25; 2 Thess 3:14)

7. If the Lord sanctifies the censure to the offender, so as by the grace

of Christ he testifies his repentance, with humble confession of his sin and judging of himself, giving glory unto God, the church is then to forgive him, comfort him, and restore him to the regular brotherly communion, which formerly he enjoyed with them.

8. To suffer those who live prophane or scandalous lives to continue in fellowship and partake in the sacraments is doubtless a great sin in those that have power in their hands to redress it and do not do it. Nevertheless, inasmuch as Christ and his apostles in their times, and the Prophets and other godly in theirs, did lawfully partake of the Lord's commanded ordinances in the Jewish church and neither taught nor practised separation from the same, though unworthy ones were permitted therein, and inasmuch as the faithful in the church of Corinth, wherein were many unworthy persons and practises, are never commanded to absent themselves from the sacraments, because of the same: therefore the godly in like cases are not presently to separate.

9. As separation from such a church wherein those who live prophane and scandalous lives are tolerated is not presently necessary, so for the members thereof, otherwise worthy, hereupon to abstain from communicating with such a church in the participation of the Sacraments is unlawful. For as it were unreasonable for an innocent person to be punished for the faults of other, wherein he hath no hand, and whereunto he gave no consent, so is it more unreasonable that a godly man should neglect duty and punish himself in not coming for his portion in the blessing of the seals, as he ought, because others are suffered to come that ought not. This is especially so considering that he himself neither consents to their sin nor to their approaching to the ordinance in their sin, nor to the neglect of others who should put them away and do not, but, on the contrary, he does heartily mourn for these things and modestly and seasonably stirs up others to do their duty. If the church cannot be reformed, they may use their liberty as is specified above (ch. XIII, sect. 4). But this all the godly are bound unto, even everyone to do his endeavour, according to his power and place, that the unworthy may be duly proceeded against by the Church to whom this matter does appertain.

Chapter XV: Of the Communion of Churches One with Another.

1. Although churches be distinct, and therefore may not be confounded one with another, and equal, and therefore have not dominion one over another, yet all the churches ought to preserve church-communion one with another, for they are all united with Christ, not only as a mystical but as a political head, whence is derived a communion suitable thereunto. (Rev 1:4; Song 8:8; Rom 16:16; 1 Cor 16:19; Acts 15:23; Rev 2:1)

2. The communion of Churches is exercised sundry ways.

i. By way of mutual care in taking thought for one another's welfare. (Song 8:8)

ii. By way of consultation one with another when we have occasion to require the judgment and counsel of other churches, touching any person or cause wherewith they may be better acquainted then ourselves. As the church of Antioch consulted with the apostles and elders of the church at Jerusalem about the question of circumcision of the gentiles and about the false teachers that broached that doctrine (Acts 15:2). In which case, when any Church wants light or peace amongst themselves, it is a way of communion of churches (according to the word) to meet together by their elders and other messengers in a synod, to consider and argue the points in doubt or difference, and having found out the way of truth and peace, to commend the same by their letters and messengers to the churches, whom the same may concern (Acts 15:6; 22:23). But if a Church be rent with divisions amongst themselves, or lie under any open scandal, and yet refuse to consult with other churches, for healing or removing of the same, it is a matter of just offence both to the Lord Jesus and to other churches, as betraying too much want of mercy and faithfulness not to seek to bind up the breaches and wounds of the church and brethren. Therefore, the state of such a church calls aloud upon other churches to exercise a fuller act of brotherly communion, to wit, by way of admonition (Ezek 34:4).

iii. A third way then of communion of churches is by way of admonition, to wit, in case any public offence be found in a church, which they either discern not or are slow in proceeding to use the means for the removing and healing of (Gal 2:11-14). Paul had no authority over Peter, yet when he saw

Peter not walking with a right foot, he publicly rebuked him before the church. Though churches have no more authority one over another than one apostle had over another, yet as one apostle might admonish another, so may one church admonish another without usurpation. In which case, if the church that lies under offence does not harken to the church which does admonish her, the church is to acquaint other neighbour-churches with that offence the offending church still lies under, together with their neglect of the brotherly admonition given unto them, whereupon those other churches are to join in seconding the admonition formerly given. If the offending church still continues in obstinacy and impenitency, they may forbear communion with them and are to proceed to make use of the help of a Synod or counsel of neighbour-churches walking orderly (if a greater cannot conveniently be had) for their conviction (Matt 18:15, 16, 17, by proportion). If they hear not the Synod, the Synod having declared them to be obstinate, then particular churches, approving and accepting of the judgment of the Synod, are to declare the sentence of non-communion respectively concerning them. Thereupon out of a religious care to keep their own communion pure, they may justly withdraw themselves from participation with them at the Lord's table and from such other acts of holy communion as the communion of churches otherwise allows and requires. Nevertheless, if any members of such a church as lie under public offence do not consent to the offence of the church, but do in due sort bear witness against it, they are still to be received to wonted communion: for it is not equal, that the innocent should suffer with the offensive. (Gen 18:25)

Yea furthermore, if such innocent members after due waiting in the use of all good means for the healing of the offence of their own church shall at last (with the allowance of the counsel of neighbour-churches) withdraw from the fellowship of their own church and offer themselves to the fellowship of another, we judge it lawful for the other church to receive them, being otherwise fit as if they had been orderly dismissed to them from their own church.

iv. A fourth way of communion of churches, is by way of participation: the members of one church occasionally coming unto another, we willingly admit them to partake with us at the Lord's table, it being the seal of our communion not only with Christ, nor only with the members of our own church, but also with all the churches of the saints, in which regard, we refuse not to baptize their children presented to us, if either their own minister be absent or such a fruit of holy fellowship be desired with us. In like case such churches as are furnished with more ministers than one, do willingly afford one of their own ministers to supply the place of an absent or sick minister of another church for a needful season.

v. A fifth way of Church-communion is by way of recommendation when a member of one church has occasion to reside in another church. If but for a season, we commend him to their watchful fellowship by letters of recommendation, but if he be called to settle his abode there, we commit him according to his desire, to the fellowship of their covenant, by letters of dismission. (Acts 18:27)

vi. A sixth way of Church-communion is, in case of need, to minister relief and succour one unto another, either of able members to furnish them with officers or of outward support to the necessities of poorer churches (Acts 11:22, 29), as did the churches of the Gentiles contribute liberally to the poor saints at Jerusalem (Rom 13:26-27).

3. When a company of believers purpose to gather into church fellowship, it is requisite for their safer proceeding and the maintaining of the communion of churches that they signify their intent unto the neighbour-churches, walking according unto the order of the Gospel, and desire their presence, help, and right hand of fellowship which they ought readily to give unto them, when there is no just cause of excepting against their proceedings. (Gal 2:1-2, 9, by proportion)

4. Besides these several ways of communion, there is also a way of propagation of churches; when a church shall grow too numerous, it is a way, and fit season, to propagate one Church out of another by sending forth such of their members as are willing to remove and to procure some officers to them as may enter with them into church-estate amongst themselves (Isa 40:20; Song 8:8-9). As bees, when the hive is too full, issue forth by swarms and are gathered into other hives, so the Churches of Christ may do the same upon like necessity, and therein hold forth to them the right hand of fellowship, both in their gathering into a church and in the ordination of their officers.

Chapter XVI: Of Synods.

1. Synods orderly assembled, and rightly proceeding according to the pattern, Acts 15, we acknowledge as the ordinance of Christ and, though not absolutely necessary to the being yet many times, through the iniquity of men and perverseness of times, as necessary to the well-being of churches for the establishment of truth and peace therein. (Acts 15:2-15)

2. Synods being spiritual and ecclesiastical assemblies are therefore made up of spiritual and ecclesiastical causes. The next efficient cause of them under Christ is the power of the churches sending forth their elders and other messengers (Acts 15:2-3), who being meet together in the name of Christ are the matter of the synod (15:6). They, in arguing, debating, and determining matters of religion according to the word (15:7-23), and publishing the same to the churches whom it concerned, do put forth the proper and formal acts of a Synod for the conviction of errors and heresies and the establishment of truth and peace in the Churches, which is the end of a synod.

3. Magistrates have power to call a synod by calling to the Churches to send forth their elders and other messengers (2 Chron 29:4, 5-11) to counsel and assist them in matters of religion, but yet the constituting of a Synod is a church act and may be transacted by the churches even when civil magistrates may be enemies to churches and to church assemblies.

4. It belongs unto a synod and counsels to debate and determine controversies of faith and cases of conscience; to clear from the word holy directions for the holy worship of God and good government of the church (Acts 15:1, 2, 6, 7; 1 Chron 15:3); to bear witness against maladministration and corruption in doctrine or manners in any particular Church; and to give directions for the reformation thereof (2 Chron 29:6, 7; Acts 15:24, 28-29). It belongs not to a synod to exercise church-censures in way of discipline, nor any other act of church-authority or jurisdiction, which that presidential synod did forbear.

5. The synod directions and determinations, so far as consonant to the word of God, are to be received with reverence and submission, not only for their agreement therewith (which is the principal ground thereof, and without which they bind not at all), but also secondly, for the power whereby they are

made, as being an ordinance of God appointed thereunto in his word. (Acts 15)

6. Because it is difficult, if not impossible, for many churches to come altogether in one place, in all their members universally: therefore, they may assemble by their delegates or messengers, as the church of Antioch went not all to Jerusalem, but some select men for that purpose (Acts 15:2). Because none are or should be more fit to know the state of the churches, nor to advise of ways for the good thereof, then elders, therefore, it is fit that in the choice of the messengers for such assemblies, they have special respect unto such. Yet in as much as not only Paul and Barnabas but certain others also were sent to Jerusalem from Antioch (Acts 15:2, 22, 23). Acts 15. and when they were come to Jerusalem, not only the Apostles and elders, but other brethren also do assemble and meet about the matter; therefore, synods are to consist both of elders and other church-members endued with gifts and sent by the churches, not excluding the presence of any brethren in the churches.

Chapter XVII: Of the Civil Magistrate's Power in Matters Ecclesiastical

1. It is lawful, profitable, and necessary for Christians to gather themselves into Church estate and therein to exercise all the ordinances of Christ according unto the word, although the consent of magistrate could not be had thereunto, for the apostles and Christians in their time did frequently thus practise, when the magistrates being all of them Jewish or pagan, and mostly persecuting enemies, would give no countenance or consent to such matters.

2. Church-government stands in no opposition to the civil government of commonwealths, does not it in any way intrench upon the authority civil magistrates in their jurisdictions (John 18:36), nor in any way weaken their hands in governing (John 18:36; Acts 25:8), but rather it strengthens them and further the people in yielding more hearty and conscionable obedience unto them. This is the case whatsoever some ill-affected persons to the ways of Christ have suggested to alienate the affections of Kings and Princes from the ordinance of Christ, as if the kingdom of Christ in his church could not rise and stand without the falling and weakening of their government, which

is also of Christ (Isa 49:23), whereas the contrary is most true, that they may both stand together and flourish the one being helpful unto the other in their distinct and due administrations.

3. The power and authority of magistrates is not for the restraining of churches, or any other good works, but for helping in and furthering thereof (Rom 13:4; 1 Tim 2:2). Therefore, the consent and countenance of magistrates, when it may be had, is not to be slighted or lightly esteemed, but on the contrary, it is part of that honour due to Christian magistrates to desire and crave their consent and approbation therein, which being obtained, the churches may then proceed in their way with much more encouragement and comfort.

4. It is not in the power of magistrates to compel their subjects to become church-members and to partake at the Lord's table, for the priests are reproved that brought unworthy ones into the sanctuary (Ezek 44:7, 9). As it was unlawful for the priests, so it is as unlawful to be done by civil magistrates. Those whom the church is to cast out if they were in, the magistrate ought not thrust into the church nor to hold them therein (1 Cor 5:11).

5. As it is unlawful for church-officers to meddle with the sword of the magistrate, so it is unlawful for the magistrate to meddle with the work proper to church officers. The acts of Moses and David, who were not only princes but prophets, were extraordinary (Matt 20:25-26) and, therefore, not imitable. Against such usurpation the Lord witnessed by smiting Uzziah with leprosy for presuming to offer incense (2 Chron 26:16-17).

6. It is the duty of the magistrate to take care of matters of religion and improve his civil authority for the observing of the duties commanded in the first table as well as for observing of the duties commanded in the second table. They are called gods (Psalm 82:2). The end of the magistrate's office is not only the quiet and peaceable life of the subject, in matters of righteousness and honesty, but also in matters of godliness, yea of all godliness (1 Tim 2:1-2). Moses, Joshua, David, Solomon, Asa, Jehoshaphat, Hezekiah, and Josiah are much commended by the Holy Spirit for the putting forth their authority in matters of religion; on the contrary, such kings as have been failing this way are frequently taxed and reproved by the Lord. And not

only the kings of Judah but also Job, Nehemiah, the king of Nineveh, Darius, Artaxerxes, Nebuchadnezzar, whom none looked at as types of Christ (though were it so, there were no place for any just objection), are commended in the book of God for exercising their authority this way (1 Kings 15:14, 22:42; 2 Kings 12:3, 14:4, 15:35; 1 Kings 20:42; Job 29:35, 31:26, 28; Neh 13; Jonah 3:7; Ezra 7; Dan 3:29).

7. The object of the power of the magistrate are not things merely inward, and so not subject to his cognisance and view, as unbelief, hardness of heart, erroneous opinions not vented, but only such things as are acted by the outward man. Neither is their power to be exercised in commanding such acts of the outward man and punishing the neglect thereof, as are but mere inventions and devices of men (1 Kings 20:28, 42), but about such acts as are commanded and forbidden in the word. Yea, such acts as the word does clearly determine, though not always clearly to the judgment of the magistrate or others, yet clearly in itself. In these he according to his right ought to put forth his authority, though oft-times actually he does it not.

8. Idolatry, blasphemy, heresy, venting corrupt, and pernicious opinions that destroy the foundation, open contempt of the word preached, profanation of the Lord's day, disturbing the peaceable administration and exercise of the worship and holy things of God, and the like, are to be restrained and punished by civil authority.

9. If any church one or more shall grow schismatic, rending itself from the communion of other churches, or shall walk incorrigibly or obstinately in any corrupt way of their own, contrary to the rule of the word, in such case, the Magistrate is to put forth his coercive power, as the matter shall require. The tribes on this side of the Jordan intended to make war against the other tribes for building the altar of witness, whom they suspected to have turned away therein from following of the Lord (Joshua 22).

FINIS

APPENDIX 2: THE BURIAL HILL DECLARATION (1865), IN MODERNISED ENGLISH

Standing by the rock where the Pilgrims set foot upon these shores, upon the spot where they worshipped God, and among the graves of the early generations, we, elders and messengers of the Congregational churches of the United States in National Council assembled,—like them acknowledging no rule of faith but the word of God,—do now declare our adherence to the faith and order of the apostolic and primitive churches held by our fathers, and substantially as embodied in the confessions and platforms which our Synods of 1648 and 1680 set forth or reaffirmed. We declare that the experience of the nearly two and a half centuries which have elapsed since the memorable day when our sires founded here a Christian Commonwealth, with all the development of new forms of error since their times, has only deepened our confidence in the faith and polity of these fathers.

We bless God for the inheritance of these doctrines. We invoke the help of the Divine Redeemer, that, through the presence of the promised Comforter, He will enable us to transmit them in purity to our children.

In the times that are before us as a nation, times at once of duty and of danger, we rest all our hope in the gospel of the Son of God. It was the grand peculiarity of our Puritan Fathers, that they held this gospel, not merely as the ground of their personal salvation, but as declaring the worth of man by the incarnation and sacrifice of the Son of God; and therefore applied its principles to purify law, to reform the Church and the State, and to assert and defend liberty; in short, to mould and redeem, by its all-transforming energy, everything that belongs to man in his individual and social relations.

It was the faith of our fathers that gave us this free land in which we dwell. It is by this faith only that we can transmit to our children a free and happy, because a Christian, commonwealth.

We hold it to be a distinctive excellence of our Congregational system, that it exalts that which is more important above that which is less, and by the simplicity of its organization, facilitates, in communities where the population is limited, the union of all true believers in one Christian church; and that the division of such communities into several weak and jealous societies, holding the same common faith, is a sin against the unity of the body of Christ, and at once the shame and the scandal of Christendom.

We rejoice that, through the influence of our free system of apostolic order, we can hold fellowship with all who acknowledge Christ; and act efficiently in the work of restoring unity to the divided Church, and of bringing back harmony and peace among all 'who love our Lord Jesus Christ in sincerity.'

Thus recognising the unity of the Church of Christ in all the world and knowing that we are but one branch of Christ's people, while adhering to our own peculiar faith and order, we extend to all believers the hand of Christian fellowship, upon the basis of those great fundamental truths in which all Christians should agree. With them we confess our faith in God, the Father, the Son, and the Holy Spirit, the only living and true God; in Jesus Christ, the incarnate Word, who is exalted to be our Redeemer and King; and in the Holy Comforter, who is present in the Church to regenerate and sanctify the soul.

With the whole Church, we confess the common sinfulness and ruin of our race and acknowledge that it is only through the work accomplished by the life and expiatory death of Christ that believers in him are justified before God, receive the remission of sins, and through the presence and grace of the Holy Comforter are delivered from the power of sin, and perfected in holiness.

We believe also in the organised and visible Church, in the ministry of the Word, in the sacraments of Baptism and the Lord's Supper, in the resurrection of the body, and in the final judgment, the issues of which are eternal life and everlasting punishment.

We receive these truths on the testimony of God, given through prophets and apostles, and in the life, the miracles, the death, the resurrection, of his Son, our Divine Redeemer, —a testimony preserved for the Church in the Scriptures of the Old and New Testaments, which were composed by holy men as they were moved by the Holy Spirit.

Affirming now our belief that those who thus hold 'one faith, one Lord, one baptism,' together constitute the on Catholic Church, the several households of which, though called by different names, are the one body of Christ; and that these members of his body are sacredly bound to keep 'the unity of the spirit in the bond of peace,' we declare that we will cooperate with all who hold these truths. With them we will carry the gospel into every part of this land, and with them we will go into all the world, and 'preach the gospel to every creature.' May He to whom 'all power is given in heaven and earth' fulfill the promise which is all our hope: 'Lo, I am with you always, even to the end of the world.' Amen.

WORKS CITED

Allison, Gregg R. *Sojourners and Strangers: The Doctrine of the Church*. Crossway, 2012.

Baxter, Richard. *The Reformed Pastor: Updated and Abridged*. Edited by Tim Cooper. Wheaton: Crossway, 2021.

Beale, G. K. *A New Testament Biblical Theology: The Unfolding of the Old Testament in the New*. Grand Rapids: Baker Academic, 2011.

———. *Handbook on the New Testament Use of the Old Testament: Exegesis and Interpretation*. Grand Rapids: Baker Academic, 2012.

———. "The Role of the Resurrection in the Already-and-Not-Yet Phases of Justification." In *For the Fame of God's Name: Essays in Honor of John Piper*, edited by Sam Storms and Justin Taylor. Wheaton: Crossway, 2010.

Blaising, Craig A., and Darrell L. Bock. *Progressive Dispensationalism*. Grand Rapids: Bridgepoint Books, 2000.

Bucer, Martin. *Concerning the True Care of Souls*. Translated by Peter Beale. Edinburgh: Banner of Truth Trust, 2009.

Burer, Michael H, and Daniel B Wallace. "Was Junia Really an Apostle?: A Re-Examination of Rom 16.7." *New Testament Studies* 47, no. 1 (January 2001): 76–91.

Calvin, John. *Commentary upon the Acts of the Apostles*. Translated by Henry Beveridge. Bellingham: Logos Bible Software, 2010.

Carson, D. A. "Matthew." In *The Expositor's Bible Commentary: Matthew–Mark*

(Revised Edition), edited by Tremper Longman III and David E. Garland, Vol. 9. Grand Rapids: Zondervan, 2010.

———. *Showing the Spirit: A Theological Exposition of 1 Corinthians 12-14*. Grand Rapids: Baker, 1987.

Chester, Tim. *Truth We Can Touch: How Baptism and Communion Shape Our Lives*. Wheaton, Illinois: Crossway, 2020.

Clifton, Cliff. *How to Start a Residency: Turning Members into Missional Leaders*. Alpharetta, GA: New Churches powered by Send Network, 2023.

Cook, Jerry. *The Monday Morning Church*. West Monroe, LA: Howard Publishing Co., Inc., 2006.

Dever, Mark, and Jonathan Leeman. *Baptist Foundations: Church Government for an Anti-Institutional Age*. B&H Publishing Group, 2015.

Erickson, Millard J. *Christian Theology*. 3rd ed. Grand Rapids: Baker Academic, 2013.

Fee, Gordon D. *The First Epistle to the Corinthians, Revised Edition*. Eerdmans, 2014.

Frame, John M. *Evangelical Reunion: Denominations and the One Body of Christ*. Grand Rapids: Baker, 1991.

———. *The Doctrine of the Christian Life*. A Theology of Lordship 4. Phillipsburg: P&R Publishing, 2008.

———. *The Doctrine of the Knowledge of God*. A Theology of Lordship. Phillipsburg: P&R Publishing, 1987.

Gentry, Peter J., and Stephen J. Wellum. *God's Kingdom through God's Covenants: A Concise Biblical Theology*, 2015.

———. *Kingdom through Covenant: A Biblical-Theological Understanding of the Covenants*. 2nd Ed. Wheaton: Crossway, 2018.

Goldsworthy, Graeme. *The Goldsworthy Trilogy*. Milton Keynes: Paternoster, 2012.

Gregory the Great. *The Book of Pastoral Rule*. St. Vladimir's Seminary Press "Popular Patristics" Series, no. 34. Crestwood, N.Y: St. Vladimir's Seminary Press, 2007.

Grudem, Wayne. *The Gift of Prophecy in the New Testament and Today*. Revised Edition. Crossway, 2000.

Harvey, David T. *The Plurality Principle: How to Build and Maintain a Thriving Church Leadership Team*. Wheaton: Crossway, 2021.

Haupt, Timothy. "Why John Was Not a Baptist: The 7 Irreconcilable Differences Between John Bunyan and the Baptists." *The Gospel Coalition* (blog). Accessed October 10, 2022. https://www.thegospelcoalition.org/blogs/evangelical-history/why-john-was-not-a-baptist-the-7-irreconcilable-differences-between-john-bunyan-and-the-baptists/.

Haupt, Timothy Mark. "The Palace Beautiful: The Evangelical Independent Ecclesiology of John Bunyan." PhD Thesis, Midwestern Baptist Theological Seminary, 2022.

Horton, Michael Scott. *The Christian Faith: A Systematic Theology for Pilgrims on the Way*. Grand Rapids, Mich.: Zondervan, 2011.

Kraft, Charles H. *Christianity in Culture: A Study in Dynamic Biblical Theologizing in Cross-Cultural Perspective*. Maryknoll, N.Y: Orbis Books, 1979.

Ladd, George Eldon. *A Theology of the New Testament*. Rev. ed., Reprinted. Grand Rapids: Eerdmans, 1994.

Littlejohn, W. Bradford. *The Two Kingdoms: A Guide for the Perplexed*. Lincoln, NE: Davenant Trust, 2017.

Long, V. Philips. *The Art of Biblical History*. Foundations of Contemporary Interpretation, v. 5. Grand Rapids: Zondervan, 1994.

Marshall, Colin, and Tony Payne. *The Trellis and the Vine: The Ministry Mind-Shift That Changes Everything*. Sydney, NSW: Matthias Media, 2021.

———. *The Vine Project: Shaping Your Ministry Culture around Disciple-Making*. Sydney, NSW: Matthias Media, 2016.

Mbewe, Conrad. *God's Design for the Church: A Guide for African Pastors and Ministry Leaders*. Wheaton: Crossway, 2020.

Metzger, Bruce Manning. *A Textual Commentary on the Greek New Testament*. 2nd Edition. London; New York, N.Y.: United Bible Societies, 1994.

Parsons, Mikeal C. *Acts*. Paideia Commentaries on The New Testament. Grand Rapids: Baker Academic, 2008.

Piper, John. *Brothers We Are Not Professionals A Plea to Pastors for Radical Ministry*. Updated&Expanded. Nashville: B&H, 2013.

Rushdoony, Rousas J. *The Institutes of Biblical Law*. 3 vols. Phillipsburg: P & R Pub, 1973.

Rutherford, J. Alexander. *God's Gifts for the Christian Life — Part 1: The Gift of Knowledge*. Airdrie, AB: Teleioteti, 2021.

———. *God's Kingdom through His Priest-King: An Analysis of the Book of Samuel in Light of the Davidic Covenant.* Teleioteti Technical Studies 1. Vancouver: Teleioteti, 2019.

———. "Is a Covering Long Hair or Veil? Interpreting 1 Corinthians 11:1-16." *Teleioteti* (blog), February 15, 2018. https://teleioteti.ca/2018/02/15/is-a-covering-long-hair-or-veil-interpreting-1-corinthians11/.

———. *Prevenient Grace: An Investigation into Arminianism.* 2nd Revised Ed. Teleioteti Technical Studies 2. Vancouver: Teleioteti, 2020.

———. "Review of The Plurality Principle – Teleioteti Book Reviews." Teleioteti, 2021. https://www.teleioteti.ca/2021/07/06/review-of-the-plurality-principle/.

———. "Review of Truth We Can Touch." *Teleioteti* (blog), April 27, 2020. https://teleioteti.ca/2020/04/27/review-of-truth-we-can-touch/.

———. *The Gift of Revelation: A Biblical Perspective on the Bible.* God's Gifts for the Christian Life - Part 2: The Gift of Truth, I. Airdrie, AB: Teleioteti, 2021.

———. *The Trinity and the Bible: How All Scripture Testifies to One God in Three Persons.* Teleioteti Technical Studies 3. Campbell River, BC: Teleioteti, 2022.

———. "Towards a Biblical Theology of Satan's Kingdom." *Teleioteti Journal for Christian Ministry* 01, no. 01 (June 15, 2023): 42–52.

———. "Whose Fall? What Hellenism? Christianity's Fall into Hellenistic Philosophy Revisited." *The Teleioteti Journal for Christian Ministry* 1, no. 1 (2023): 1–40. https://doi.org/10.60080/cliw1201.

Sande, Ken. *The Peacemaker: A Biblical Guide to Resolving Personal Conflict.* Baker Books, 2004.

Strauch, Alexander. *Biblical Eldership: An Urgent Call to Restore Biblical Church Leadership.* Rev. and Expanded. Littleton, CO: Lewis and Roth Publishers, 1995.

VanDrunen, David. *Divine Covenants and Moral Order: A Biblical Theology of Natural Law.* Emory University Studies in Law and Religion. Grand Rapids: Eerdmans, 2014.

———. *Living in God's Two Kingdoms: A Biblical Vision for Christianity and Culture.* Crossway, 2010.

———. *Natural Law and the Two Kingdoms: A Study in the Development of Reformed Social Thought.* Emory University Studies in Law and

Religion. Grand Rapids: Eerdmans, 2010.

Walker, Williston, ed. *The Creeds and Platforms of Congregationalism*. New ed. New York: Pilgrim Press, 1991.

Wilson, Douglas. *Empires of Dirt: Secularism, Radical Islam, and the Mere Christendom Alternative*. Moscow, Ida.: Canon Press, 2016.

Windsor, Lionel. "Preachers and Leaders." In *Women, Sermons, and the BIble: Essays Interacting with John Dickson's Hearing Her Voice*, edited by Peter Bold and Tony Payne. Sydney: Matthias Media, 2014.

Witt, William G. *Icons of Christ: A Biblical and Systematic Theology for Women's Ordination*. Baylor University Press, 2021.

ABOUT TELEIOTETI

Teleioteti (Τελειοτητι, te-ley-o-tey-tee)—meaning "unto maturity"—is dedicated to faithful, thoughtful ministry. We create resources for Christian discipleship, resources that address theological and pastoral concerns from a Biblical worldview. Our purpose is to see Christ's Church mature in its understanding of God and His Word. We do this through the production of Gospel-centred materials that connect the Bible with the heads, hearts, and minds of Christians. We hope to enable Christians from all walks of life to better understand and glorify God through service in His Church.

To achieve this purpose, Teleioteti publishes online materials and books researched with academic rigour yet based upon Biblical presuppositions. That is, we are neither academic nor lazy. We use methods, or epistemology, informed by the Bible along with the hard work usually associated with professional research and study. We produce resources directed towards all Christians, but most of our resources are directed towards students, pastors, and theologically inclined lay Christians.

To learn more about us and what we are doing, please visit us at https://teleioteti.ca or contact us at info@teleioteti.ca. If you have found this resource helpful, prayerfully consider supporting us by giving a review on the web (e.g. Amazon, Goodreads, etc.), praying with and for us, or giving financially so that we can produce more resources like this one. For more information on how you can support us, visit us at https://teleioteti.ca/about/partner/ or at our page on Patreon, https://www.patreon.com/

teleioteti.

Other Books by J. Alexander Rutherford

God's Kingdom through his Priest-King: An Analysis of the Book of Samuel in Light of the Davidic Covenant (Teleioteti, 2019)

Though many studies have probed the significance of the Davidic Covenant (2 Sam 7:1-17) within the biblical canon, few have endeavoured to explore its significance within the narrative of Samuel. This thesis argues that by weaving references to God's promises made to David (collectively known as the Davidic Covenant) throughout his narrative, the author of Samuel reveals God's will to strip away all human pretension by bringing his promises to fulfilment through the lowly David, whose ascension to kingship and endurance therein is owing all to God. In this way, the author fulfils his purpose to demonstrate God's sovereign working in history to establish his kingdom on earth through his chosen priest-king, a descendant of David, in fulfilment of the promises he made beforehand. Engaging in a literary close-reading of the text of Samuel, the author shows how the narrative of Samuel is shaped towards this end.

Endorsements:

In the present environment of high interest in the Book of Samuel, this contribution by James Rutherford is most welcome. Rutherford is well versed in current scholarship on Samuel, but his work moves well beyond this scholarship to contribute fresh insights, not least in respect of the priestly character of King David. And concerning its structure, Rutherford argues that the Book of Samuel as a whole is arranged and narrated so as to draw attention to the centrality of the Davidic Covenant of 2 Samuel 7. Having myself studied 1 and 2 Samuel for decades now, I was nevertheless benefitted at numerous points from Rutherford's creative interpretive suggestions. His is a work well conceived, well written, and worthy of a serious read.
- V. Philips Long, PhD Cambridge
  Professor of Old Testament, Regent College

This thesis argues that by weaving references to God's promises made to King David throughout his narrative, the author of Samuel reveals God's will to strip away all human pretension by bringing his promises to fulfilment through a lowly man whose ascension to kingship and endurance therein is entirely owing to God. In this way, the Samuel author fulfils his purpose of demonstrating God's sovereign working in history to establish his kingdom on earth through his chosen priest-king, a descendant of David. The thesis represents an excellent piece of work that does a great job of bringing together into one coherent argument, focused on the Davidic covenant, much of the best recent narrative-critical research on 1-2 Samuel, and from this point of view represents a distinctive contribution to the field of Samuel studies.

- Iain Provan, PhD Cambridge
  Marshall Sheppard Professor of Biblical Studies, Regent College

Prevenient Grace: An Investigation into Arminianism, 2ⁿᵈ Revised Edition (Teleioteti, 2020)

When a building is built on a poor foundation, the inevitable result is its collapse. But this isn't a book on architecture; foundations are found in thought structures as well as in material structures. In theology, a bad foundation will produce results as catastrophic as a bad foundation in architecture. How we think about God and His work in the world will profoundly affect how we live and work out our Christian faith; is your foundation strong? This book evolved from the conviction that a prominent theological system rests on a fragile foundation.

Endorsements:

This book is a fine piece of scholarship. Rutherford presents his arguments with admirable clarity. His intention is to offer guidance for pastors and teachers who may be faced with questions about whether human beings have the freedom to accept or reject God. The great strength of Rutherford's book is his knowledge of Biblical texts and an appropriate interpretation of them. He successfully shows that the claims of Arminianism with its view that prevenient grace allows an acceptance or rejection of God are not supported by Biblical texts. Nor are they justified by philosophical arguments. They layout of the book and its careful treatment of arguments both for and against prevenient grace is a model of excellent writing. His chapters are supplemented by a Glossary that explains all specific terms and Appendices where detailed theological discussions are given. Most helpful is his Index of Scripture passages discussed.

- Dr. Shirley Sullivan, FRSC (elected), Professor Emeritus of Classics, University of British Columbia

Habakkuk: An Exegetical-Theological Commentary (Teleioteti, 2019)

It is all too common to find commentaries that miss the forest for the trees, commentaries that get so caught up in the minutiae of scholarly controversies that they miss what God is saying for His church today. This is especially evident when it comes to the book of Habakkuk.

The Teleioteti Old Testament Commentaries series is an attempt to attain theological depth, to pay attention to the forest, without neglecting the details of the text, without missing the trees. To do this, a Teleioteti Old Testament Commentary seeks to bring scholarly rigour and thoughtfulness together with faithful attention to the purpose and significance of each book for God's people today. It strikes a balance between technicality, working through the Hebrew text and its difficulties, and practicality, applying each major section of the text to contemporary needs.

Reviews:

Habakkuk is a solid commentary. The emphasis upon the text of Habakkuk and its address of key theological issues presented in the text make it a worthy addition to the collection of commentaries on Habakkuk already in print. Habakkuk will fit nicely on the bookshelf in the pastor's library.

- Daniel Wiley, Adjunct Professor Clarks Summit University in Journal of Ministry and Theology, Spring 2020, Vol. 24, No. 1.